OXFORD STUDIES IN AFRICAN AFFAIRS

THE
WESTERN SLAVE COAST
AND ITS RULERS

Oxford University Press, Ely House, London W. 1

GLASGOW NEW YORK TORONTO MELBOURNE WELLINGTON
CAPE TOWN SALISBURY IBADAN NAIROBI LUSAKA ADDIS ABABA
BOMBAY CALCUTTA MADRAS KARACHI LAHORE DACCA
KUALA LUMPUR HONG KONG

THE
WESTERN SLAVE COAST
AND ITS RULERS

EUROPEAN TRADE AND ADMINISTRATION
AMONG THE YORUBA AND ADJA-SPEAKING PEOPLES
OF SOUTH-WESTERN NIGERIA
SOUTHERN DAHOMEY AND TOGO

BY

C. W. NEWBURY

OXFORD
AT THE CLARENDON PRESS

TO MY PARENTS

PREFACE

THERE is a Yoruba proverb which warns that 'It is easy to cut to pieces a dead elephant.' Now that West African historiography has embarked on the necessary detailed monographs to correct or substantiate earlier regional studies, there is perhaps a danger that academic partition may faithfully follow international partition. Yet the ethnic march-lands cut by boundaries are broad; and historically they are as significant as the great ritual and political centres of Africa—if only to illustrate the confusion in perspective between ethnography and post-colonial nationalism.

This is not to say that West Africa was a frontierless society. Nineteenth-century Yoruba did not pass into the kingdom of Dahomey unless they were captives or slaves; and before 1914 the mid-Volta or the Mono river boundaries, laid down in Europe, recognized to some extent political divisions existing between the Akan and Ewe, or between the Ewe and the Fon.

Equally important is the international nature of European economic and cultural contact, both before and after partition. Traders tended to follow the best markets, not the flag; and the early literate African groups in the coastal towns were not rigidly divided into German, French, or English-speakers. The Togo protectorate treaty of 1884 was drawn up in English with the help of two native traders; the earliest farm-school and plantation in Lagos Colony was run by a French missionary; and the language of business and diplomacy in southern Dahomey was for long Portuguese—a reminder of earlier European contacts dating from the fifteenth century.

It is the purpose of this book to survey the history of a coastal area the name of which was derived from the principal aspect of early Eur-African relations, and where contiguous groups of Adja and Yoruba-speakers fell under three different European administrations. The similarities and contrasts in the colonial period of Lagos, Togo, and Dahomey stem not merely from differences in metropolitan and local policies, but also from ethno-political factors which had to be taken into account by alien rulers. In one sense West African history is Atlantic and Caribbean history; in another the coast was only the back door to a continent whose sub-savanna peoples looked inland for some of the most important elements in their ritual and political organization, for part of their trade, and for their enemies. But by the nineteenth century the coastal zone was an economic and cultural crossroads; and since the historical 'elephant' that flourished there is still vigorously alive, the task of demarcating the area for study in depth presents problems of which anachronism and omission are only two.

The difficulty for the historian of West Africa is not simply size and definition, but the international character of the sources—both African and European—for works embracing more than one tropical dependency. It is a pleasure, therefore, to record my gratitude to those whose help and patience have done something to diminish the parochial bias of a British student—not least to my wife whose intelligent and unstinting work on German materials saved me many hours of drudgery.

For supplementing German colonial records in Potsdam which could not be examined, both my wife and I would like to thank Fräulein Finck, Librarian of the *Institut für Auswärtige Politik*, Hamburg, Dr. v. Vietsch and Dr. Winter of the *Bundesarchiv*, Koblenz, Dr. Ewald of the *Staatsarchiv*, Hamburg, Dr. F. Prüser and Dr. Schwebel, *Staatsarchiv*, Bremen, the librarians of the *Handelskammer* in Hamburg and Bremen, and Dr. E. Hieke of the *Wirtschaftsgeschichtliche Forschungsstelle*, Hamburg, whose own work on German trade in Africa is a model of impartiality. I am also grateful to Dr. Otto Diehn for allowing me to read his unpublished thesis on German colonial policy before 1914.

In Paris M. C. Laroche and M. Jean Baillou permitted access to relevant materials in the archives of the former *Ministère de la France d'Outre-Mer*, and in the *Ministère des Affaires Étrangères*. At the Library of the *Musée de l'Homme* Mlle Heyum tracked down a number of useful references to obscure publications and journals.

In Rome the Superior General and the Rev. Father Guérin of the *Missions Africaines de Lyon* kindly made available records of the early French missions on the coast.

In Africa Professor Théo. Monod, Director of the *Institut Français d'Afrique Noire*, and M. R. Mauny materially assisted my stay in Dakar, while the energetic and courteous help of M. J. Charpy, then Conservator of the Government-General Archives, enabled me to read a maximum in the time available. At Porto-Novo M. J. Lombard, Director of the I.F.A.N. centre, and M. Serpos Tidjani of the *Service des Archives*, permitted me to work on a mass of

uncatalogued documents during several visits. At Ibadan Professor
K. O. Diké, as Director of the Nigerian Record Office, kindly allowed
me to read material on British Colonial Administration, when this
was housed in the University College Library. I am also grateful
for the grant of £30 from the Department of History, contributed
towards my travel expenses in French West Africa. At Badagri field
work was assisted by Chief Mobee, Chief Williams Abass II, *Seriki*
of Badagri, and Mr. T. Ola Avoseh whose own work on local oral
history deserves better recognition than it has so far received.

In England the archivists of the Public Record Office, the Methodist Missionary Society, aided me in countless ways; and Mr. L.
Frewer, Superintendent of Rhodes House Library, was instrumental
in procuring microfilms of German documents and books.

I am grateful to Professor V. Harlow, Dr. R. Oliver, and Miss
M. Perham for their comments on various chapters, and to Professor
Daryll Forde for reading the manuscript. Finally, I have been
enabled to write up this material with the help of an Oppenheimer
grant from Queen Elizabeth House and the unfailing encouragement
of Mrs. E. M. Chilver, Director of the Institute of Commonwealth
Studies, Oxford.

C. W. NEWBURY

Oxford, June 1960

CONTENTS

LIST OF MAPS

LIST OF ABBREVIATIONS

C.O.	Colonial Office
F.O.	Foreign Office
I.F.A.N.	Institut Français d'Afrique Noire
M.A.É.	Ministère des Affaires Étrangères, Paris
M.F.O.	Ministère de la France d'Outre-Mer, Paris
M.M.A.	Methodist Missionary Society Archives
N.R.O.	Nigerian Record Office, Ibadan
P.N.	Porto-Novo Archives, Dahomey
P.P.	Parliamentary Papers
U.C.I.	University College, Ibadan

Introduction

AMONG the royal insignia of the kings of Dahomey is a bas-relief dating from the reign of Agaja depicting a two-masted caravel to celebrate the extension of the Abomey kingdom to the sea in the early eighteenth century. Another is a royal staff designed to commemorate the boasting phrase of a later king, Behanzin, by representing him as a shark denying the French access to the Dahomey port of Cotonou towards the end of the nineteenth century. Together these two symbols roughly define a period in the history of the Western Slave Coast. In the time scale of African history it was a relatively short period—a mere one and a half centuries—from the most intensive phase of the Atlantic slave trade till the advent of European administration. Long before that the Slave Coast had been charted by the Portuguese; and the peoples of the area west of Benin between the Volta river and Lagos had much older origins and a cultural history which linked them with the earliest Yoruba settlements to the north and east. On the whole, however, the inhabitants of the Volta–Lagos plain were on the far periphery of the great savanna states, away from the main caravan routes, unknown to the Arab geographers and travellers, and to a certain degree isolated from continuous maritime contact by the hazards of a surf-bound coast and a notorious climate. There is a sharp division in the materials available for their history: before the eighteenth century their records are mostly legend and a few archaeological sites; later their sources are partial and European, furnished in the main by those who followed in the wake of King Agaja's heraldic caravel.

To describe Agaja's subjects, their origins, or their neighbours entails a serious risk of ethnographical anachronism, if post-eighteenth-century materials are used to project sub-tribal divisions back over two hundred years. It is not even certain what changes in environment, both natural and man-made, took place prior to the seventeenth century. The term 'forest-kingdoms', if taken to refer to the urban paramountcies of Allada, Abomey, or Ketu, may well be a misnomer: for by the eighteenth century the plateaux sites of these political centres were undulating bush and scrub land, separated by thickly wooded, swampy depressions, untypical of the areas of heavier precipitation west of the River Mono and east of Lagos. Yet it was a region suitable for both hunting and settled subsistence economies, for fishermen, foragers, root-croppers, and grain-growers alike, rising gradually from the coastal lagoons to merge with the granitic outcrops of the Agu hills in Togo and the savanna country of the Attagora massif north of the seventh parallel in Dahomey.

On the coast the lagoon system which is the main feature of the long alluvial plain from the Volta estuary to Lagos probably changed considerably in detail, though the lagoons themselves provided a constant avenue of communication and a means of protection for the residual peoples who inhabited their banks and islands. One of the earliest topographical accounts of the coast by the Portuguese explorer, Pereira, described in the first years of the sixteenth century the stretch from Cape St. Paul to east of Lagos as low and sandy 'with clumps of woodland, and the shore . . . composed entirely of beach'.[1] The only important break east of the Volta was the *Rio do Lagua* which had a dangerous entrance noted by Pereira in terms not so very different from those used in mariners' guides three hundred years later—with 'shallows of sand on which the sea breaks during the greater part of the year, so that the channel is rarely seen'.[2] To the east the surf barrier gave way to mud-flats; and there at Gwato, near Benin, the Portuguese had made their first settlement on the Slave Coast in 1486.

Their charts of the coast suggest that little more was known than sailors' landmarks and anchorages, though the picturesque *Terra Gazellas* and the more prosaic *Terra alagada* were not inaccurate descriptions of the fauna and flood-lands behind the beach west of Lagos.[3] By 1570 Ijebu is noted on the Benin maps; but not till 1602 does the Ardra river (Weme) appear; and 'Cradoo' (Ikorodu), Allada, and other market towns are late seventeenth- and early

[1] Duarte Pacheco Pereira, *Esmeraldo de Situ Orbis* (trans. and ed. G. H. T. Kimble, Hakluyt Society, Series II, lxxiv, London, 1937), p. 123.
[2] Ibid., p. 124.
[3] The earliest charts dating from 1489 were drawn by Cristofaro Soligo and are usually known as the 'Ginea Portogalexe'. See Youssouf Kamal, *Monumenta Cartographica Africae et Aegypti*, v (Cairo, 1951); and maps by Gaspar Viegas (c. 1537), Georges Reinel (c. 1540), Luis Teixeira (1602), in Armando Cortesão and Avelino Teixeira da Mota (eds.), *Portugaliae Monumenta Cartographica*, i (Lisboa, 1960); Luis Silveira, *Portugal: Colonies. Collection of Plans and Views* (London, 1956), p. 28, c. 35; J. Dennée, *L'Afrique au XVIe siècle et le commerce anversois* (Anvers, 1937), p. 110; John W. Blake, *European Beginnings in West Africa 1454–1578* (London, 1937), p. 82.

eighteenth-century additions. By 1602, however, the Portuguese had certainly contacted Allada—the earliest-named kingdom between the Volta and Lagos.[1] Later Dutch and French maps, while consolidating and extending this knowledge, often exaggerated the deep northward bend of the Bight coastline—a mannerism absent from the coastal charts of their predecessors.[2] A possible reason for this exaggerated indentation is the increased familiarity of the Dutch and French with the interior lagoon system which in the Lake Nokué sector may well have been open for a period to small sailing vessels through a flooded sea channel, thus placing the 'shoreline' farther inland than the usual sand-spit.

There were other characteristics, too, that have altered. A map of 1775 shows twin channels from Lagos to Grand Popo;[3] and there were (and still are during floods) a number of secondary lateral lagoons besides the old Volta–Lagos waterway which was open to canoes for its entire length in the early nineteenth century before it silted up at Godomey near Lake Nokué. It also seems established that there was, as late as the end of the eighteenth century, a watercourse just south of Allada connecting the Mono and Weme, and which the traveller, Robert Norris, refers to as a 'pretty deep and rapid river . . . formerly the Northern boundary of the Whydah Kingdom'.[4] The silting up of the lagoons and the opening and closing of temporary outlets to the sea was part of the long process by which the alluvial plain of the Western Slave Coast was built up.[5] But apart from the seaward frontier no natural barriers impeded population movements in an area where bush, alluvial soils, and strategic sites on low plateaux supported a close-knit variety of subsistence and specialization.

The descriptive terminology used to distinguish the various ethnic groups of the West Benin–Volta region is a mixture of linguistic, tribal, and sub-tribal classifications devised and applied by authorities from the eighteenth century to the present day.[6] Within the major linguistic divisions of Adja and Yoruba speakers a diversity of dialects

[1] See below, p. 17.
[2] S. H. Moll (c. 1710), in Kamal, v (1951), 1569; D'Anville (1775), ibid. 1577.
[3] Cf. Robert Norris (based on D'Anville), Fig. 1.
[4] Robert Norris, *Memoirs of the Reign of Bossa Ahádee, King of Dahomy, An Inland Country of Guiney* (London, 1789), pp. 68–69.
[5] U.C.I., J. C. Pugh, 'The Porto-Novo–Badagri Sand Ridge Complex', 'Research Notes', No. 3 (Department of Geography, 1953); and for evidence from more recent hydrographic surveys, A. Monnet (ed.), *La Mise en valeur de l'A.O.F. et du Togo* (Casablanca, 1955), pp. 92–94. [6] Fig. 3, below, p. 33.

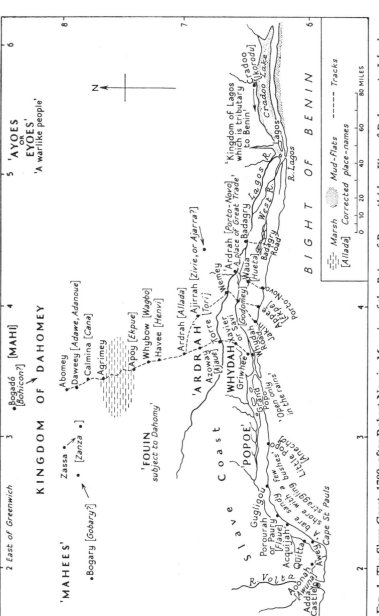

FIG. 1. The Slave Coast, 1789, after Robert Norris, *Memoirs of the Reign of Bossa Ahádee, King of Dahomy, An Inland Country of Guiney* (London, 1789)

abounds. How far this diversity is a product of the absorbtion of small migratory groups into 'an early cultural continuum over much of the forest belt' or the result of localized sound-change is a problem for the linguist.[1] It is worth noting, however, that the term 'Adja', adopted in preference to 'Ewe' to comprehend the dialect cluster between the Akan and Yoruba speakers, has one if not two other meanings. It may be used to denote the ruling lineages of Tado, Allada, Abomey, and Porto-Novo; and it denotes a small residual group in the Mono-Athiémé area—the Adja proper—from whom these lineages may derive. Similarly, for the Adja-speaking people as a whole three or four centuries of cultural infiltrations from the north and east and uneven contact with later Yoruba states and maritime aliens resulted in a remarkable range of political structures.

Les systèmes de parenté sont partout à dominante patrilinéaire; mais les organisations politiques vont d'une poussière de petites chefferies où le rôle des conseils d'anciens était de première importance (*Ewe*) au royaume sans doute le plus centralisé de toute l'Afrique de l'Ouest (Dahomey); et les systèmes religieux sont plus ou moins complexes et plus ou moins composites. Il s'agit donc d'un bloc très diversifié, et dont la relative unité n'apparaît dans bien des domaines que par opposition aux deux autres blocs qui l'encadrent.[2]

The distribution of ethnic groups of the Adja and western Yoruba is complicated rather than clarified by the large corpus of myth collected during the last decades of the nineteenth century and expanded since by town and lineage legends. It is probably true that, as among the Tallensi of northern Ghana, these 'myths and legends counterfeit history; they do not document it'.[3] They have undoubtedly been used to validate the existence of an institution or the claims of senior lineage families by postulating sacred derivation or uninterrupted descent from a divine lineage-founder in the distant past. But they contain a good deal of circumstantial evidence about migratory origins—that is to say, the origins of lineage-founders, not the origins of the tribe or sub-tribe as a whole with its numerous and unsung ramages built up by intermarriage with neighbouring groups or lost by dispersal, conquest, and absorbtion into other sub-tribes.[4]

---

[1] Daryll Forde, 'The Cultural Map of West Africa: Successive Adaptations to Tropical Forests and Grasslands', *Transactions of the New York Academy of Sciences*, Series II, xv (1953), 209. See, too, Paul Mercier, 'Note de présentation', in *Cartes ethno-démographiques de l'Afrique occidentale*, No. 5 (Institut Français d'Afrique Noire. Dakar, 1954), pp. 9–10, 18–21.   [2] Mercier, pp. 18–19.
[3] M. M. Fortes, *The Dynamics of Clanship among the Tallensi* (1945), p. 26.
[4] More evidence—particularly from archaeology—would be needed to decide

The Ewe sub-tribes have legends of a common ancestral migration centre at Nuatyi (Notsie) in Togo and vaguer references to a prior migration from somewhere east near the Niger. The Allada and Abomey royal lineages trace their origins from Tado north-west of Nuatyi on the Togo border. The Adja rulers of Porto-Novo also looked to Tado for their semi-divine origins. For the Yoruba kingdoms of Ketu and Shabe and for secondary towns in Egbado and Egba territory there are legendary connexions with Ile-Ife, Oyo, and ultimately with the polymorphous ancestor of the Yorubas, Oduduwa. It may well be, as has been suggested, that there is a close ethnic parentage between the Yoruba and their Adja neighbours.[1] But the Allada and Abomey legends look no farther back than Tado. And to plot schematically the *Völkerwanderung* of Yoruba and Adja from the Niger to Ife and Tado assumes too often a mammoth exodus led by kings for what may have been merely the work of a few hunters, adventurers, or political exiles.

The sub-tribal histories of non-ruling lineages are usually more modest in their claims. Of the thirty-nine lineage myths recorded for the inhabitants of the Abomey kingdom, only seven are of Adja origin (including the royal lineage), two or three are Yoruba, while most of the others that are identifiable belong to a shifting stratum of riverine and plateau inhabitants who looked upon themselves (and were considered by their neighbours) from the early seventeenth century as Fon, under the military paramountcy of Abomey.[2]

to what degree and at what period the Adja and Yoruba have been culturally homogeneous to merit the term 'Benin civilization'. But for an ethnohistorical reconstruction of unusual time-depth suggesting the persistence of social structure, ritual, agricultural, and craft techniques over four centuries among the Gwambe of Mozambique, see Charles Edward Fuller, 'Ethnohistory in the Study of Culture Change in Southeast Africa', in William R. Bascom and Melville J. Herskovits (eds.), *Continuity and Change in African Cultures* (Chicago, 1959), pp. 113–29.

[1] Jacques Bertho, 'La Parenté des Yoruba aux peuplades de Dahomey et Togo', *Africa*, xix, No. 2 (1949), pp. 121–32, and map 125.

[2] Melville J. Herskovits, *Dahomey An Ancient West African Kingdom* (2 vols. New York, 1938), i. 165–91; A. Le Herissé, *L'Ancien Royaume du Dahomey* (Paris, 1911), pp. 373–6. The pre-Fon groups and their post-Fon residuals have been termed Watyi (Wo-Tchi), closely related to the Ewe proper, Wemenu, the Wa-We (or Gedevi), and possibly the Efon (with Yoruba scarifications). See, too, E. Dunglas, 'Contribution à l'histoire du Moyen-Dahomey (Royaume d'Abomey, de Kétou et de Ouidah)', *Études dahoméennes*, xix, xx, xxi (I.F.A.N. Porto-Novo, 1957–8), 1, 75–76, 78–79; Rev. Samuel Johnson, *The History of the Yorubas From the Earliest Times to the Beginning of the British Protectorate* (4th ed. Lagos, 1957), p. 105.

Similarly, the ward histories of Porto-Novo indicate a strong admixture of Yoruba with local Gun, particularly before the demise of the Oyo empire in the 1830's. Yet the legends of the ruling lineage and its associated religious institutions point west to Tado, as admitted by one of their historians:

C'est une manie chez nous de tout rapporter au pays Adja, que la foi de nos mystiques vénère, parcequ'il est le berceau des *voudoun* de la race des conquérants. Tout ce dont l'origine est mystérieuse pour les indigènes, tout ce qui se perd dans la nuit des temps est venu d'Adja.[1]

The ruling lineages of Abomey and Porto-Novo have histories which indicate a common origin from the Adja kings of Allada and Tado.[2] These legends are subject to reservations: they were recorded late in the nineteenth century by Europeans and educated Africans and with subsequent additions refer to events and persons three to four hundred years ago; chronology for the earliest period is not merely defective, it is non-existent; and the fact that the Abomey genealogy of the Tado and Allada kings is considerably foreshortened makes it impossible to reconcile the two stories in detail.

It was not the purpose of the court chroniclers of Abomey or Porto-Novo to recount the past with accuracy, but to account for the present—the *Dahomenu*, the people and things of Dahomey, and the *Alladanu* institutions of Porto-Novo—whose living protectors, sacred kings, royal officials, and priests were essential to ritual which preserved the links between the living and the dead, between the children and the fathers of the descent group. Both stories agree that the kings of Allada were descended from the kings of Tado through a female not a male ancestor; and at some time, probably in the fifteenth century, the male descendants of the Tado princess migrated with their families and followers to found Allada. From there, towards the end of the century, succession disputes between the chiefs of the senior ramages of the Adja-Tadonu in Allada caused two of

---

[1] Paul Hazoumé, *Le Pacte de sang au Dahomey (Transactions et mémoires de l'Institut d'Ethnologie,* xxv, Paris, 1937), pp. 139–40; Herskovits, ii. 171 and n.

[2] Le Herissé, pp. 271–352; Dunglas, i. 80–82; A. Akindélé and C. Aguessy, *Contribution à l'étude de l'histoire de l'ancien royaume de Porto-Novo* (I.F.A.N. Dakar, 1953), pp. 19–21. Akindélé and Aguessy used in addition to oral accounts from officials of the royal dynasty the *Iwé itan Ajasé* ('History of Ajasé'), by A. Akindélé, based on earlier manuscripts collected by the Wesleyan coloured pastor Thomas J. Marshall who may have used Portuguese or Brazilian documents as a guide to his chronology. A search in the archives of the Methodist Missionary Society failed to throw any light on this source.

them to strike out north and east, one to found the ruling lineage of Abomey, the other the ruling houses of Porto-Novo.

It is in the explanation for the first 'migration' from Tado to Allada that the Abomey version moves into phantasy. Agassu, the father of the Adja-Tado kings, was born of a Tado princess and a male leopard. As the Porto-Novo version has it this totemic progenitor was simply a wandering Yoruba hunter who won his way to a position of influence in the Tado court under King Aholuho, married his daughter, and founded a lineage whose senior male line encountered understandable opposition from the direct descendants of Aholuho when they laid claim to the royal stool of Tado. According to the Abomey story, the sons of Agassu (the *Agassuvi*), insulted by the aspersions cast on their ancestor, left Tado and migrated by way of Lake Han (Athiémé) to found a new settlement at Allada where the sacred remains of Agassu were buried and the ancestor himself promoted to the highest place in the Adja-Tado pantheon. The cult of Agassu, as an ancestral divinity, was in the charge of an *Agassunon* priest who presided over the enthronement rites of the kings of Allada. From then on the ruling lineage, known as the Adja-Tadonu (or Allada-Tadonu), enforced claims to tribute on the Hueda inhabitants of the coastal villages of Savi and Jakin from the beginning of the seventeenth century.

The Porto-Novo version is the more likely of the two stories. For the Abomey Adja, after two centuries of tributary relationship and intermittent war with the Yoruba, the creation of a totemic ancestor was a convenient way to forget the Yoruba parentage of the Adja-Tadonu. But to the rulers of Porto-Novo with Yoruba wards in the town and close trading connexions with Oyo, it was no disgrace that the Yoruba hunter, Adimola, rather than his son Agassu (not named in their story) should be the ancestral divinity of the Allada kings. Indeed his services to the King of Tado were recognized, according to the Porto-Novo historians, by the title of *Oba-Ajo* (Gun: *Avajo*)— the 'stranger-king'; and his male descendants supplied no less than sixteen of the kings of Tado before some of the lineage departed for Allada. True, the sons of Adimola (or *Avajo*) were not accepted at Tado without ritual purification—a ceremony carefully preserved during the enthronement rites of the kings of Porto-Novo; and ultimately some of them were banished as usurpers. But *Avajo* Adimola also acquired the title of *Zu-non* which (whatever its original meaning) was handed down through Adimola's Yoruba brothers and their descendants, taken to Porto-Novo, and firmly established as a sacred oracle attached to the *Avajo* shrine whose priest symbolized the 'father of the kings'.[1] The two versions may be compared thus:

The Adja-Tado Lineage

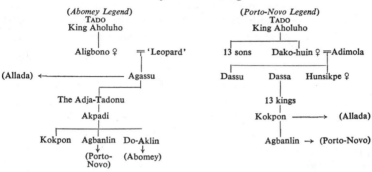

The chronology of the two accounts cannot be reconciled;[2] and whether the 'migration' to Allada took place under Agassu or Kokpon is immaterial. Politically, Tado faded in importance after the rise of Abomey, though it retained more than legendary significance for the Abomey kings. The first European to visit the town in 1889 recorded that the 'fetish king' (*Avajo?*), one Pohenzon, claimed direct descent from the early rulers; and he was told that the kings of Abomey regularly made ritual sacrifices at Tado, after enthronement, though Pohenzon himself was at that time no friend of the Abomey court.[3]

Common to both stories are accounts of secondary 'migrations' to villages founded by Tado Adja on the banks of Lake Han. And at least one of Kokpon's partisans (or sons) founded a settlement at Huete (or Seme) on the lagoon opposite the site of Porto-Novo, where Agbanlin followed him, via Ganvié and Abomey-Calavi. Exchange of women between Adja, Fon, and Hueda must have been

[1] Akindélé and Aguessy, p. 29. The *Zu-non* is sometimes called 'king of the night' from the fact that the *Avajo* priest did not walk abroad in daylight to avoid encountering his 'son' the Adja King of Porto-Novo. The title and office are reported to have been introduced via Allada during the reign of Lokpon (1739–46) by one Vode who founded an Ijebu Yoruba ward (Zebu) at Porto-Novo.

[2] Akindélé and Aguessy, following Marshall, give 1688 as a date for the arrival of Agbanlin at Porto-Novo. Kokpon reigned at Allada at the beginning of the seventeenth century. Allowing an average reign of ten years for each of the legendary kings of Tado they arrive at about 1440 for the reign of Aholuho.

[3] M.F.O., Senegal, vi/22, d'Albéca to Bayol, 1 Nov. 1899.

commonplace (Kokpon's mother is reported to have been a Yoruba from the Porto-Novo area). Only for the Abomey Adja and its ramages was there a theory of 'pure' agnatic descent from a totemic ancestor; and this was invented many centuries after the event.

It is also indicated in the Porto-Novo legend that the Adja-Tado, already at Tado, and later at Allada, created ministers and officials from followers of merit, whatever their origins, rather than princes who were left with the alternatives of fratricidal succession disputes or adventuring forth to farm new lands and occasionally to found dynasties of their own. Of the two princes who left Allada for the Abomey plateau and Porto-Novo (then called Hogbonu),[1] the former founded the more centralized and politically sophisticated kingdom. Yet their early fortunes were not dissimilar. The followers of Do-Aklin and his two sons, like those of Agbanlin at Hueta, were roving bands of raiders under war-chiefs who acquired land-rights by the generosity of their hosts or by force. Do-Aklin settled on the Abomey plateau near Bohicon, paying tribute originally to Yoruba and Wemenu inhabitants. At his death, in about 1620, his body was returned to Allada—the last of the Abomey-Adja chiefs to be buried there. His sons separated: one returned to Allada to be consecrated by the *Agassunon* as head of the northern Adja lineage; the other, Dakodonu, joined by other Allada migrants, staked out a *de facto* claim to paramountcy by his qualities of leadership in the struggle of the Agassuvi of the plateau for new land and water rights in the Wa-We area. The local chiefs yielded to the new-comers and were reduced to tributary status between 1620 and the 1640's. Dakodonu's son, Aho, who was particularly successful in these exploits succeeded his father as head of the lineage in about 1645 and took the 'strong name' of Wegbaja. Further land disputes resulted in the seizure of an important watering-place west of Abomey and in the assassination of a local chieftain, Dan—which gave rise to the Abomey-Adja legend of the origin of the name 'Dahomey'.[2] By the 1650's Wegbaja was paramount over all the Wa-We area and over the Adja villages on the west of the plateau where the capital of the Agassuvi lineage was built, a small fortified town called Agbomey which, for the remainder of the seventeenth century, was attacked by the local enemies of

---

[1] Later Ajashé ('conquered by the Adja').

[2] There are several possible translations for 'Dan-homey' the most likely of which is simply 'in the house of Dan'. Dunglas, i. 88.

the Agassuvi and was in tributary relationship to Oyo from about 1747.

In the south-east at Porto-Novo the Agbanlin ramage of the Adja-Tado fared more easily, though the same features of expansion by force, treachery, and compromise are present in the legend. By the end of the reign of Agbanlin in 1729, the Adja migrants were firmly established in Hueta and the villages on the opposite side of the lagoon. But by the time of his death Allada was in the hands of Abomey which had broken through to the sea-kingdoms and the advantages of European contact.

Officials at Porto-Novo are stated to have been derived from the example of court government at Allada. There were about five in the early eighteenth century, increased to about a score by the time of Tofa's reign a hundred years later.[1] Their offices were hereditary, and they appear to have been drawn from Adja families whose members were not direct descendants of Agbanlin.

Succession to kingship at Porto-Novo seems to have been a source of political instability rather than strength, and there is no evidence that authority was exercised outside the town beyond a radius of about twenty miles. Selection of the royal candidate was at first based on a rotary principle among the five families founded by the sons of Agbanlin. But other factors—particularly wealth from trade—played an increasingly important part.

Tè Agbanlin eut cinq fils, qui donnèrent souche à cinq lignées royales à Porto-Novo. Ces rameaux fournirent tour à tour des rois. Quand le tour est terminé, le cycle recommence, de telle sorte que l'héritier direct d'un roi défunt ne peut pas toujours succéder immédiatement à son père. De temps à autre, cependant, il se produit quelques irrégularités: Gbèyon est couronné après la mort de Houyi, alors que c'est le tour d'Ayaton, fils héritier de Hiakpon. La popularité, la richesse, l'audace, jouent beaucoup en pareil cas. Dès que la mort d'un roi est rendue officielle, les candidatures affluent de tous côtés: à tort ou à raison, tous les princes veulent régner. Certains étalent leur fortune, essayant d'acheter les voix des ministres influents.[2]

The pattern of succession among the ramages of the Adja lineage at Porto-Novo, from Agbanlin till the time of Tofa, was as follows:

[1] Akindélé and Aguessy, pp. 43–56; and for later descriptions of Porto-Novo, its officials and priests (c. 1870), 'L'Histoire dahoméenne de la fin du xixe siècle à travers les textes', *Études dahoméennes*, ix (1953), pp. 21–26.
[2] Akindélé and Aguessy, p. 35.

Kings of Porto-Novo

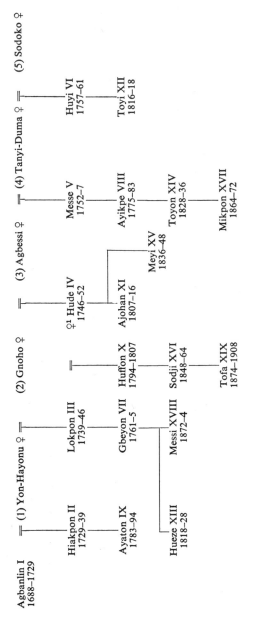

¹ Second wife of Lokpon.

The regular rotation stopped after the sons of Agbanlin had each been enthroned in turn and had reigned for short periods till the middle of the eighteenth century. The break in regularity coincided with the advent of numerous slave traders and the importation of arms through Porto-Novo for the Yoruba interior. Thereafter, in the struggle for paramountcy between the five ramages, the house of Lokpon provided six out of the thirteen rulers of Porto-Novo, while its principal rival the house of Messe provided three. The remaining three royal houses provided only two or three rulers each (including their founders). The patronage extended by the princes to Portuguese, Brazilians, Oyo, Yoruba, and Hausa slave merchants was at once a source of wealth and political opposition from those who awaited their own opportunity to bribe and manipulate ministers, priests, and elders for support. It was a system of kingship with parallels at Badagri and Lagos.[1] Possibly it was the system at Allada before its fall.

At Abomey, however, the royal lineage, constantly under pressure from enemies, refined the institution to suit the need for superior statecraft and military leadership and produced a succession of long-ruling autocrats whose kingdom was matched at the end of the eighteenth century only by the numbers and cavalry of the Oyo empire. The history of the Adja dynasty at Abomey from the time of Wegbaja indicates serious succession disputes between the sons of a dead king, but not between the ramages founded by the sons of the first ruler.[2] Princes with a claim to succession were born of royal wives during their father's reign. Those descended from royal collaterals do not seem to have been eligible—not even for ministerial office from which members of the royal lineage were rigidly excluded, at least till the reign of King Ghezo.[3]

Since the number of sons born to a king during his reign was limited—particularly if he came to the throne late in life after a long reign by his predecessor, competitors for the title were relatively few and generally bound by their father's selection. Akaba was not

[1] See below, pp. 30–32, 46.

[2] For a discussion of title-succession at Abomey see Herskovits, ii. 31–32.

[3] Ibid. ii. 33, 37–41. The chief minister, or *Migan*, was also governor of Allada from the 1730's. The better-known *Yovogan* was chief of the Whites on the coast and dates from the reign of Agaja. The *Meu* or financial officer dates from the reign of Tegbessu and was also used at a later date to control the coastal territory. The 'Caboceers' or subordinate officials performed the same functions as the *Lari* at Porto-Novo—messengers, custodians, and tax-collectors. See C. W. Newbury (ed.), *A Mission to Gelde, King of Dahome* (London, 1966), pp. 26–36.

Kings of Abomey[1]

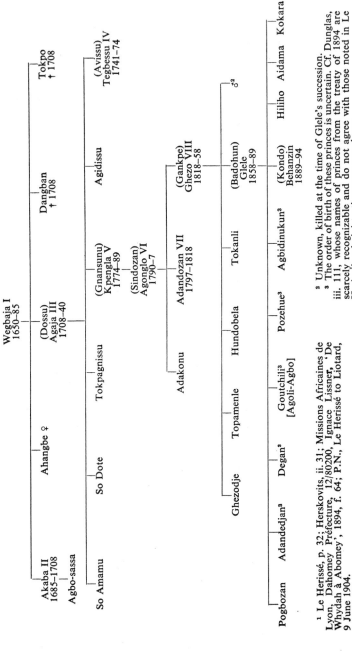

[1] Le Herissé, p. 32; Herskovits, ii, 31; Missions Africaines de Lyon, Dahomey Préfecture, 12/80200, Ignace Lissner, 'De Whydah à Abomey', 1894, f. 64; P.N., Le Herissé to Liotard, 9 June 1904.

[2] Unknown, killed at the time of Glele's succession.

[3] The order of birth of these princes is uncertain. Cf. Dunglas, iii. 111, whose names of princes from the treaty of 1894 are scarcely recognizable and do not agree with those noted in Le Herissé's administrative correspondence.

followed by his son—a mere youth; and effective power passed to the boy's uncle, Dossu, who took the strong name of Agaja. Other possible competitors were eliminated by the death of his two brothers in battle in about 1708. Primogeniture was not the rule. Of the sons of Agaja, the youngest, Avissu, the child of a favourite wife and a distinguished warrior against the Oyo, took precedence. When this decision of the dead king was made known, it was challenged by the eldest son, So Amamu, who was seized on the order of the officials, *Migan* and *Mehu*, taken to Whydah and drowned. His brother Tokpa was restrained by force: the need for leadership outweighed precedence by birth. Logically a son of Tegbessu should have succeeded at his death; but a brother was chosen (with Tegbessu's assent) as *Vi-Daho*, since it was suspected the dead king was probably sterile. The last case of brother succeeding brother before the French conquest occurred in the nineteenth century when Ghezo overthrew the erratic and unstable Adandozan and seized power.

Of Abomey's immediate neighbours, the oldest was the kingdom of Ketu, sited between the Weme and Ogun rivers, whose kings traced their origins back to Ile-Ife. In the absence of archaeological evidence it is impossible to verify the antiquity of Ketu, though the remarkably long list of forty-eight kings (*Alaketu*) suggests a foundation in the late fifteenth or early sixteenth century.[1] From the reign of the twenty-fifth king, the *Alaketu* appear to have been selected from one of five ramages of the royal lineage. It is claimed in the oral histories of the town that there was a strict rotation of office, but the genealogical connexions between the successive rulers of each royal family are uncertain.[2]

From Ketu, tradition has it that the early *Alake* of the Egba Yoruba were derived, first at Ake—a town in the Egba forest which served as capital for one of the three Egba sub-tribes, and later in the nineteenth century at Abeokuta.[3]

The hegemony of Oyo over the Yoruba provinces, against which the Egba revolted towards the end of the eighteenth century, and which was broken finally by the Fulani, curbed the expansion of the

---

[1] E. G. Parrinder, *The Story of Ketu An Ancient Yoruba Kingdom* (Ibadan, 1956), pp. 4–24.

[2] Ibid., pp. 85–86. The long reign of the *Alaketu* would last about ninety years before any one of the five families had their turn again to supply a king. Also it is not stated whether the names of the *Alaketu* were 'strong names'.

[3] Saburi O. Biobaku, *The Egba and their Neighbours 1842–1872* (Oxford, 1957), pp. 3–8. The Egba Agura, the Egba Oke-Ona, and the Egba Agbeyin (Ake).

Abomey kingdom. The weakening of Oyo over-rule left open the way in the south-west for a series of emergent 'successor-states' at Abeokuta and Ibadan, and a number of weaker urban chiefdoms among the Shabe, Ketu, Egbado, and Awori Yoruba. Between these and the Akan to the west lay the Adja military paramountcy—'a small black Sparta—hedged in by hostile accolents'[1]—admirably organized to profit from the weakness of landward rivals, less able to meet the ultimate demand for change made by seaward foes.

[1] R. F. Burton, *A Mission to Gelele, King of Dahomey* (2 vols. London, 1893), ii. 155.

CHAPTER I

European Contact and the Rise of the Abomey Kingdom

THE Portuguese who first charted the coast from the Volta to Benin derived little commercial advantage from their knowledge of the area west of Lagos. By the middle of the seventeenth century, when the long quest for gold and spices was surpassed by an increasing demand for slaves for the Americas, Portuguese power to exploit their old discoveries for a new market was at an end. First French, then English and Dutch privateers had challenged their precarious monopoly of West African trade; the union of Portugal with Spain in 1580 sacrificed the Gold Coast settlements to wider interests; the eclipse was complete when Mina was lost in 1637 and Axim in 1642—two years after the introduction of sugar-cane into the West Indies. Not for another eighty years did the Portuguese win back a prominent place on the Western Slave Coast; and when they did, the commercial initiative and finance for their venture was supplied not from Lisbon but Brazil.

By then, the conditions of trade between the Volta and Lagos had been modified by the establishment of permanent factories and by intense international competition. The change had begun as the Portuguese position in the Bight of Benin declined. At the end of the sixteenth century the staple exports from the Slave Coast were native cloth, peppers, and ivory, exchanged for cotton goods, corals, and iron.[1] The entrepôt for this trade was the island of San Thomé where Portuguese vessels provisioned on their way to the Americas from the Costa da Mina or from Benin.[2] Raided by the French and the Dutch in 1567 and 1590, the settlement suffered the loss of many of its colonists who emigrated to Brazil, but it still remained a Portuguese

[1] Capt. Gaspar da Rosa [1618], in Luciano Cordiero (ed.), *Viagens, Explorações e Conquistas dos Portuguezes 1516–1619. Escravos e Minas de Africa* (Lisboa, 1881), pp. 22–25.

[2] Luciano Cordiero (ed.), *Viagens . . . 1593–1631. Terras e Minas Africanas segundo Belthazar Rebello de Aragão* (Lisboa, 1881), p. 6; Antonio José de Aranjo, *Colonies portugaises d'Afrique. Colonisation, émigration, déportation* (Lisbon, 1900), pp. 12–13.

outpost with a handful of soldiers and a population of some 800 Europeans and 2,000 creoles. From this base Portuguese vessels had made occasional visits to the markets between the Volta and Lagos rivers. The lack of gold and spices had been disappointing; but contact had been established with the King of Allada about the beginning of the seventeenth century. He was familiar enough to the Portuguese to be placed in the same class as the chiefs of Ijebu and Benin—friends and allies—by the adventurer and trader, Branco, who was engaged in supplying San Thomé with ivory, native cloth, palm-oil, and yams from Allada.[1] It is clear from Branco's account that there was no European factory in or near Allada at this period, though one had been recommended as early as 1607 by a captain in Portuguese service who claimed that the kingdom would provide an annual market for at least 800,000 *reis* worth of imports from Lisbon and Bahia.[2] This proposal went unheeded. It was left to other nations to establish the first factories on the coast south of Allada; and the Portuguese who gave the Slave Coast its trading language became the poorest of its merchants. In 1698 the Dutch factor, Bosman, whose countrymen were the principal instruments of the Portuguese decline, noted scornfully that they were forced to accept other traders' leavings at Little Popo which wealthier slavers avoided because of the sharp practice of the Mina middlemen. 'The Portuguese are cheated by them more than any nation; notwithstanding which they cannot avoid trading with them by reason they are loaded with such sorry goods, that they can scarcely get slaves any where else.'[3]

Bosman and his kind could afford to jeer. For by the 1690's, the Dutch, French, and English, together with an occasional Dane, were firmly established at the Allada and Hueda markets on the coast. In 1663 the Chartered Company of Royal Adventurers opened a factory at Jakin (Godomey), a few miles south-east of Allada. The Dutch already had a post at the neighbouring market of Offra, where

---

[1] Luciano Cordiero (ed.), *Viagens . . . 1574–1620. Da Mina ao Cabo Negro segundo Garcia Mendeo Castello Branco* (Lisboa, 1881), p. 27. Branco was in the pay of de Novaes, the Angola *conquistador*. The palm-oil, like the native cloth, was destined for the population of San Thomé, not Europe.

[2] Luciano Cordiero (ed.), *Viagens . . . 1607. Estabelecimentos e Resgates Portuguezes na Costa Occidental de África* (Lisboa, 1881), p. 17. The *real* (pl. *reis*) was a money of account. About 2,000 *cruzados*. Benin was judged to be good for imports worth half this amount.

[3] William Bosman, *A New and Accurate Description of the Coast of Guinea*, in John Pinkerton (ed.), *A General Collection of the Best and Most Interesting Voyages and Travels in all Parts of the World*, xvi (London, 1814), 475.

they were joined by French factors of the *Compagnie des Indes Occidentales* in 1670 and by English factors of the Royal African Company (successor to the Adventurers) in 1678. All these early markets seem to have been under the control of Allada. Their position inland, several miles from the coast, must have been a serious disadvantage. Though the Dutch remained under their Allada protectors, the English and the French by 1685 had turned to the Hueda chiefs of Savi for land and chose the village of Grehue nearer to the beach for their later factories. Other traders followed their example; and the village, known to all European traders according to their corruption of the word 'Hueda',[1] expanded into one of the principal slave markets of the Bight, the site for European forts, and a convenient centre for canoe traffic along the interior lagoons which ran from the Volta to Benin.

With the possible exception of the Dutch East India Company, the monopoly enterprises which invested in the Slave Coast factories and forts during the last half of the seventeenth century were unsuccessful.[2] The promising beginnings of the Royal Adventurers were wrecked by the Dutch Wars. The Royal African Company was robbed by its factors, by its captains, and by private interlopers. The privileges of the slave trade brought poor returns, compared with trade in gold dust, ivory, and dyewoods. But the mirage of enormous profits persisted; and the triangular voyage of the company vessels from England to Africa, the West Indies, and back became a regular feature of the Atlantic trade. On the Slave Coast at Whydah the company was forced to employ as its agent an interloper—Captain Petley Weyborne—for lack of anyone with sufficient experience of conditions east of Cape Coast. It was an unsatisfactory arrangement; and after 1690 captains of the company's vessels dealt directly with native brokers for a commission of four slaves in a hundred (and the chance of shipping cargoes for themselves).[3] Finally, as the company sank steadily into debt, an effort was made to protect its interests against foreign competition. A fort was built in 1702 between Whydah

---

[1] Cf. Juda, Fida, Whida, Whydah, or the Hueda name of Grehue (Gregory, Grewhe). The modern orthography is Ouidah.

[2] K. G. Davies, *The Royal African Company* (London, 1957), pp. 17–22, 42–44; P. Chemin-Dupontes, *Les Compagnies de colonisation en Afrique occidentale sous Colbert* (Paris, 1903), pp. 89–90, 102; Pierre Bonnassieux, *Les grandes compagnies de commerce. Étude pour servir à l'histoire de la colonisation* (Paris, 1892), pp. 225–33, 369.

[3] Davies, pp. 229–30.

and the beach and was placed under the nominal control of the company's agent-general on the Gold Coast. After 1730 when the decline of the Royal African Company as a trading monopoly was complete, it continued for a period to own and administer the fort with the help of a government subsidy. Shortly before its affairs were finally liquidated, control of the fort passed to the Merchant Adventurers.

French companies were even more transient. Between 1664 and 1684 the privileges of the *Compagnie des Indes Occidentales* on the African coast were inherited by three short-lived successors, passing finally to the *Compagnie de Guinée* which lasted from 1685 till 1713. The latter company was accorded the *assiento* in 1701, only to lose it to the English by the treaty of Utrecht. It had been a doubtful advantage: the *Compagnie de Guinée* never fulfilled the terms of its monopoly—namely, to furnish 4,800 slaves annually to the Spanish colonies and an additional 3,000 to the French Antilles.[1] Its sole achievement at Whydah was the construction of the fort of Saint-Louis in 1704, taken over later by the *Compagnie des Indes* in 1720 till the ruin of its trade by the Seven Years War. From then till it was eventually abandoned in 1797, the fort was owned and administered by the French Crown.

The evidence of the early traders suggests that Whydah thrived best on the slave trade during the half-century before the town came under the control of the Abomey kingdom. Both Bosman and the French officer Du Casse agree that the Gen markets to the west were good for no more than about 300 slaves a year.[2] But Whydah, according to Du Casse, supplied some 14,000 or 15,000 slaves a year to English factors in the 1680's. Another French observer a decade later saw 2,300 slaves sold there in six months, and claimed that at least 200 a month might be obtained, if transport was available.[3] However good the market, the roadstead was a dangerous one, surf-bound with a strong easterly current, particularly between April and July when, noted Bosman, 'dismal accidents are very frequent . . . great quantities of goods are lost, and many men drowned; for the sea-burning is so violent, and rolls so, that a canoe full of people is

---

[1] André Du Casse, *Les Négriers ou le traffic des esclaves* (Paris, 1938), pp. 31–32, 35.

[2] André Du Casse in Paul Roussier (ed.), *L'Établissement d'Issiny 1687–1702* (Paris, 1935), p. 14; Bosman, xvi, 473–4. Lieutenant Du Casse was ordered to survey the commerce of the Guinea Coast in 1687 and 1688. He was followed by the Chevalier d'Amon on a similar mission in 1698 and 1701–2.

[3] D'Amon in Roussier, pp. 82–83.

over-turned, and the canoe shattered into splinters in a minute'.[1] But to the experienced Bosman the natural hazards were well worth risking at Whydah where the brokers were 'so diligent in the slave-trade, that they are able to deliver one thousand slaves every month, if there are no ships at Jakin'.[2]

Rivalry between the Hueda kingdom of Savi and Whydah and the Adja dynasty at Allada which controlled the market at Jakin is a feature of the pre-Abomey period and an early indication of one of the permanent results of European contact for the coastal lineages— competition for the role of middleman. Alternative supplies of slaves at Jakin could make 'a very considerable alteration' to the amount of business done at Whydah; and the generous terms of trade offered by the King of Allada to encourage the Frenchman d'Amon to open factories there in 1698 suggest that the European traders derived great advantage from the rivalry between the Hueda and the Adja.[3] But the animosity appears to have been confined to the merchant chiefs on either side:

the King of Great Ardra, through whose territories most of the slaves are obliged to pass, when ships are there, to favour his own subjects, very commonly shuts up all the passes to Fida by a very strict prohibition; upon which his subjects are obliged to deal by stealth with those of Fida (against whose King he is an irreconcilable enemy), which yet they continually do, seeming not much concerned at their Kings' disputes.[4]

On the other hand, King Agbangla of Savi in Bosman's time seems to have been even weaker than his rival and the victim of his own officials who robbed him as shamelessly as Europeans. He had been enthroned by European factors, in preference to his elder brother, and presumably could be dethroned by them. His only respite in the commercial feud with Allada came in about 1680 when the northern kingdom was invaded by Oyo Yoruba: 'and these all being horsed, and a war-like nation, in a short time mastered half of the King of Ardra's territories', before retiring after great carnage.[5] It does not appear that the Yoruba at this date wished direct access to the mari-time markets. But it was a sign that the arrogance on the part of Allada that had provoked the war would not be tolerated in the Fon

[1] Bosman, xvi, 476.   [2] Ibid., p. 479.
[3] Cf. the early embassies sent by Tohonu of Allada to the court of Phillip IV of Spain in 1658 and to Versailles in 1670. Henri Labouret and Paul Rivet (eds.), Le Royaume d'Arda et son évangélisation au XVIIᵉ siècle (Paris, 1929), pp. 14, 19.
[4] Bosman, xvi, 479.   [5] Ibid., p. 506.

and Yoruba interior, and that trade had in no way strengthened the coastal kingdoms or supplied a noticeable advantage from European firearms. There was, however, a considerable fiscal advantage for the Hueda king whose own slaves were sold at 25 per cent. above the market price. There was a general duty of one rix-dollar on every slave sold in the kingdom of Savi, levied by three officials. In the case of slaves sold in the king's presence at Savi there was a royal duty of three rix-dollars; 'yet some of his subjects are so fly as to fetch their money for their slaves by night, or at unseasonable times, and consequently cheat him', confessed Bosman; 'and on account that we have continual occasion to make use of them, we cannot deny them their money whenever they demand it'.[1]

These lax controls in the Whydah slave market and the steady supply locally and from markets 'sometimes two hundred miles deep in the country' help to explain the heavy investments made there by the companies. In 1685 exports by the Royal African Company to the Whydah factories were second only to the Windward Coast in value; and in 1701 the £14,878 worth of goods destined for the Slave Coast exceeded the value of goods sent to any other region where the company traded. By about 1716 the slave trade at Whydah probably reached its zenith, when the French were exporting nearly 6,000 slaves a year, the English and Portuguese nearly 7,000 together, and the Dutch 1,500.[2] The price of slaves cannot be accurately determined, except in terms of the trade 'ounce'; and this unit of account, as on the Gold Coast, was made up of assorted European goods—cloths, cowries, beads, guns, powder, rum, tobacco, and iron bars—valued locally in ounces, but varying greatly in their original purchase price. The cost of a slave in European goods in the 1650's and 1660's was about £3 (or eight ounces).[3] After 1669 the price of slaves in European goods increased to about £8, partly because of the increased price in Europe for certain items of trade—notably gunpowder—but more perhaps because of increased competition from privateers.[4] The Frenchman d'Amon blamed the latter for the reckless over-bidding and payment of presents and bribes to the brokers which had raised local prices for

[1] Bosman, xvi, 488.
[2] Simone Berbain, *Le Comptoir français de Juda* (*Ouidah*) *au XVIIIe siècle* (Mémoire de l'I.F.A.N., No. 3, Paris, 1942), p. 52 n.
[3] Davies, p. 236.
[4] On the Gold Coast the price of a slave rose to £16 or £17 by 1712. Davies, p. 237.

slaves by the time of his second visit in 1701: 'les grands nombres d'interlopes anglois qu'on nomme les dix pour cent, qui négocient sur cette coste ont mis la traite sur ce mauvais pied, il me paraît qu'il sera difficile d'y remédier et de remettre les choses en l'estat ou elles estoient'.[1] Against the interlopers the forts were useless except as storehouses. And in 1721 the Portuguese from Bahia brought fresh competition and constructed a fort of their own, as the companies which had supplanted them in the Bight of Benin gave up the pretence of monopoly, and the Savi and Allada kingdoms yielded ground to the Fon.

Seizing the opportunity provided by the death of the King of Allada in 1725, King Agaja intervened in a contested succession and made the southern kingdom tributary to Abomey.[2] Tempted further by this easy success and the stocks of arms and cannon taken and angered by the sharp practices of the Hueda middlemen, Agaja invested Savi in 1727 and captured the Whydah market, the factors, and the forts. While the war continued, the Dutch, French, English, and Portuguese traders established subsidiary posts at Keta, Grand Popo, and Jakin. Whydah was retaken in 1729 by the Hueda, and lost when the French fort was blown up. Encouragement of the Hueda by the director of the English fort, Testesole, resulted in a third attack on the town, when Testesole himself was lured into a trap, taken to Allada and tortured to death.[3] The Fon, by then, had entered into the slave trade as brokers, as well as suppliers, and had begun to sell directly to ships anchored off-shore. The rival market of Jakin was sacked in 1732.

The struggle for the control of Whydah market continued for another forty years as a three-cornered dispute between the European factors who had lost their dominance over the weak kings of Savi, the Hueda who drifted back to found new settlements under the shelter of the forts, and the Fon who found it easier to gain a foothold on the coast than to assure the peaceful conditions necessary to trade there.

---

[1] D'Amon in Roussier, p. 106. The 'Ten per cent.' interlopers were separate traders who by an Act of 1698 were required to pay a duty of 10 per cent. *ad valorem* to the Royal African Company on all exports to Africa for the privilege of trading and using the company's forts. Davies, pp. 134–5.

[2] Dunglas, i. 149; Archibald Dalzel, *The History of Dahomey, An Inland Kingdom of Africa; compiled from Authentic Memoirs, with An Introduction and Notes* (London, 1793), p. 7; Pruneau de Pommegorge in A. Walckenaer (ed.), *Collections des relations de voyages*, xi (Paris, 1842), 183–211; William Snelgrave, *A New Account of Some Parts of the Guinea Coast* (London, 1734), pp. 19, 112–20.　　　　　　　　　　　　　　　　　[3] Snelgrave, p. 123.

During the reign of Agaja's successor, Tegbessu, the Fon gradually enforced their conditions on the directors of the forts who were weakened by rivalries between themselves, lack of naval support from Europe, and by the position of the Portuguese in the local market. Despite regulations to the contrary, the staples of trade from Bahia to the Slave Coast were gold and tobacco. The first item tempted the personnel of other European factories to sell slaves to the Bahia merchants on their own account, rather than to the declining companies; the second, a coveted article of consumption in the native markets, could be imported cheaply from Brazil and sold at about six times its original price to the French and English who found it essential for their trade. Tegbessu at the beginning of his reign cut short an attempt on the part of the director of the Portuguese fort to decrease the amount of gold and tobacco flowing into the Whydah market by limiting the number of vessels permitted to trade from Brazil.[1] In June 1743 the fort was destroyed and its director Bazilio and his deputy were expelled to Bahia. During the next five years, before another official was sent, Tegbessu assumed the right to appoint two Portuguese directors himself—one a chaplain, the other an adventurer.

The French fort between 1704 and 1779 was in the hands of no less than twenty-three directors. Six of these died on the coast; six others were expelled by the Fon authorities at Whydah on various charges arising from their resentment of Abomey jurisdiction over their Hueda labourers or, more frequently, from ill-judged attempts to prevent their European personnel from trading with Fon brokers on their own account. This tendency towards open privateering was well summed up by the French director, Levet, in 1745.

La désunion et le désordre que je trouvay à mon arrivée en ce fort ne me permirent pas d'abord de remédier à un nombre d'abus qu'une longue pratique sembloit avoir donné force de loy, entr'autres le commerce particulier . . . il se faisoit icy comme dans un marché public: chaque chambre était autant de cantine où l'on abreuvoit les négres marchands que les officiers s'arrachoient les uns aux autres.[2]

In effect by the 1760's all officials were private merchants in league

---

[1] It was intended by the authorities at Bahia to allow only twenty-four ships every two years to sail to the Mina Coast. A. F. C. Ryder, 'The Re-establishment of Portuguese Factories on the Costa da Mina to the mid eighteenth century', *Journal of the Historical Society of Nigeria*, i, No. 3 (1958), p. 171.

[2] Levet in Berbain, p. 65 n.

with one or more of the native brokers, buying up slave lots with goods from the forts and selling them at the highest price to ships' captains. At least one of the French directors, d'Olivier de Montaguère, went into partnership with a Bordeaux captain, supplied merchandise on credit, and levied a personal tax on all transactions carried on in the fort. His commercial sleight of hand carried him too far; and when his agents sold better goods to Oyo traders at the Cana market than to King Kpengla of Abomey (who had been fobbed off with inferior articles at the same price), they were seized and murdered and d'Olivier himself was expelled.[1]

There were over thirty English directors at Whydah between 1700 and 1807, when the fort was abandoned. After the example of Testesole, none of them offered any opposition to the Fon. One of the last of them, Lionel Abson, remained there for the unusually long time of thirty-six years, his movements carefully sanctioned by the King of Abomey.[2]

By the 1740's Whydah became a Fon colony: settlers populated three wards in the town, two of which were under the authority of an Abomey official, the *Yovogan*, and the third under a war chief. They were quickly unpopular because of their private exactions on trade. An early *Yovogan* was killed in 1744 during an attack on the English fort; another was driven out by the Hueda in 1763, but restored—this time with the help of English cannon. A formal truce between the Hueda and the Fon was concluded with the help of Lionel Abson in 1772.

The period of most active slave-trading under Abomey rule coincided with the first phase of the long struggle between the Hueda and the Fon in the late 1720's and early 1730's when ready exports were provided by the war at Whydah and Jakin. For the rest of the 1730's some 6,000 slaves were shipped annually to Bahia alone.[3] During the remainder of the century French and English exports from Whydah probably declined, while Portuguese shipments remained fairly high. It has been shown that French privateers from Nantes between 1729 and 1733 sent eight vessels to Whydah out of a total of sixty-one trading on the African coast—more than to any other

---

[1] Dunglas, ii. 23; cf. Hazoumé, p. 31 n., where a different history of the d'Olivier family is given.

[2] Capt. John Adams, *Remarks on the Country extending from Cape Palmas to the River Congo, including observations on the Manners and Customs of the Inhabitants* (London, 1823), pp. 52–53.

[3] Ryder, pp. 169, 180.

single point.[1] But as the wars which provided this harvest continued, the port received a decreasing proportion of Nantes privateers. The French slaver, Labarthe, who made many visits to the Slave Coast, observed a decline in Whydah exports from 10,150 slaves in 1776 to only 3,605 in 1787, which he attributed to increased customs and the monopoly of Fon brokers over sales.[2]

The evidence is not conclusive as regards total numbers, but it seems likely that stricter customs, the rise of alternative ports outside Abomey control, and fluctuations in supplies from the interior were the three principal factors influencing the volume of slave exports from Whydah.

The question of regular supply was of the utmost importance not merely for the Fon but also for their neighbours. From the reign of Agaja till the early nineteenth century, the Fon themselves remained in tributary relationship to Oyo, and it is probable that despite wars with the outlying Yoruba provinces, diplomatic relations between Oyo and Abomey were sufficiently good to ensure that the Cana market was one steady source of slaves for Fon brokers on the coast. They were also purchased from the Bariba and Djugo in northern Dahomey via the Mahi at the Ombadjo market.[3] Apart from this peaceful supply, the principal source was raiding. By the reign of Ghezo in the nineteenth century annual military campaigns had become a complementary feature to the institution of annual ancestral 'customs' for which sacrifices were required. The wars fought by Tegbessu and the two kings who succeeded him, Kpengla and Agonglo, were fought for many reasons of which the sale of prisoners to the coast was only one. The principal targets of Fon campaigns in the eighteenth century after their conquest of Savi were the Mahi to the north, the Za Yoruba on the upper Weme, the Wemenu on the lower Weme, the Tchi and Watyi on the Mono, and the Gun of Porto-Novo, Ekpe, and Badagri. Revenge for insults (real or imagined) was the motive for raids on the Za in the 1740's,

---

[1] Gaston Martin, *Nantes au XVIIIᵉ siècle. L'Ère des négriers (1714–1774) d'après des documents inédits* (Paris, 1931), pp. 207, 218.

[2] P. Labarthe, *Voyage à la Côte de Guinée, ou Description des Côtes d'Afrique, depuis le cap Tagrin jusqu'au cap de Lopez-Gonsalves* (Paris, 1803), p. 136. Cf. E. Donnan (ed.), *Documents Illustrative of the History of the Slave Trade to America* (4 vols. Washington, 1931), ii. 598 n. From a Privy Council report for 1789 it was estimated that a total of 74,200 slaves were exported annually from the Gambia to Loando. Of the ports, Keta and Grand Popo were attributed an export of 100 a year, Whydah 4,500, Porto-Novo and Badagri 3,500, Lagos and Benin 3,500.

[3] Dunglas, ii. 8.

and against the Wemenu in 1775 and again, in alliance with Oyo, in 1786. From 1775, too, in the reign of Kpengla, are recorded the first instances of raids to supply labour for royal plantations, which may have been convenient stock-piling for trade with Whydah, but more likely was an effort to increase the food-supply for the population of the Abomey plateau from farmlands on the right bank of the Cuffo river. Raiding for supplies during not infrequent periods of drought on the plateau may also be counted as a reason for the military activity of the Fon kingdom. Finally, commercial rivalry with the Gun and a desire to preserve for Whydah a market monopoly of trade with Europeans were strong incentives for the elimination of Jakin as a slave-port in the 1730's and for campaigns against Porto-Novo and the villages to the south-east. In 1778 the Ekpe slave market was destroyed on the sand-spit opposite Porto-Novo. Badagri was raided twice, in 1783 and again in 1784 (with the permission of Oyo), when the town defences were breached and 6,000 heads taken to Abomey. Two years later, without the permission of the *Alafin* of Oyo, a Fon army descended on the remaining 'free' port at Porto-Novo and took prisoner a large number of French traders who were ransomed to the director of the French port at Whydah for £4,600. For his temerity, King Kpengla was warned by the *Alafin* that Porto-Novo was an Oyo 'calabash' and the greater part of the ransom was sent to the Yoruba capital.[1]

By the last quarter of the eighteenth century the Abomey kingdom under Agonglo had reached the limit of its territorial power, though not the end of its vitality as a military state. Apart from gifts and taxes levied at the time of the annual 'customs' at Abomey, the principal source of revenues was at Whydah. Duties there were numerous. From the time a slave ship anchored in the roadstead, the master was required to pay the value of twelve slaves, or about £100, if the vessel was three-masted, the value of nine slaves if two-masted.[2] With the permission of the *Yovogan* captains landed their goods on the beach; and once ashore, the trader was burdened by the necessity to employ a host of messengers, porters, and servants provided by the *Yovogan* and to pay fixed duties to officials and the King of Abomey. Servants guarded his goods; messengers put him

---

[1] Dunglas, ii. 18, 21; Dalzel, pp. 190–1, 194–8.

[2] Paul Erdmann Isert, *Voyages en Guinée et dans les îles caraïbes en Amérique* (Paris, 1793), p. 135. 'Cette circonstance a souvent engagé les Français à abattre leur mât de derrière avant d'arriver à la rade, pour épargner les cinq esclaves' (*sic*); Labarthe, p. 136.

in touch with slave brokers; guides conducted slaves to the shore; carriers, small boys, and washerwomen attached themselves to the trader's retinue. And the *Yovogan* or his spies were present at all stages to see the official channels were not by-passed. In 1791 the English slaver, Johnston, recorded in his journal the details of his payments to local authorities. The *Yovogan* received two slaves, rum, cloth, and a Dane gun, 'as Customary on opening trade'.[1] A guide and two messengers cost equal measures of rum and cloth; miscellaneous boys and servants were paid goods to the value of £13. 4s. To the King of Abomey were sent two slaves, cloth, twenty-five Dane guns, powder, cowries, and rum, to the value of thirty-eight trade ounces, or about £40. All this gave Johnston the right to embark only 148 slaves whose price averaged eleven ounces, or between £11 and £20, depending on the type of goods used to make up the ounce. The slaves were bought from six different Fon brokers. It is noticeable that only the king was paid in powder, and none of the brokers were given guns. The insistence on a royal monopoly of the arms traffic has also been commented on by another trader at this period: 'Car si l'on trouve chez un Nègre plus d'un chapeau plein de poudre à la fois on le regarde comme un rebelle; et il est vendu sans autre forme de procès pour le compte du roi.'[2] So long as the *Yovogan* of Whydah (also spied on by the king's agents) remained viceroy, diplomat, and market-master, the chances of Europeans circumventing the system were small.

Apart from furnishing slaves, Whydah in the last two decades of the eighteenth century had recovered its old position as a market centre for lagoon traffic from the Mina and Gen territory to the west. Cloth, salt, and foodstuffs were ferried from Little Popo, Gridgi, and Grand Popo. These latter ports, because of their good defensive position on the creeks, had escaped from Abomey control. The slave trade, however, had made its mark there: the Dutch had had a small fort at Little Popo in the 1690's, and the Danes built one at Keta as late as 1784. The trader Isert, in Danish service, who visited the area in 1785 found a large native market at Gridgi, evidence of wealth in the houses of the lineage chiefs, and worldly trading connexions in the person of a native merchant named Lathe who spoke

---

[1] Jeorge A. Plimpton (ed.), *The Journal of an African Slaver, 1789–1792* (Worcester, Mass., 1930), pp. 22–23. Cf. Labarthe, p. 265, who lists charges paid by French slavers.

[2] Isert, p. 137.

English, Portuguese, and Danish and had two sons abroad, one in England and the other in Portugal.[1] But by the end of the eighteenth century wealth came from ivory rather than slaves and the area was singled out as an oasis of 'legitimate' trade on the Slave Coast, both by Captain Adams and by the naval editor of *The Merchants' and Mariners' African Guide* whose remarks apply to the coast in the late eighteenth and early nineteenth centuries respectively.

The houses are well constructed and generally two stories high with stone steps. There is a good market with the most abundant supplies of stock of every species, and a diversity of fruits the most delicious. The natives and chiefs are respectful, honest, and desirous of trade. Ivory abounds here in endless quantities, which is constantly sent from the inland towns to the Northward by corresponding traders to the coast; few vessels call here which makes them tractable and easy to trade with.[2]

Trade goods in demand in the Popo towns were the same as at other ports to windward and to leeward—silks and Manchester cottons, guns and powder, valued in ounces—but more highly than on the Gold Coast or elsewhere in the Bight. The method of conducting business at Little Popo or Grand Popo was pleasantly unsophisticated compared with the strict regulations at Whydah.

The mode of proceeding is thus on arriving, it is necessary to go on shore, (for the natives will not bring their trade to the ship) with samples of each of your articles of merchandize, and pronounce before an assembly of the Caboceers their various prices, which you must maintain as high as possible, (though obliged sometimes to abate.) When the prices are agreed on, by both parties, a piece of cloth and a few gallons of rum are paid to each Caboceer, for custom; upon which you open trade.
The owner of a tooth of ivory sells it through the medium of a broker, who according to its size makes a demand, which never fails to be exorbitant, however you must patiently abate until he reduces it to a price you can afford to give; observe, that independent of the assortment that is given, the broker on commencing will desire you to hold back a certain number of ackeys in proportion to the size of the tooth, which afterwards are to be paid to him.[3]

The commercial development of Porto-Novo also dates from a relatively late period. In the history of the Gun paramountcy, the

[1] Isert, p. 120.
[2] Lieut. Edward Bold, R.N. (ed.), *The Merchants' and Mariners' African Guide; containing an accurate description of the Coast, Bays, Harbours, and adjacent Islands of West Africa* (London, 1822), p. 62.
[3] Bold, p. 62.

first slave trader, one de Campos, does not arrive till the 1750's, and the founding of a Yoruba quarter and a Brazilian quarter—two indications of the direction of trade to and from the town—did not take place till the reign of King Ayikpe in the late 1770's.[1] Captain Adams in the next two decades considered Porto-Novo the most populous of the Bight towns next to Benin with 7,000 to 10,000 people. The major trade route inland was to Oyo, a journey of about nine days, where the Gun, like the Fon, paid tribute. In the local market, held every six days, he found an abundance of European goods— cloths, tobacco, iron, corals, cowries, and beads alongside African cloth from Oyo and Ijebu, hides, potash soap, and livestock.[2]

To the south-east of Porto-Novo, Badagri is first mentioned as a slave-mart in 1740. A refugee town for Hueda, Wemenu, and Gun, the confusions of its unhappy history are explained partly by these mixed origins, and partly by its geographical position on the left bank of the Porto-Novo and Lagos lagoon which made it an uneasy site for defence and alliance, a prey to stronger neighbours, and a key market on the trade route between the Gun and Yoruba, and later between the Egba and the sea.

Of the eight wards existing at Badagri, two—Jegba and Awanjigo— still trace their lineage chiefs back to the 1730's when they were founded by Hueda driven out of the Savi and Jakin area by the Fon.[3] During or shortly after this foundation, Jegba tradition has it that a Portuguese slaver[4] arrived with a Hueda interpreter and went into partnership with the senior lineage chief, or *Akran*, of the Jegba ward. His barracoons were built on the other side of the lagoon near the beach, and his supplies of slaves were bought through Badagri middlemen from Yoruba markets to the north and from Porto-Novo. Further Fon pressure on the coastal Hueda and raids on the Wemenu drove a number of other refugee groups to settle on the high ground near the town with the lagoon and low, swampy terrain for protection. Three distinct Hueda lineages founded Ahoviko, Boeko, and Asago wards, between the 1750's and early 1780's; refugees from the Weme area were given land by *Akran* Sobu and by *Akran* Jiwu on the sites of Ganho ward in about 1740 and in Possuko ward in 1775. The latter group provided title-holders for the position

[1] Akindélé and Aguessy, pp. 72, 73.　　[2] Adams, pp. 82–84, 90.

[3] The material for this section was collected during field work among the Gun and Yoruba of Badagri, 1956–7. See, too, T. A. Ola Avoseh, *A Short History of Badagri* (Lagos, 1938).

[4] Called 'Freemingo', 'George', or 'Huntokonu'.

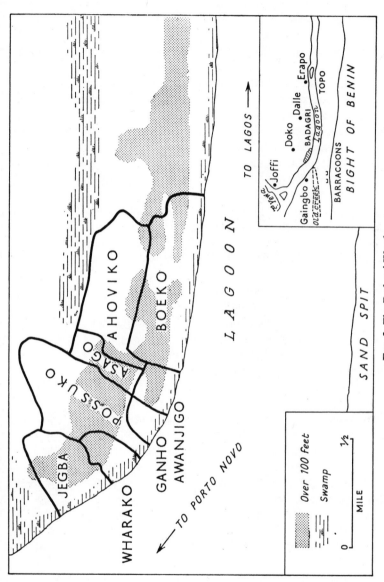

Fig. 2. The Badagri Wards.

of *Possu* or war-chief of the *Akran*, when they occupied the most vulnerable quarter of the town open to attack from the north-west. The last of the ward-founders to maintain a distinct tradition came from Porto-Novo in the 1750's and settled under the protection of the *Akran* in Wharako ward on the lagoon front.

Throughout its history the town wards occupied by Gun and Hueda in the west and east, and by Wemenu in the centre, intermarried among themselves and with the Yoruba. There were two sources of division from connexions outside the town: the *Finhento* title-holders of Wharako ward went to Porto-Novo for consecration and remained sensitive to politics in that quarter; a number of Lagos chiefs married Badagri women from Ahoviko ward; and these alliances were contributory factors to the civil wars that plagued the town in the early nineteenth century.[1] An additional source of weakness was the limited authority of the *Akran*. There is some evidence that he had a judicial function as president of a court of ward elders. But succession to the *Akran* title itself was complicated by a rotary system of election from among the six segments of the Jegba ward lineage. There is a record of thirteen *Akran* from the 1730's till the 1860's. Till the time of *Akran* Soba V, only four families are mentioned in Jegba tradition. When Soba was killed during a Fon raid in 1783, his war-chief, *Possu*, usurped the title, only to loose it when the town fell a second time in 1784. Thereafter, the *Akran* title was restored to the Jegba families, but their exact genealogical connexions with the founding families are tenuous and possibly confused by the efforts of individual claimants to trace descent from previous title-holders by the most direct means. In any case, after the devastation of 1784, three of the original families no longer seem to have supplied title-holders; and since that time the *Akran* are provided from the Jigboko family, counted as direct descendants of the original founders, and the Ganyiko family which segmented from the senior line (it is claimed) before 1784.

By the end of the eighteenth century Badagri still had not fully recovered from the Fon attacks. Like Lagos, where there was only a small domestic market for slaves and where the major export was cloth, Badagri awaited the impetus of events in the Yoruba interior and the arrival of Europeans opposed to the slave trade before becoming ports in the Bight equal in historical importance to Whydah.

[1] See below, p. 48.

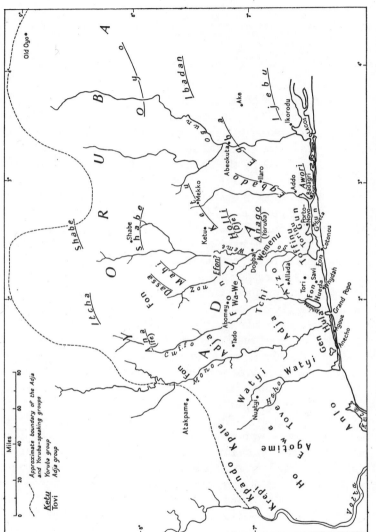

FIG. 3. Distribution of ethnic groups on the Western Slave Coast and interior, nineteenth century.

CHAPTER II

The Decline of the Slave Trade

THE abandonment of the forts at Whydah marked the end of a century and a half of continuous contact by Europeans with the markets of the Western Slave Coast. Nearly four decades elapsed before a semblance of 'castle' trade revived. The French fort was reoccupied in 1842 by the agents of the firm of Victor Régis of Marseilles; and three years later the remains of Fort William provided a base for the factors of the Gold Coast trader, Thomas Hutton. The symbols of the protection of European commercial interests around which had grown the French and English quarters quickly decayed. A French officer wrote in 1856: 'Aujourd'hui les bastions s'écroulent, les vieux canons de fer, enfouis dans l'herbe au milieu des débris de leurs affûts, sont condamnés à un éternel silence, et la luxuriante végétation des tropiques a envahi et comblé les fossés.'[1] The market had changed. The last vestiges of the old monopoly companies housed the stores, weights, and measures of the palm-oil merchants; the inner courtyard of Fort Saint-Louis was cluttered with gear for making casks; and the officers' rooms were turned into a counting-house.

It was not an easy or particularly profitable change before the 1850's. The transition period from slaves to palm-oil in the coastal markets of the area between the Volta and the Ogun rivers was accompanied by intense political and economic rivalry between great and small lineages with a stake in the material wealth and the firepower that accrued from European contact, and by the advent of new types of settlers—both African and European—who were not to be hemmed into the small quarter of a company concession. Between the Abolition Act of 1807 and the destruction of the slave factories at Lagos in 1851, there were scarcely more white traders on this section of the coast than in the days of Bosman; and apart from a few explorers and a handful of missionaries, there was little depth to European penetration of the forest kingdoms. But if European

---

[1] A. Répin, 'Voyage au Dahomey, par M. le Dr Répin, ex-chirurgien de la marine impériale, texte et dessins inédits', *Le Tour du monde. Nouveau journal des voyages* (Paris, 1863), p. 70.

business was still on the whole confined to the coast, its purpose was to suppress by persuasion or by force the slave trade conducted with Africans since the sixteenth century. It was a challenge to which the Fon, the Gun, and the Yoruba responded in their own ways. And the reaction of indigenous authorities to European demands in the first half of the century explains much in the course and results of alien settlement, administration, and expansion beyond the coast during the second.

Equally important for the future of the coastal markets were events north of Old Oyo. The Fulani invasion of the Oyo empire in the 1820's threw the Yoruba paramountcies into an 'era of anarchy and disruption'[1] from which there emerged a new war-camp at Ibadan and a densely populated settlement of Egba remnants at Abeokuta after 1830. Moreover, the decline of Old Oyo, the pressure of the Fulani, and the Yoruba wars released the kingdom of Abomey from its humiliating tributary obligations to the *Alafin*. The Fon army was free to attack the Mahi, the Yoruba of Save, and the Ewe of Atakpame with impunity and able to enforce tribute from Porto-Novo, Badagri, and the petty chiefdoms south-west of the Mono river.[2] The weakening of Oyo suzerainty over the Egbado and Awori towns lying between the Ogun and the kingdom of Ketu, encouraged the Gun of Porto-Novo and Badagri and the Yoruba of Lagos and Ijebu to raid for slaves on their own account and offer alternative slave markets to Whydah with lower export duties and less rigid controls. But after 1830, as the Egba consolidated their position at Abeokuta, the Gun and Ijebu markets were threatened by a new rival and purveyor. Harried by Ibadan and by the Yoruba of the south-east, the Egba under the leadership of Shodeke fought for their share of the arms traffic to the interior and for a safe route of their own to the coast. This entailed no less than reducing the Egbado and Awori towns to acknowledge Abeokuta as the new successor to Old Oyo. It entailed, too, containing the Ijebu on the one hand, and on the other, the Fon, both of whom were keen competitors for slaves, as the caravans that had formerly brought large numbers of Hausa and others were cut off.

The Ijebu threw in their lot with Ibadan; and in 1832, operating from Egbado country, they blockaded Egba supplies from the coast

[1] Saburi O. Biobaku, *The Egba and their Neighbours 1842–1872* (Oxford, 1957), pp. 18, 19–26.

[2] Dunglas, ii. 73–76; Forbes, i. 16–17.

through Badagri and Porto-Novo. They were routed by Shodeke with the assistance of Adele, the *Ologun* of Lagos, who was rewarded with a present of 300 slaves for his help. The Egba had entered into the commercial and political rivalries of the coastal chiefdoms. Henceforth, the fortunes of the ruling lineages of Porto-Novo, Badagri, and Lagos were made or unmade by the policies of their two powerful and mutually hostile neighbours at Abeokuta and Abomey. Of the two, the former was the immediate menace.

From the first, the Egba sought to establish their control of the key market town of Okeodan on the right bank of the Yewa river. As their raids on other Egbado towns intensified between 1832 and 1836, and Ilobi, Ilaro, Erinja, and Eyo were attacked in turn, Okeodan filled with refugees who founded wards under their own lineage chiefs.[1] When the incentive for gain overcame their animosity, they acted as brokers for the Egba slave trade to Porto-Novo and Badagri; and growing wealthy and ambitious, they enforced tribute of their own from Shagbo, Okebode, Ipokia, and Ihumbo, till their town was sacked by the Fon in 1848. But its commercial importance did not decline; and in the early 1860's Okeodan was still described as 'the great slave market of the Egbas'.[2]

The Awori Yoruba, caught between the Egba and the Ijebu, fared similarly. In 1842 Otta acknowledged a tributary relationship with Abeokuta and opened a trade route for the Egba to Ebute Metta on the Lagos lagoon. For a period, till 1845, an Egba force stationed near Addo prevented the Awori there from interfering with the supply line from Badagri.

Lagos, unlike the ports to the west, was hardly a thriving centre for the slave trade before the 1830's, though the purchase of domestic slaves from Porto-Novo, Badagri, and Ijebu had been noted by Captain John Adams at the turn of the century.[3] Its rise to commercial significance owed much to the interior struggles which provided its material for export, and still more to the presence of a new type of slave factor from Brazil who appeared on the Western Slave Coast towards the end of the eighteenth century and kept the slave trade vigorously alive. Unlike the interlopers of previous years, the Brazilian

[1] E. V. S. Thomas, 'Historical Survey of the Towns of Ilaro, Ilobi, Ajilite and Ilashe in the Ilaro Division' (typescript, 4 Jan. 1933), ff. 5–6. Okeodan is of early nineteenth-century origin, though the precedence of the different ward-founders is disputed.

[2] C.O. 147/3, Glover to Russell, 6 Nov. 1863.

[3] Adams, p. 96.

creoles were permanent settlers in the ports of the Bight of Benin.[1]
Their origins were diverse; their language was Portuguese; and they
had in common commercial abilities, as well as in most cases part-
African parentage which enabled them to rise to positions of confidence and influence in the coastal chiefdoms, while their business
connexions in Bahia and Havanna made them ideal entrepreneurs
during the last intensive phase of the Atlantic slave trade.

Such was Francisco Felix Da Souza who drifted in from Brazil
about 1788 and was for a time commander of the Portuguese fort
at Whydah.[2] Turning to the slave trade, he worked on his own account
as a broker at Badagri and Anecho where he became a creditor of
the King of Dahomey, Adandozan. While trying to reclaim his debts
he was imprisoned at Abomey; and there he entered into an alliance
(cemented by a blood-pact) with Prince Gangpe—later King Ghezo.
Released with Gangpe's help, he supplied his 'brother' with rum and
tobacco to increase the number of the prince's partisans and enable
him to seize power at Abomey in 1818. Ghezo reciprocated by in-
stalling Da Souza at Whydah as a Fon customs official with the title
of *Chacha*, and with the privilege of conducting the king's own business with visiting vessels. He was, in effect, the royal broker with
ample occasion to supplement his share of the revenues by private
imports and exports of his own. His riches and hospitality became
the legend of the coast;[3] and he charmed even missionary opponents
with manners that were 'easy and graceful and exhibited the highly
finished gentleman'.[4] The stricter organization of tolls at Whydah
province during Ghezo's reign probably owes much to him; and he
was instrumental in encouraging the king to divert slave labour to
palm-oil production in which he and his sons engaged as conditions
of trade were modified.

There were others, Brazilians and ex-slaves who had travelled
abroad, who appear briefly in the records in positions of affluence

[1] Pierre Verger in *Les Afro-Américains* (Mémoires de l'Institut Français
d'Afrique Noire, Dakar, 1952), pp. 11–104. The best account of the Portuguese
Brazilians is by J. F. de Almeida Prado, 'Les Relations de Bahia (Brésil) avec le
Dahomey', *Revue d'histoire des colonies*, xli (1954), 167–226; but it suffers from
a lack of source references.

[2] Hazoumé, pp. 4–5, 27–30; Dunglas, ii. 40–41; de Almeida Prado, p. 183.

[3] Brantz Mayer (ed.), *Captain Canot; or, Twenty Years of an African Slaver.
Being an Account of His Career and Adventures on the Coast, in the Interior, on
Shipboard, and in the West Indies* (New York, 1854), pp. 262–3.

[4] M.M.A., Thomas Birch Freeman, ['History of West Africa'], (untitled typescript, n.d.), f. 248.

and power. The wealthiest merchant at Porto-Novo in John Adams's day had been a certain 'Tammata', a former Hausa slave who had been to France. At Little Popo (Anecho), George A. Lawson, a Fanti from Accra who had been a steward on a slave vessel, returned to West Africa in 1812 to found the Lawson lineage and build his compound of 'New London', where he dealt in slaves and palm-oil alike, saluted all flags, and supplied false information to naval officers. Also at Anecho, on the opposite side of the lagoon, was a colony of Brazilians headed by one 'Pedro Kogio' who raided for slaves and bought Manchester cottons from the Gold Coast firm of F. and A. Swanzy. In the 1820's Domingo Martinez succeeded 'Tammata' at Porto-Novo. He exhibited a similar willingness to rival Da Souza in the slave business and traded, at the same time, 'on palm-oil account' with the respectable Gold Coast firm of Forster & Smith.[1]

For, as the vigilance of the Preventive Squadron increased and legal ways were found to enable it to prosecute its task, the slave traders devised methods of their own to elude detection. The methods of the 1820's were described by Lander:

As soon as a vessel arrives at her place of destination, the crew discharge her light cargoe, with the manacles intended for the slaves, and land the captain at the same time. The vessel then cruises along the coast to take in country cloth, ivory, a little gold dust etc., and if a British man-of-war be near, the crew having nothing on board to excite suspicion, in most cases contrive to get their vessel searched whilst trading with the natives. . . . They return to the place where the cargoe had been loaded, and communicate with the captain on shore . . . who then takes the opportunity of acquainting his crew with the exact time in which he will be in readiness to embark. The vessel then cruises a second time up and down the coast, till the appointed day approaches, when she proceeds to take in her living cargoe.[2]

Fast clippers sailing under Spanish, Portuguese, or American flags, defied the naval patrols. There were still rich pickings to be had for commission firms and their agents. Slaves, bought for between £15 and £20 at Whydah and Lagos in the 1830's and 1840's fetched on auction in Brazil (and after import duty) £50 to £80 a head in 1844, rising to as much as £120 in 1846, and declining to £80 in 1847.[3] Professional renegades, like Captain Canot, continued to risk

[1] P.P., 1852, liv (221), Forbes to Fanshawe, 5 Nov. 1849, Encl. 13 in No. 3, p. 19.

[2] Richard Lander, *Records of Captain Clapperton's Last Expedition to Africa* (2 vols. London, 1830), ii, 238–9.

[3] Prices for slaves fluctuated a good deal on both sides of the Atlantic market.

mutiny, prison, and the hazards of other competitors to supply Havanna and Bahia. And if they were eliminated, the Brazilian and Portuguese merchants from Fernandez Zulueta & Co. of Cuba, down to the smaller fry—da Cruz Rios, Gomes Bello, Guerino Antonio, or Lopez Guimaraes of Bahia—were not.

The insertion of the equipment clause in international anti-slavery conventions and the Act of 1839 which authorized the detention of Portuguese (and in practice Brazilian) slave vessels made some difference, however, to the scale of the trade in the western sector of the Bight of Benin. It is difficult to estimate how much. Evidence presented to the Parliamentary Committee of 1842 suggested that trade from Whydah had been 'very much broken up' since 1839: there were no longer to be seen a score or so of vessels waiting for shipments through the surf.[1] But the proceedings of the Mixed Courts and Vice-Admiralty Court at Freetown indicate how few ships operating on the Western Slave Coast were captured and condemned in relation to the coast as a whole.[2] During the twenty years from the establishment of the courts till 1838, the number of vessels prosecuted and condemned numbered 282. In the next decade, following the application of the equipment clause, the annual average of cases heard doubled: some 284 vessels were condemned between 1839 and 1849. A quarter of this total was taken in the first year the clause was enforced. Thereafter, there was a decline in the number of vessels captured, a sharp increase to thirty in 1845, and again a low annual average till the end of the 1840's. Only thirty of the vessels condemned during the decade were bound for, or had loaded at Lagos, Whydah, or Anecho; and half of these were captured in 1845. It is possible that others frequenting these markets were taken on the South American coast; and there is no way of estimating those that eluded capture. The figures merely show that the trade of the Western Slave Coast was not suppressed by naval action; and the

Excessive imports into Brazil between 1846 and 1847 caused the auction price to fall from $600 to $400. The price at Whydah in 1847 for a slave was $70 to $80, and at Lagos £20 in 1849, paid in goods, *pesos*, or cowries. De Almeida Prado, p. 194; Verger, pp. 75–76; Report of the British Commissioner of the Mixed Courts, Rio de Janeiro [1844], *The British and Foreign Anti-Salvery Reporter*, i, No. viii (new series, 1846), p. 117.

[1] P.P., 1842, xi (551), Qq. 769–76, 3969–80.

[2] Commissioners' reports in *The British and Foreign Anti-Slavery Reporter*, iii. 3 (1842), p. 18; v. 16 (1844), pp. 153–4; vi. 14 (1845), p. 128; i. No. viii (new series, 1846), pp. 114–15; ii, No. xx (1847), p. 113; iii, No. xxxiii (1848), pp. 141–2; iv, no. xlii (1849), pp. 98–99; v, No. lviii (1850), p. 151.

capture of vessels shipping slaves from that region was low in proportion to the number of slaves estimated to have been exported from there to Bahia, Cuba, and Rio.[1] From the slavers' point of view 1845 was a particularly bad year: three ships out of Anecho and Lagos were seized with full cargoes; the papers of at least twelve others showed that they were destined for the same area.

But this was not a crippling blow. The business correspondence passing between one of the smaller Brazilian traders at Whydah, José Francisco dos Santos, and the commission firms at Bahia and Rio, indicates that his shipments increased, rather than declined, in the 1840's.[2] His principal difficulty was not obtaining slaves, or exporting them, but importing rum, tobacco, molasses, cottons, knives, and specie for payment—'patacons, onces mexicaines ou pesos, ce qui pour moi est indifférent'.[3] By 1842 the practice of leisurely coasting for several months to make up a cargo had ceased. The better-known beach market of Whydah was avoided; and slaves were marched or transported in canoes to prearranged collecting points to the west and to the east. Transactions were completed as quickly as possible and payment made in 'dollars and dubloons', rather than in goods.[4] The demand for coin increased. The papers of a slave ship captured in 1844 revealed that she had carried a 'consignement, consisting of 1,830 dollars in gold' for Da Souza.[5] And the French palm-oil factor, Blancheley, had no difficulty in getting ready specie to the amount of 2,000 dollars in 1847 from Dos Santos.[6] Cowries were imported in bulk into the Slave Coast market from 1847 by the Hamburg trader Lorenz Diedrichsen.[7] A dollar was worth about half

---

[1] Estimated at about 10,000 a year in 1848 by naval officers. *The British and Foreign Anti-Slavery Reporter*, iv, No. xlii (new series, 1849), pp. 98–99.

[2] Verger, pp. 53–86. The dos Santos letters, Nos. 6–83, show that the numbers of slaves exported by him from Whydah and Anecho, as an agent for merchants in Bahia and Rio, and on his own account, were:

	1844	1845	1846	1847
Males . .	20	32	87	208
Females . .	7	15	78	88
Total . .	27	47	165	296

[3] Dos Santos to da Cruz Rios, 25 May 1845, in Verger, No. 9, p. 63.

[4] P.P., 1842, xi (551), Q. 735.

[5] *The British and Foreign Anti-Slavery Reporter*, vi. 14 (1845), p. 128.

[6] Dos Santos to Francisco Lopez Guimaraes, 22 Dec. 1847, in Verger, No. 83, p. 86.

[7] Dos Santos to Guerino Antonio, 20 Jan. 1847, in Verger, No. 49, p. 74.

a head of cowries (1,000 shells) in 1847; but as the imports increased, the rate for a dollar altered to one and a half heads by 1849; and there was some resistance to using large quantities of them as a medium of exchange at Whydah even in 1847, when Dos Santos reported to a commission firm in Bahia: 'Les nègres font déjà mauvaise figure à recevoir les cauries et ne se donnent guère le travail de se les procurer.'[1]

The dispersal of the slave markets was helped by the topography of the region. Apart from the Lagos estuary, the heavy surf made an outright attack on the barracoons difficult, if not impossible; and the thick bush obscuring the lateral creeks enabled 'the trader in human flesh to ship his cargo where and when least expected'.[2] Such conditions explain the expansion by the Fon of a secondary slave port at Cotonou in the late 1830's.[3] They explain, too, the incentive given to the smaller brokers from Anecho to Lagos to make a precarious but profitable living as agents (or rivals) for Da Souza and Domingo, and the efforts of Domingo himself between 1845 and 1850 to shift his barracoons farther east from Porto-Novo to Ajuda. The argument of those who claimed that the Preventive Squadron could not end the trade (particularly in the Niger Delta) was undoubtedly supported by these facts;[4] and even those who were opposed to the possible withdrawal of the squadron in 1849 admitted that the trade would not be given up so long as it was 'the only means of obtaining that supply of European merchandise which has been made necessary to the peoples' welfare'.[5]

It did not follow, however, that 'fair trade' was an easy remedy or anything more than a supplement rather than an alternative to the

Capt. Lorenz Diedrichsen was a freelance trader who was on the coast in a Flensburg brig from about 1843. He was instrumental in opening up the East African cowrie trade with West Africa. See E. Hieke, *Zur Geschichte des deutschen Handels mit Ostafrika. Wm. O'Swald & Co., 1831–1870* (Hamburg, 1939), pp. 71–72; and below, p. 57.

[1] Dos Santos to Guerino Antonio, 20 Jan. 1847, in Verger, No. 49, p. 74; Forbes, i. 36. There were 2,000 cowries to a head. The cowrie units and exchange rates usually cited from R. F. Burton, *Wanderings in West Africa: from Liverpool to Fernando Po* (London, 1863), pp. 40–45, should not be read as typical of the Bight of Benin markets.

[2] R. F. Burton, *A Mission to Gelele, King of Dahome* (2 vols. London, 1864), i. 69.

[3] J. Lombard, 'Cotonou ville africaine', *Études dahoméennes*, x (1953), 30–31.

[4] For the debate in England on the effectiveness of the Preventive Squadron, see W. L. Mathieson, *Great Britain and the Slave Trade 1839–1865* (London, 1829), chap. iii.

[5] 'Letter from the Rev. H. Townsend to Captain Trotter, R.N. on the African Coast Blockade,' [31 Jan. 1849], F.O., *Slave Trade* (Confidential Print), 403, p. 4.

slave trade, though the belief that the former would in some mysterious way 'be the means of putting an effectual stop' to the latter was expounded as an article of faith by the chief spokesmen of the traders and the Church Missionary Society alike.[1]

With the exception of the agents of Victor Régis, the small number of palm-oil factors on the Western Slave Coast made little progress till the end of the 1840's. By then, there were signs that the African demand for goods rather than specie at Whydah placed the Brazilian slave brokers in the position of having to organize supplies of palm-oil to purchase European cottons, powder, and arms, as the shipments of cheap tobacco and rum from Brazil ran short. Palm-oil was shipped to Bahia by Dos Santos as early as 1846 in the 'pipes' used for the import of rum. Three years later, when Commander Forbes visited Whydah, he saw several new palm-oil plantations belonging to native merchants and a small casking-plant owned by Dos Santos whose 'yard was filled with traders,—some with only a gallon, others having slaves loaded with large calabashes of oil; while dozens of his own slaves were counting out cowries to pay for the produce'.[2] Only by encouraging the production of a new cash crop—and thus an alternative use for captives—can it be said that 'legitimate' trade diminished the number of those who were otherwise destined 'sans cette industrie, à être, comme tant d'autres, entassés pêle-mêle sur des navires négriers, puis jetés sur le littoral du Brésil ou de Cuba'.[3]

The 'legitimate' traders on the Western Slave Coast numbered no more than half a dozen before the capture of Lagos. The agent of Victor Régis at Whydah and Thomas Hutton's men at Anecho, Whydah, and Badagri were joined in 1849 and 1850 by Legresley, acting for the Gold Coast firm of Banner Brothers, and by J. Sandeman with two or three employees, acting for the firm of Stewart & Douglas. Where they could not supplant the Brazilians (as they eventually did at Badagri and Lagos) they were obliged to trade with them. The agent of Régis, Blancheley, had no qualms about this; and the missionary, Freeman, wrote of Hutton that he 'was not supposed, as a merchant, to be practically an active adversary to the slave trade; and however strong might his private feelings against

[1] *Slave Trade*; P.P., 1842, xi (551), Q. 10329.
[2] Forbes, i. 114.
[3] E. Bouët-Willaumez, *Commerce et traite des noirs aux côtes occidentales d'Afrique* (Paris, 1848), p. 125.

that trade, as a moral question, his opposition could only, as a matter of prudence be of a negative kind'.[1]

The amount of palm-oil shipped from Whydah to France before 1850 was small—not more than 800 tons a year after 1845—and represented only a fraction of the Delta trade to Great Britain.[2] But it was sufficient for Victor Régis to decide in 1847, after some debate, to maintain a factory there, pay the exorbitant bribes and presents to Ghezo and the Fon officials, and risk rising insurance rates, as trading vessels were seized and delayed at random.[3] The economic incentive for investing in the palm-oil trade west of the Delta was directly related to the improved prices on the European market in the 1840's. In England, after the high duty on the import of oil had been lowered in 1817, total imports rose to 16,000 tons in 1840 and nearly doubled by 1851. Imports of the commodity into France grew at a similar rate, but in bulk were no more than one-twentieth of the amount shipped to British ports.[4] Comparison of market prices in the two countries reveals that palm-oil fetched £2 to £3 more per ton at Marseilles than at Liverpool. In the latter market prices rose from £20 per ton in 1816 to an average of £42 in the late 1840's, and to a maximum of £48 per ton in 1854. Prices in the African market are harder to evaluate, given the different units of account used in the coastal trading centres. But here, too, British and French figures for the Western Slave Coast are reasonably consistent. The average local price (*valeur réelle*) for palm-oil shipped from West Africa to France in the late 1840's from Whydah and the Congo was £20 per ton—which parallels the Delta prices of the early 1850's. At Whydah the purchase price of oil by 1851 was slightly higher than the average for the Delta and stood at one head of cowries per gallon (1*s*. 8*d*.), or £25 for a ton of 300 gallons.

Dahomey control over the Whydah market did not change, whatever the exports. After the death of Da Souza in 1849, one of his sons succeeded to his title and remained like his father 'the principal agent to the king in all matters of trade'. His function, as described by Forbes, was as follows:

[1] M.M.A., Freeman, ['History'], f. 417.
[2] M.F.O., Gabon, i/1, Régis to Ministère de la Marine, 1 July 1849. Cf. P.P., 1854, lxv (296).
[3] P.P., 1847–8, xxii (272), Second Report, Q. 4859.
[4] M.F.O., Sénégal et Dépendances, xiii/72 (trade reports, 1845–9); 'Commerce de la France avec la côte occidentale d'Afrique jusqu'en 1854', *Revue coloniale*, xvi, 2ᵉ série (1856), pp. 70–73.

To him must be subjected all commerce, whether in slaves or palm-oil, that he may have the refusal. The price is laid down by law, subject to his alteration if concurred in by the viceroy and six traders or superintendents of trade appointed by the king. . . . One or the other of these must be present at all sales to take the royal duty, which in palm-oil is about a gallon in a measure of eighteen.

These men are not paid, but have the advantage of trading at the royal price, or ten per cent. under the market. They are besides political spies on the viceroy, and attend all conferences, reporting directly to the king any infringement on the royal prerogative.[1]

Another type of trader arrived in the early 1840's—the liberated African from Sierra Leone—whose economic significance was hardly, even by 1851, proportionate to the amount of attention the 'migration' attracted first from the missionary societies, and ultimately from the Foreign Office. The first small groups of freed slaves made their way back through Badagri to Abeokuta in 1838 and 1839 and revealed to the surprised Egba that there existed 'a race of white people who did not trade in slaves, but who actually rescued them when captured'.[2] Many more, mostly Yoruba, together with a few Hausa and Nupe, left the crowded settlement of Freetown and made the same journey till, by 1844, it was estimated there were about 3,000 emigrants from Sierra Leone settled within the vast fortified Egba capital. Those who had come by way of Badagri were allowed to pass in safety; the few hundred who tried to pass through Lagos were robbed of all they possessed. The four vessels that brought them were condemned slave ships, bought and fitted out by the migrants themselves with the financial help of leading members of the liberated community at Freetown and the Methodist mission. The greater part of the returned Yoruba were petty traders and farmers with a miscellaneous collection of skills picked up during their travels. A few were products of Freetown mission schools. And where their converts lead, the missionaries soon followed.

Thomas Birch Freeman, a coloured pastor and superintendent of the Cape Coast Wesleyan mission toured the Whydah and Abeokuta area and established a station at Badagri at the end of 1842 which he left in the charge of a series of assistants.[3] The Church

[1] Forbes, i. 111.

[2] Ibid., p. 392; *Church Missionary Intelligencer*, vi. 6 (1853), p. 128.

[3] Freeman, *Journal of Various Visits to the Kingdoms of Ashanti, Aku, and Dahomi, in Western Africa* (2nd ed. London, 1844), pp. 204–14. The assistants at Badagri were the Rev. W. de Graft, Samuel Annear, and John Martin.

Missionary Society, impressed by the character of 'King' Shodeke of Abeokuta and his reception of the Sierra Leone contingents, ordered the Rev. H. Townsend, C. H. Gollmer, and Samuel Crowther to begin a Yoruba mission, laying emphasis on the promotion of agriculture and trade, which, in the view of the C.M.S. committee, 'expands the minds of those engaged in it . . .'.[1] In January 1845 the expedition arrived at Badagri; and there they were drawn into the tangled web of Gun and Yoruba political and economic rivalries.

The death of Shodeke in 1845 removed the semblance of paramountcy at Abeokuta and left the Egba a prey to divided counsels in the *Ogboni* association of chiefs and elders.[2] The policy of unrestricted access to the coast was never lost sight of; but there was rarely unanimous consent on the type of alliances with Lagos or Badagri needed to achieve this. And while the senior lineages, headed by Apati, the *Bashorun*, and Okukenu, the *Sagbua* of Ake, hesitated between supporting rival contestants and trading interests in the coastal towns, the *Ologun* association of war chiefs pursued its slave raiding activities and bartered for guns and powder at Okeodan and Porto-Novo.[3] From the missionaries' point of view the route to the interior was unsafe as soon as the Egba relaxed their hold on Addo by withdrawing the force stationed there in 1845. The C.M.S. missionaries made the best of it for over a year and established themselves in Ahoviko ward alongside the Wesleyan mission at Badagri 'while the inhabitants of that apparently devoted place, were in daily apprehension of a hostile attack from Lagos, on the one hand, and from Porto-Novo and Dahomey on the other'.[4] Not till July 1846 did the Townsend party achieve their objective, build their houses and chapels at Abeokuta, and drive the first thin wedge of British humanitarian and commercial interests into the Yoruba interior. Like the Egba they grew to appreciate the necessity for an open road to the sea. And from their isolated position 'in the heart of the Slave Trade', they found that the tasks of redemption and self-preservation were thwarted and imperilled by the closing of that road during a conflict that embroiled the entrepreneurs of Badagri and had its origins further back in Lagos history.

[1] N.R.O., ECC 1/524, 'Instructions of the Committee', 24 Oct. and 25 Jan. 1844.

[2] For an analysis of Egba political associations, see Biobaku, 'An Historical Sketch of Yoruba Traditional Authorities', *Africa*, xxii. 1 (1952), pp. 35–49.

[3] Biobaku, *The Egba and their Neighbours 1842–1872*, pp. 22–23.

[4] Freeman, ['History'], f. 395.

The struggle at Lagos in the early nineteenth century for the *Ologun* title and the right to collect revenues from the slave trade was fundamentally another example of the way in which the presence of aliens (in this case the Brazilian merchants) aggravated the difficulties of selecting title-holders by rotation from among the segments of a senior ruling lineage. The problem had its parallels at Porto-Novo where the support of the Hausa and Egba merchants, and later the creoles, for one or another faction had become an increasingly important factor; and even at Abomey the wealth of Da Souza had assisted Ghezo to overcome the opposition of other princes in 1818.

The sources for early Lagos history are slender, and at some points conflicting.[1] But it seems clear that paramount authority over the nineteen or so local lineages, headed by the *Idejo*, or White Cap Chiefs, was derived ultimately from the *Oba* of Benin whose emissaries and settlers contacted the Lagos Yoruba towards the end of the sixteenth century. The paramount title *Oloriogun* (abbrev. *Ologun*), and the responsibility for collecting and paying tribute to Benin was vested in the senior *Idejo* by the *Oba*'s officer of state and representative—the *Eletu*;[2] and the first *Ologun*, according to tradition, had been a certain Ashipa at the turn of the seventeenth century. No rigid succession principles can be deduced from the surviving lists of *Ologun* title-holders. They are all members of what one source calls a 'Family Dynasty'; descent from Ashipa is traced at least at one point through a female ancestor; and they are recognizable, within the last two generations before the capture of Lagos, as members of the *Akarigbere* class of chiefs—the male heads of lineage segments—who competed with each other for the lineage title. From the beginning of the nineteenth century evidence of this competition accumulates. Adele, the seventh *Ologun*, was driven out of Lagos by his brother and spent some years in exile at Badagri in the 1820's where Richard Lander saw him.[3] He was called back by the *Eletu* in 1832 and regained the title from his brother's agnates. At his death in 1834, one of these, Kosoko, put up a claim; but he was ignored by the *Eletu* in favour of one of the sons of Adele. Kosoko, in turn went into

[1] N.R.O., CSO 33/1776, Herbert Macaulay, 'Inquiry into the House of Decemo', n.d.; Rev. Buckley Wood, *Historical Notices of Lagos, West Africa* (Lagos, 1878), pp. 24–25. See, too, Chief Egharevba, *A Short History of Benin* (Lagos, 1953), pp. 31–32.

[2] Macaulay lists ten descendants of the first *Eletu*, Akiwon.

[3] Lander calls him 'Adooley'. *Journal of an Expedition to Explore the Course and Termination of the Niger* (3 vols. London, 1832), i. 7–14, 45.

exile at Whydah for about six years and found new supporters from among the Brazilian slavers who were anxious to shift the base of their operations away from a port which was too well known to the Preventive Squadron to the safer network of lagoons to the east. On the death of the reigning *Ologun* in 1841, Kosoko returned to the contest, only to see the title pass to his uncle, Akitoye. Supported by the dollars and arms of his new allies, he drove out both Akitoye and the *Eletu*, in 1845, breaking with the traditional sanctions of Benin, and capturing and expanding the local slave market.

The exiles took refuge at Badagri with the *Wawu* of Ahoviko ward. At the same time, another exile, the Gun chief, Mewu, who had been driven out of Porto-Novo by King Meyi, associated himself with the *Finhento* chief of the Wharako ward. The two factions combined to disrupt the shipment of produce and slaves down the Ossa lagoon; and they made a bid for English assistance.

The Wesleyan and C.M.S. missionaries who were also associated with the chief of Ahoviko ward tended to simplify the Porto-Novo and Lagos-Badagri quarrels in terms of those who were for, and those who were against the slave trade.[1] Enemies of Kosoko and King Meyi were loosely included among the latter; and the fact that Akitoye also had a few allies among the Egba and made a profession of his willingness to end the slave trade if restored, gave strength to their belief that the principal obstacle to the spread of lawful commerce and civilization was Kosoko at Lagos. For their part, Akitoye and Mewu gave little real proof that they subscribed whole-heartedly to the anti-slavery thesis. They were anxious to be numbered among the 'English' chiefs at Badagri;[2] but they could not change overnight the principal source of the town's economic wealth; and they steadily created an opposition to themselves among the other ward chiefs whose livelihood depended on good relations with Porto-Novo and Lagos. Furthermore, when English intervention did not take place,

---

[1] They also over-simplified the ward structure at Badagri in the 1840's, readily confusing the names and titles of chiefs, an error followed by later authors. For example, Freeman lists only four wards for the town and their chiefs, according to their trading associations with different European nationalities:

'French' under 'Gingy' [Chief Sinji, *Jengen* of Awhanjigo ward].

'English' under 'Wawu' [Chief Mesi, *Wawu* of Ahoviko ward].

'Portuguese' under 'Ekra' [Toyi, *Akran* X of Jegba ward].

'Dutch' under 'Possu' [Chief Agongoro, *Possu* of Possuko ward].

M.M.S., Freeman, ['History'], f. 415; and *Journal of Various Visits*, p. 237. See, too, above, p. 31.

[2] M.M.S., Samuel Annear, 'Journal', entries for Oct. 1844.

Akitoye turned in 1847 to the arch-slaver Domingo Martinez who had designs of his own. As Whydah was the province of Da Souza, so might Lagos, under Akitoye, become the realm of Martinez.[1] His wealth was used freely in 1847 to enlist military support from the Fon, and a few of the Egbado and Awori towns. But his campaign against Lagos in March failed; the breach between Akitoye and Kosoko widened; and the Badagri chiefs were incensed that the presence of a handful of missionaries, returned Egba, and English factors caused Domingo to establish a new slave market at Ajuda, half-way between Badagri and Lagos.

In 1851 the Akitoye and Kosoko dispute resulted in civil war at Badagri. A fight broke out in the centre of the town; buildings were set on fire, including the factory of the British trader Hutton, and 'two large compounds of the Sierra Leone people'; and by nightfall on 12 June 1851, the majority of Badagri chiefs had been defeated by Mewu and Akitoye, and had fled to neighbouring villages.[2] In the background were the forces of the Egba, who, according to a trader of the time, used the occasion to attack the Awori for slaves, under the pretence of holding Kosoko at bay.[3] Less ambiguously situated were the missionaries, Townsend and Gollmer, the palm-oil factors, naval officers, and, by 1851, a consul, all of whose humanitarian, commercial, and officious interests in the area complicated the issues still further.

[1] M.M.S., Samuel Annear, 'Journal', entries for 12 July and 25 Nov. 1846, 2 Mar. and 17 May 1847.

[2] *Church Missionary Intelligencer*, ii (1851), 252–4; *Proceedings of the Church Missionary Society* (1851–2), pp. 50–52.

[3] J. Sandeman, cited in P. A. Talbot, *The People of Southern Nigeria* (4 vols. London, 1926), i, 93.

CHAPTER III

European Intervention at Lagos and Porto-Novo

THE road to empire in West Africa is paved with treaties. The use that was made of these varied with the motives of the signatories—both European and African—and the degree to which they could be enforced. Commercial and humanitarian reasons prompted the earliest French and British attempts to extract guarantees from African authorities in the Bight of Benin; and as the former motive steadily displaced the latter, both powers acquired interests and a measure of jurisdiction which were weighed in the sum of their respective policies towards West Africa as a whole. If the years of the 'scramble' for the interior were, as yet, three or four decades in the future, the preliminary manœuvres on the coast had already begun as the slave trade declined.

The advent of consular and colonial jurisdiction to the Western Slave Coast in the mid-nineteenth century is usually treated as a by-product of the anti-slavery campaign into which Britain had cajoled or bribed most of the maritime nations of Europe. But Lagos which was placed under consular and naval protection in 1851 and added later to the West African settlements was not the only slave port between the Volta and the Ogun rivers. Nor was it the most impor-tant. Its selection for 'reduction' and the installation there of the puppet ruler, Akitoye, as a pliable signatory to an anti-slavery treaty, owed much to the balance of power between the Fon, Gun, and Yoruba chiefdoms to the north and west of Lagos and still more to the alignment of missionary and Egba interests some seventy miles up the Ogun at Abeokuta. To the Foreign Office, and to the consular and naval officers who acted as envoys, diplomatists, and finally as administrators, the Egba were accessible and amenable, so long as the threat of Fon invasion and pressure from the Ijebu were dangers that required a steady supply of powder and arms. The Gun of Badagri, the principal port for missionary and Egba supplies, were weak but strategically placed entrepreneurs on the creek system, as well as unhappy hosts to returned slaves, the Porto-Novo renegade,

Mewu, the exiled Akitoye, the missionaries and traders. Farther west at Abomey, King Ghezo, whose ancestors had pursued an un-remitting course of aggrandisement in the interior and dictated the terms of trade at Whydah for just over a century, was unconvinced by the thesis that the substitution of palm-oil exports for slaves would ever provide 'from moderate and reasonable customs duties a much greater and more certain revenue' than his dynasty had collected from Europeans in the past.[1] Nor was this argument ac-ceptable to Kosoko and the Brazilian slavers at Lagos, to the majority of the Gun chiefs at Badagri, or to the Egba war chiefs at Abeo-kuta. But Lagos was open to naval action; Abomey was not. Any occupation of Whydah would have inevitably entailed a protracted campaign against the Fon kingdom which no British government of the day would sanction.

The idea of military posts on parts of the Western Slave Coast was kept alive, however, and even put into effect in 1843 by Captain Maclean, governor of Cape Coast, on the suggestion of the mission-ary, Freeman.[2] A small detachment under a sergeant of the Gold Coast Corps was sent to Badagri in August of that year and hoisted the British flag over Ahoviko ward, where it remained for a few months to protect Hutton's agents, the Wesleyan mission, 'and con-vince the slave-dealers that the eye of the British Government' was on the town.[3] Maclean was prepared to do the same at Whydah; and he forwarded his own, and Freeman's proposals, to England, where they were rejected by the Foreign Office in favour of treaty-making.[4] The object of British policy in the 1840's was not to secure a colony, but a contract with native authorities to stop the slave trade at source.

Efforts in this direction were not encouraging. Freeman's private embassy to Whydah and Abomey at the end of 1842 and early in 1843 was an occasion for polite pageantry and evasive replies to questions about the slave trade. Received at Cana and interviewed by Ghezo, he spent much time explaining the purpose of the Wes-leyan mission on the coast; but he could obtain no assurances that the Fon dynasty was willing to sacrifice its principal source of in-come in order to meet the novel and puzzling proposals of aliens.[5]

[1] P.P., 1852, liv (221), Palmerston to Beecroft, 23 Jan. 1850, No. 3, p. 4.

[2] M.M.S., Freeman, ['History'], ff. 423–4.

[3] Ibid., f. 421.

[4] Ibid., Maclean to Freeman, 24 May 1843, 422; F.O. 84/493, F.O. to Admiralty, 20 Sept. 1843.

[5] Freeman, *Journal of Various Visits*, pp. 235–61.

Nevertheless, the illusion that a treaty could be made with Ghezo persisted. Governor Hill (Maclean's successor) went to Whydah to remonstrate, and at length to threaten, in vain. Governor Winniett, in 1847, concluded a treaty of friendship from which anti-slavery clauses were excluded.[1] Again, in 1848 Brodie Cruickshank, chief magistrate at Cape Coast, made a fourth attempt. He was the first of the ambassadors to estimate the importance of Ghezo's revenues from the slave trade. On the assumption that the Fon kingdom exported about 8,000 slaves a year, Cruickshank calculated that the royal income from duties and the sale of slaves on the king's own account could not be less than about £60,000. Whether this was accurate or not, his own 'paltry offer' of an annual compensation of £400 was unacceptable; and Cruickshank, in his report, was obviously impressed by Ghezo's arguments.[2]

The state which he maintained was great; his army was expensive; the ceremonies and customs to be observed annually, which had been handed down to him from his forefathers, entailed upon him a vast outlay of money. These could not be abolished. The form of his government could not be suddenly changed, without causing such a revolution as would deprive him of his throne, and precipitate his kingdom into a state of anarchy.

Ghezo admitted that the palm-oil trade might have promising beginnings.

But it was a slow method of making money, and brought only a very small amount of duties into his coffers. The planting of coffee and cotton had been suggested to him; but this was slower still. He held his power by an observance of the time-honoured customs of his forefathers; and he would forfeit it, and entail upon himself a life full of shame, and a death of misery, if he neglected them.

A further candid outline of Fon policy was forwarded to Queen Victoria.[3] Slave-raiding would not stop; but a British consul would be welcomed at Whydah to learn 'the manner in which the King governs his people'. It was conceded that the slave trade at Porto-Novo, Badagri, and Lagos ought to be prohibited; and to this end King Ghezo humbly begged the queen 'to make a law that no ships be allowed to trade at any place near his dominions lower down the

[1] Treaty, 5 Apr. 1847, Hertslet, xii (1905), 33.
[2] Cruickshank, Report, 9 Nov. 1848, in *The British and Foreign Anti-Slavery Reporter*, iv, No. xiv (new series, 1849), pp. 125–6.
[3] P.P., 1852, liv (221), Ghezo to Queen Victoria, 3 Nov. 1848, Encl. 2 in No. 3, pp. 5–6.

coast than Whydah, as by means of trading vessels the people are getting rich, and withstanding his authority'. Fon customs revenues were diminished by the dispersion of slave shipments from other ports, and Fon hegemony over the Egbado interior was challenged by the Egba whose supplies of arms could not be cut off. The palm-oil trade, Ghezo urged, should be similarly restricted, 'as the trade that is now done at these places can be done at Whydah, and the King would then receive his duties, and be able to keep these people in subjection; and also in the event of his attacking these places he would not run the risk of injuring Englishmen or their property'.[1] A polite request for a cargo of guns, cannons, and cowries concluded the royal dispatch.

Only the suggestion for a consul was taken up. When, in June 1849, John Beecroft was appointed to the Bight of Benin with instructions to regulate the conduct of trade in the Delta and 'in the territories of the King of Dahomey', John Duncan was posted as unpaid vice-consul at Whydah.[2] The attention of the Foreign Office had not yet turned to Lagos, and the fruitless negotiations for a treaty continued. But Duncan's influence at Whydah, where he made little impact on Fon and Brazilian officials whose favours were dispensed according to the sums they received, was 'nugatory'.[3] His mission to Abomey with Commander Forbes in October 1849 elicited no more from Ghezo than a promise to reflect on the economic advantages of the palm-oil trade. To help his reflections Palmerston ordered Beecroft to accompany Forbes in a final attempt to persuade him that the days of the slave trade were over.

Before Beecroft reported the failure of his mission, a deputation from the Church Missionary Society and a letter containing the views of the trader Thomas Hutton deflected Palmerston's attention away from Dahomey to the problem of keeping open communications with Abeokuta. The Foreign Secretary was impressed with the Missionary Society's proposition (inspired by Townsend) that better commercial relations with the Egba would help to end the slave trade and perhaps open a way to the Niger via the Ogun. Entry to the Ogun was through Lagos: 'Lagos is therefore said to be the natural port of Abbeokuta; but the Slave Trade being carried on at Lagos with great activity, the Yoruba have been obliged to use the port of

[1] P.P., 1852, liv (221), p. 5.
[2] Ibid., Palmerston to Beecroft, 30 June 1849, No. 1, p. 1.
[3] Ibid., Forbes to Fanshaw, 1 Nov. 1849, Encl. 12 in No. 3, pp. 13–18.

Badagry, between which and Abbeokuta communications are carried on by a difficult road by land.'[1] The news that Ghezo was planning to attack the Egba capital was an additional argument for supporting the centre of missionary contact. Hutton supplied a third reason for concentrating naval and consular efforts on clearing a passage to the Yoruba interior. Only when lesser mortals among the slavers had been crushed would Ghezo condescend to come to terms: 'One thing alone is wanting to compel him to stop the trade, that is, to get possession of Lagos, and either by treaty or force utterly extinguish the Slave Trade there.'[2]

That Abomey might welcome this as a chance to revive the Whydah trade does not seem to have occurred either to Hutton or the Foreign Office. The agents of Hutton, at odds with the authorities of Whydah and unable to compete for limited palm-oil supplies with the French firm of Régis, looked to a Lagos free from rivals to pursue their trade. Their position was similar to the slaver, Domingo Martinez, who was unable to break the Da Souza monopoly at Whydah and turned to the markets of the eastern creeks. Domingo enlisted the support of the Badagri and Awori chiefs to break the control of Kosoko and his allies; Hutton enlisted the support of the Foreign Office and the navy. Finally, Beecroft, despairing of Ghezo and impressed by Townsend's work at Abeokuta, made the same point in his report of July 1850: the Fon would not be persuaded till slave trading at the secondary ports had been stopped.[3]

The blueprint for action against Lagos had been supplied in 1840 and again in 1849 by the successful destruction of the slave factories at Gallinas.[4] Kosoko was to be made to accept a similar treaty and the Brazilian factors driven out. If he refused he was to be removed and Akitoye set up in his place.[5] In February 1851 a model treaty was forwarded to Beecroft together with the news that the importation of slaves into Brazil was about to cease. This evidence was to be used by Beecroft in his effort to persuade Kosoko that 'lawful commerce is more advantageous to the nations of Africa than the Slave Trade . . .'.

---

[1] Ibid., Palmerston to Beecroft, 25 Feb. 1850, No. 4, pp. 29–30.

[2] Ibid., Thomas Hutton to William Hutton, 7 Aug. 1850, Encl. 8 in No. 4, p. 39.

[3] Ibid., Beecroft to Palmerston, 22 July 1850, pp. 40–43.

[4] A slave market between Liberia and Sierra Leone. For the naval action there, see Lloyd, pp. 94–95; 99; J. J. Crooks, *A History of the Colony of Sierra Leone Western Africa* (London, 1903), pp. 168–9.

[5] P.P., 1852, liv (221), F.O. to Admiralty, 11 Oct. 1850, p. 45.

And if he did not recognize this advantage, he was to be warned that the navy might be called in.[1]

Beecroft, after visiting Badagri and Abeokuta, had already made up his own mind, before receiving the above dispatch. Akitoye, as a useful pawn in the consul's manœuvres, was taken to Fernando Po away from the dangerous and mounting opposition to him at Badagri. The consul's policy towards the Gun and Yoruba ports was clear: 'they all want coercion—the Porto Novans as well as others; but Lagos ought not to be allowed to escape; place the right person there, all is well'.[2]

In March 1851 the Fon assault on Abeokuta failed—but not disastrously enough to allay Egba and missionary fears of a second attempt. In July the Badagri area came under attack from Kosoko, and the town was plunged into civil war. The Admiralty was requested to blockade the coast in September and ordered Admiral Bruce to consider the possibility of an expedition against Kosoko.[3] Bruce was busy transporting arms for the Egba from Sierra Leone when he received this dispatch. In his absence Beecroft and Forbes began the final negotiations with Lagos on their own initiative; and when these were rejected, the consul enlisted Forbes to use force by showing him Palmerston's dispatch of February 1851.[4] After the first assault from the sea ended in defeat, it was left to Bruce who was doubtful of the value of destroying Lagos to repair the humiliation and push the action home. The blockade began on 6 December 1851; Kosoko and his Brazilian allies were driven out; and Akitoye signed the treaty after his installation on the first day of February 1852.[5] It was agreed that human sacrifices and the sale of slaves were ended at Lagos. And as the naval blockade was extended for another five months, naval officers concluded treaties with Ghezo. at Cana, with King Sodji at Porto-Novo and with Mewu at Badagri.[6] The Gallinas policy seemed to have been vindicated in the Bight of Benin.

The treaties with the Gun and the Fon were broken immediately;

[1] P.P., 1852, liv (221), Palmerston to Beecroft, 21 Feb. 1851, No. 25, pp. 85–86. Estimated at 62,000 in 1846, the number of slaves shipped annually to Brazil had declined by about two-thirds four years later, and fell to less than 3,000 a year after 1851, till the revival of the trade 1858–63. Lloyd, pp. 140–6.

[2] Ibid., Beecroft to Palmerston, 24 Feb. 1851, 96.

[3] Ibid., F.O. to Admiralty, 29 Sept. 1851, No. 43, p. 136.

[4] For the details of the action at Lagos, see A. C. Burns, *History of Nigeria* (3rd ed. London, 1942), pp. 129–33); Geary, pp. 25–26.

[5] Burns, Appendix C, pp. 313–15.

[6] Treaties in Hertslet, ix (1856), 14, 29, 41.

and the Badagri treaty was never signed by any chief of the town. Kosoko was still at large at Epe, east of Lagos. Moreover, naval blockade could not be continued indefinitely, however effective as an arm of naval diplomacy. Badagri had been omitted from the list of closed ports, being the only avenue for missionary supplies and arms for the Egba at Abeokuta.[1] This omission confirmed the suspicion of the agents of Victor Régis at Whydah that the suppression of the slave trade was a pretext for ensuring commercial advantage for the British traders at Badagri and Lagos.[2] No cargoes of slaves had been loaded at Whydah between 1850 and 1852, argued the French firm, not because of the Preventive Squadron, but because the governments of Brazil and Cuba had prohibited further imports. When these points were raised through the French embassy in London, Granville replied that Badagri had been excepted because the chiefs there had given assurances they were not selling slaves and were allied with 'another anti-slavery tribe' at Abeokutá.[3]

Both the accusation and the excuse were unfounded. Commodore Bruce simply needed more time to get his treaties signed, to arm the Egba and to make sure that Kosoko would not immediately return. The problem as Bruce saw it was not encouraging the growth of legitimate commerce, but making sure that both legitimate and slave trade were not carried on at the same time. He suggested, as a check, full consulates for Lagos and Whydah and no less than nine consular agents stationed in towns from Anecho to Ijebu Ode, each of whom could call on naval support.[4] The plan was not accepted; and within a decade Lagos had to be annexed and the treaties of 1852 renewed.

Bruce's fear that a single consulate at Lagos would not prove sufficient was justified. The inefficiency of Vice-Consul Fraser, appointed in May 1852, allowed Kosoko to land on the island; and only vigorous measures taken by his successor, Consul Benjamin Campbell, prevented the overthrow of Akitoye. Furthermore, in addition to the difficulty of maintaining an imported paramount chief, the development of legitimate trade brought with it problems that required greater powers of jurisdiction for their solution than the consuls

---

[1] P.P., 1852, liv (221), Bruce to Admiralty, 6 Dec. 1851, p. 162.
[2] M.A.E., Afrique/51, Régis to Turgot, 24 Jan. 1852.
[3] Ibid., Granville to Walewski, 20 Feb. 1852. Bruce gave a similar explanation to French naval officers. Baudin to Ducos, 27 Mar. 1852. Ships engaged in legitimate trade were eventually permitted to pass through the blockade in Apr. 1852.
[4] P.P., 1852, liv (221), Bruce to Admiralty, 17 Jan. 1852, p. 213.

possessed. As the decade passed, they were called on to act as administrators over a society whose composition changed rapidly in a few years and whose trading communities improvised ways of securing and defending their interests in what became a British protectorate, in fact, if not in title.

There were two sections of the Lagos population over whom the *Idejo* chiefs, King Akitoye, or his son Docemo, had no authority: the returned liberated slaves from Sierra Leone and Brazil, and the European traders.[1] Of these, only the British traders were strictly entitled to the little armed protection the consuls could call in. In practice, many of the Sierra Leoneans were regarded as British protected subjects—a habit encouraged by the missionaries and by the more prosperous of the freed slaves themselves, when such protection was useful. A formal agreement placed the Brazilians under Akitoye's care; but they, too, tended to look to the consuls for advice, and remained socially aloof from the bulk of the indigenous population. Both immigrant groups from Brazil and Sierra Leone had some education, a smattering of European skills, and 'the outward stamp of freemen'.[2] With these advantages they set up as traders, acquired domestic slaves of their own, and used their knowledge of European and African society to further their interests at Lagos and at Abeokuta. Having departed as slaves and returned as more than the equal of the *Idejo* chiefs, those who were literate became land-owners and men of substance. Those who were not became artisans, retailers, hawkers, or, at the lowest level, farmers whose lot was scarcely distinguishable from the original inhabitants. The most enterprising of their leaders were successful middlemen in the highly competitive conditions of trade at Lagos in the 1850's. In this economic competition the *Idejo* chiefs who had nothing to sell but their land and knew little trade but in slaves were gradually left behind.

Among the European traders and the missionaries, the former group had the stronger influence on consular policy, though the latter could never be entirely discounted, because of their connexions with the returned slaves and the Egba at Abeokuta. The C.M.S., led by Gollmer, moved in with the traders in 1852; and like the principal firms it took up a strategic position on the Lagos waterfront, where

[1] There was no census at Lagos before the 1860's. Freeman estimated the population of the island at 25,000 to 30,000. Freeman, ['History'], f. 400. At the beginning of the consular period there were only about 200 to 300 Sierra Leoneans and 130 Brazilian families. F.O. 2/28, Campbell to Clarendon, 28 Dec. 1853.

[2] Campbell, cited in Geary, p. 32.

the Wesleyan mission and the German, British, and French factories flanked the unpretentious consulate. No aspect of trade or consular jurisdiction escaped the attention of one faction or another; and on the cramped unhealthy island, the conviction grew that the consuls were inadequatè to serve their interests.

The principal palm-oil factors arrived in the first months of the consular period. William McCoskry, Legreseley, and J. Sandeman had already been prospecting the market at Badagri for the firms of Hutton, Banner Brothers, and Stewart & Douglas. They were joined in March 1852 by Captain Lorenz Diedrichsen from Whydah who, the following year, persuaded the Hamburg firm, O'Swald & Co., to open a factory, selling out his own concern to their agent, Hermann Grote.[1] After 1856 these pioneers yielded ground to the Italian, G. B. Scala, the agents of Chillingworth & Co., two Germans, Meyer and Johannsen, and the numerous employees of Victor Régis. The establishment of a steamer line to the Bights in 1852 enabled the smaller factors to consign their palm-oil regularly to British commission houses from whom they received goods which they sold on credit to the Sierra Leone and Brazilian middlemen. A few of these, too, began to consign produce on their own account; and by the end of the decade about a dozen of the Sierra Leoneans and two of the Brazilians had entered the export trade alongside the Europeans. Régis and O'Swald had transport of their own. Moreover, till 1856 O'Swald's monopoly of the cowrie trade from Zanzibar placed their agents in a strong position; and two of the five vessels of the firm were used to ensure a steady flow of this currency from East Africa, while the others were engaged exclusively in shipping traders' palm-oil to Hamburg.[2]

Lagos, in the 1850's, exported between 4,000 and 5,000 tons of palm-oil a year. A peak was reached in 1857. Thereafter, till 1861, there was a slow decline in the tonnage and value of exports, attributed by the consuls to a revival of the slave trade and disruptive wars in the interior. The staple export was supplemented by shea-butter, ivory, and a little cotton from the Abeokuta region. The great hopes of Consul Campbell, the missionaries, and the Manchester Cotton Supply Association who looked to the Yoruba for a new

---

[1] Hieke, pp. 119–20.

[2] The rudimentary consular trade statistics do not indicate how much the German share was, though Campbell thought they had most of the palm-oil, before 1856. N.R.O., Consulate Letter-Book, Campbell to Clarendon, 1 June 1856. The Hamburg archives are silent on this point.

cash-crop were not fully realized; and the export of baled cotton, after reaching a figure of 236,500 lb. in 1858, fluctuated wildly before recovering in the 1860's.[1] Compared with other ports of the Western Slave Coast, Lagos was not greatly superior in its volume of exports.

*Lagos Exports**

				Palm-oil (tons)	Ivory (lb.)	Cotton (lb.)
1856	.	.	.	3,884	16,057	34,491
1857	.	.	.	4,942	24,118	114,848
1858	.	.	.	4,612	5,776	236,500
1859	.	.	.	3,980	31,639	198,305
1860	.	.	.	2,752	..	1,735
1861	.	.	.	3,865	..	153,754

* N.R.O., Consulate Letter-Book, Campbell to Clarendon, 7 Feb. and 1 Apr. 1859; *Blue Book*, 1862; P.P., 1862, lxi (339), 21; P.P., 1865, v (1), Appendix No. 8, p. 467. Consular returns were at best intelligent estimates. A good deal of ivory, for example, was smuggled out of Lagos to avoid customs. Cf. Geary, p. 38.

Palm-oil exports

Estimated annual average, 1856–8 (tons)			
Lagos	Palma	Badagri	Porto-Novo, Whydah, Agege*
4,479	2,580	1,250	7,160

Ibid.;* M.F.O., Sénégal et dépendances, xiii/72.

In 1856 Whydah, Badagri, and Porto-Novo between them exported as much as Lagos; and the following year their exports more than doubled, while those of Lagos increased by about one-third. They, too, suffered a decline in the late 1850's, when the sale of slaves revived at Whydah. But the palm-oil trade did not stop: the two activities, as in the 1840's, were not mutually exclusive.

The basis of the oil market at Lagos was credit and cowries. While most of the European traders and the Sierra Leone middlemen operated the former system, O'Swald's agents traded directly with the native suppliers and secured the bulk of palm produce, till the monopoly was broken by Victor Régis in 1856. Both firms imported cowries directly from Zanzibar; and between 1856 and 1861 the number of sacks of cowries landed at Lagos quadrupled, compared

[1] For the cotton experiment at Abeokuta, see Biobaku, pp. 57–60.

with the first five years of the decade.[1] Cowrie currency devaluated to such an extent that, for a period in 1859, the German factors complained that it was impossible to have them accepted at all. A sack of cowries was worth about 48s. in 1851 and purchased 36 gallons of palm-oil at Lagos. Despite an agreement between the two firms in 1858 to fix the exchange of oil at 18 or 19 gallons for a sack, the truce was quickly broken as each strove to outdo the prices of the other; and by the end of 1859, when the glut of currency had eased a little, a sack of cowries was worth only 18s. and would buy no more than 14 or 15 gallons of palm-oil.[2] O'Swald, for this and other reasons, began to prospect for new markets at Godomey and Palma, and finally withdrew from Lagos altogether in 1869.

Those who purchased on credit through middlemen had problems of their own. The Egba resented the sharp practice and faulty measures of Sierra Leone and European traders, and boycotted the Lagos market for five months in 1855. The estimated loss of about 20,000 gallons of palm-oil crippled exports for the year, and the debts of the middlemen piled up.[3] The Egba complained that they were not paid enough for their oil; they demanded an improvement in the quality of cottons, spirits, and arms exchanged; and they asked for an explanation of the wide variation in measures and market prices that existed between Lagos, Badagri, Porto-Novo, and Epe. Consul Campbell confessed that he was powerless to regulate palm-oil prices.[4] He pointed out patiently that the market price for oil at Epe in 1855 was nine heads of cowries for a measure of 15 gallons, while at Lagos the measure was only 10 gallons, and the price, therefore, only six heads of cowries. Elsewhere the system was different: 'The Porto-Novo Oil is sold at Badagry Market and the measure there is 30 gallons which is sold for what is called an ounce

---

[1] Shipments of cowries from Zanzibar to the Bight of Benin (mainly Lagos and Whydah) were as follows:

	O'Swald | Régis ('000 sacks)	
1851–5 . . .	58·6	. .
1856–61 . . .	148·6	126·

See Hieke, p. 283.

[2] F.O. 2/28, Lodder to Malmesbury, 30 May 1859; Hieke, pp. 73, 132.

[3] N.R.O., Consulate Letter-Book, Campbell to Clarendon, 30 Aug. 1855.

[4] Ibid., Campbell to the *Alake* of Abeokuta, 4 Apr. 1856. One sack contained 12 heads of cowries (24,000 cowries).

which ounce represents so much cloth, rum and two heads of cowries.' This explanation and Campbell's injunction to work harder to compensate for loss of revenues from the slave trade were not well received by those among the Egba who considered that men's work was war, and marketing was for women.[1] A visit by Campbell to Abeokuta in November 1855 was necessary to heal the breach between the suppliers and the merchants.

The European palm-oil prices which had attracted the traders to Lagos rose from about £40 a ton at the beginning of the decade to a peak of £48 at the outbreak of the Crimean War, and slowly declined to about £38 per ton at the beginning of the 1860's.[2] Campbell estimated that in 1855 a ton of palm-oil f.o.b. was worth £20 at Lagos of which at least £15 represented the cost of transactions between the middlemen and the European factors as repayment for credit.[3] As the margin of profit for the exporters narrowed (despite cheaper freight rates), traders like McCoskry viewed with alarm the slightest interruption to the flow of produce from the interior which left him and his fellows without return for the credit extended to the middlemen, and, under the consulate, without means of legal redress. The credit system with its long and uncertain periods of accumulated debts was the core of European dissatisfaction with both the consuls and King Docemo.

Akitoye and his son who succeeded him in 1853 were, by treaty, granted fixed revenues from customs levied on the export of palmoil and ivory in return for guarantees that the freehold and leasehold rights of traders would not be disturbed and that debtors would be brought to book.[4] In practice it proved impossible to determine the price on which an *ad valorem* duty for Akitoye was to be collected. When his son was installed as *Ologun*, a new treaty between the leading traders and the king offered a fixed duty on the volume of exports, to be paid in cowries. In return, the king agreed 'to relinquish trading on his own account'.[5] Debtors and thieves were to be

[1] N.R.O., Consulate Letter-Book, Campbell to Clarendon, 20 Oct. 1855.

[2] Hieke, p. 125; Allan McPhee, *The Economic Revolution in British West Africa* (London, 1926), pp. 32, 33 n. 1.

[3] N.R.O., Consulate Letter-Book, Campbell to Clarendon, 2 June 1855. This would agree with the cowrie purchase-price for oil in the early 1850's. By 1859 the local market price (in cowries) was equivalent to £18 per ton f.o.b.

[4] P.P., 1862, lxi (339), 2–4. Art. II of the Agreement of 28 Feb. 1852 laid down the customs duty at 3 per cent. on imports and 2 per cent. on exports.

[5] Hamburg Staatsarchiv, CL vi/2/4a, Agreement, 27 Mar. 1854, copy encl. in O'Swald to Senate, 8 Apr. 1857. It was signed by Campbell, Docemo, and the

caught and punished; and merchants doing business with middle-men who were already loaded with debts were to be fined 1,000 gallons of palm-oil. Moreover, the treaty recognized unrestricted transfer of land—'in any spot previously unoccupied'—by purchase from a useholder or from one of the *Idejo* chiefs.

The advantages for the traders were striking, if the clauses could be enforced. For Docemo, they were less obvious: he was excluded from the market; and customs were easier to contract than to levy. Collection was at first the responsibility of the king's own officials who robbed him. Then, with Campbell's permission, the customs were farmed out to the consulate interpreter, S. B. Williams, a Sierra Leonean who was cheated by the whole trading community, European and African alike. Finally, the task of extracting duties was taken on by Signor Scala whose familiarity with smuggling aroused the bitter resentment of those who found it hard to defraud one of their own kind.[1] Scala's position as agent for the African Steamship Company gave him an advantage which none of the traders dared to challenge openly. Instead their anger at efficiency was vented on Campbell who, they claimed, was undermining Docemo's authority.[2] Docemo, for his part, was content to receive between £1,300 and £1,600 a year. In 1859 the contract with the traders was renewed: the duties were extended to exports of shea-butter; the same requests for police action against debtors were repeated; and William McCoskry who tried his hand at the customs farm 'made something out of it' in 1859 and 1860.[3]

It was a contract that the king was never able to keep without the support of the consul. The Sierra Leone traders formed their own tribunal in 1855 for hearing debt cases among themselves. In theory, if Lagos Yoruba were involved, Docemo was to be a final court of appeal; if Europeans were involved, the case was to be referred to the

traders J. G. Sandeman, William McCoskry, G. B. Scala, W. R. Hansen, W. J. Austin. The customs duties were two heads of cowries (8s.) on every puncheon (120 gals.) of palm-oil, and two strings of cowries (2½d.) on every pound of ivory.

[1] N.R.O., Consulate Letter-Book, Campbell to Clarendon, 14 May 1856.

[2] Ibid., Petition signed by McCoskry, Sandeman, Hansen, H. Woodhead, Legreseley, and the Sierra Leoneans, F. Thomas, W. E. Cole, J. M. Turner, John Macaulay, and James Davis, encl. in Campbell to Clarendon, 25 Oct. 1856.

[3] Ibid., Agreement signed by nine Europeans, sixteen Sierra Leoneans, and three Brazilians, 10 Feb., encl. in Lodder to Clarendon, 30 May 1859; P.P., 1865, v (1), Qq. 1558–63, 1872. The duty on shea-butter was 2 heads of cowries (3s.) per ton. McCoskry's fee as collector was 2,000 sacks of cowries a year which, even at the devalued rate, must have netted him at least £250 during the first twelve months.

consul.[1] But it was difficult to apprehend a small debtor; and it was nearly impossible to take action against an important one, like Madam Tinubu, a trader from one of the *Idejo* families, whose removal from Lagos by Campbell represented a loss of about £5,000 to her European and African creditors.[2] Docemo could, if pressed to it, exercise sanctions against theft—to the extent of executing four Lagos Yoruba in 1859. But fines imposed on traders like McCoskry, and upheld by Campbell, made influential enemies.[3] On the other hand, when Signor Scala, detested for his zealous collection of customs, was summoned to appear before the Sierra Leone tribunal, Campbell annulled its proceedings.[4] The Foreign Office was at last made to see the futility of leaving jurisdiction to Docemo, the consul, or the Sierra Leoneans—none of whom had any powers over non-British subjects in a predominantly non-British settlement.[5]

There was a danger that, in these circumstances, European traders might call in foreign consular or naval support. The firm of Régis, in the face of local opposition, had established its factory in 1856 under the guns of a French man-of-war. The following year, when the agents of O'Swald were arbitrarily fined by Docemo, the Hamburg firm forwarded a list of complaints through the Hamburg Senate to the British Foreign Office, requesting British consular and naval protection.[6] Clarendon would not promise the help of a naval vessel; but he gave an assurance that the government would take 'particular pleasure' in meeting the request by instructing Campbell to intervene in future.[7] Campbell furnished a different version of the affair: the German agents were disliked for their monopoly of the cowrie trade; their attitude to native authority had been 'disrespectful, offensive and overbearing'; and he feared that their long and close trade relations with Kosoko and his chiefs at Epe and Palma might encourage further attempts on the part of that 'African Nero' to regain control of Lagos.[8]

[1] F.O. 84/976, Campbell to Clarendon, 2 Aug. 1855.
[2] Biobaku, p. 57. She was expelled to Abeokuta for her part in an alleged plot against Campbell.
[3] P.P., 1865, v (1), Qq. 1655–69. McCoskry was fined 120 sacks of cowries (£80 or £90) for trading with Kosoko.
[4] F.O. 2/20, Campbell to Clarendon, 2 June 1857.
[5] Ibid., Campbell to Clarendon, 22 Aug. 1857.
[6] Hamburg Staatsarchiv, CL vi/2/4a, Rücker to Clarendon, 11 May 1857.
[7] Ibid., Rücker to Merck, 12 May 1857; Clarendon to Rücker, 15 May 1857, encl. in Rücker to Senate, 16 May 1857.
[8] F.O. 2/20, Campbell to Clarendon, 29 June 1857; Hieke, pp. 152–3. The

The external relations of the consulate with the Ijebu, Gun, and Egba illustrated how indecisive were the results of the early treaties. The consistent effort of the consuls to cajole and browbeat the chiefs of Epe, Porto-Novo, Badagri, and Abeokuta into the belief that legitimate trade could only be carried on to the exclusion of the slave trade was marked by a lack of demonstrable proof. Kosoko was bribed in 1854 to remain at Epe and to refrain from robbing canoes crossing the lagoon from Ikorodu market to Lagos.[1] But this did not prevent him organizing a clandestine slave trade with the Brazilian, Carvalho, and King Sodji of Porto-Novo. In the same year the Badagri chiefs were restored from their exile; and Mewu, so long the ally of the Egba and friend of the missionaries, was removed by force, in order to appease Sodji and to open the Ossa lagoon to palm-oil traffic between Porto-Novo and Lagos. McCoskry was appointed unpaid vice-consul to Badagri to see that the Gun chiefs kept to legitimate commerce. But he was rarely there; and Campbell could only warn the Badagri chiefs against permitting Carvalho to buy slaves in the town.[2] When the restored chiefs turned a blind eye on this and on repeated thefts from Hutton's factory, Campbell angrily admonished them.

The Consul therefore thoroughly disgusted with the Chiefs now sends them this letter to tell them that all this robbing and plundering must cease and be put a stop to, that the large quantities of Palm Oil stolen from Mr Hutton's factory must be restored and the Consul holds the Chiefs responsible and calls on them to get Mr Hutton's Oil back from the thieves.[3]

He went on to regret that he had not left them in exile 'to perish in the Bush' instead of assisting them to regain the town from Mewu. 'For Badagry without trade under Mewu was preferable to Badagry with trade under such drunken worthless chiefs as Wawu and the others and the thieves and robbers their people.'

Powerless to enforce his threat to remove all traders from the town, Campbell appealed in vain to King Sodji to compel the unruly

Hamburg Senate was sufficiently impressed by the consul's version to call before it the representatives of O'Swald for explanations and cautioning. Hamburg Staatsarchiv, CL vi/2/4a, Rücker to Clarendon, 20 Oct. 1857.

[1] Biobaku, p. 50.

[2] N.R.O., Consulate Letter-Book, Campbell to the chiefs of Badagri, 1 Mar. 1856; Campbell to 'Chief Okara' [the *Akran*], 16 Apr. 1856; Campbell to Clarendon, 23 June 1856.

[3] Ibid., Campbell to the Chiefs of Badagari, 14 June 1856.

Gun to restore Hutton's losses.[1] But Sodji, under the influence of the Brazilian, Carvalho, who in 1858 acted as Régis agent at Porto-Novo, pursued an economic policy of his own. For better prices, and for a share in the revival of the export of slaves at Cotonou and Whydah, he diverted palm-oil canoes from the Weme, So, and Porto-Novo area across Lake Nokué, rather than down the Ossa lagoon to Badagri and Lagos. This diversion of produce coincided with the outbreak of the Ijaye War in the Yoruba interior; and this latter event combined with the French 'immigration' scheme to 'raise the hopes of Kosoko and the whole Slave Trade fraternity even at Abeokuta'.[2] Campbell lived just long enough to see the trade routes through Egbado and Egba territory close. After his death in April 1859, no less than five consuls tackled the task of opening them again.

Consul Brand, faced with a decline in Lagos exports, and a dangerous threat to the Egba from Dahomey, attempted to mediate between Ibadan and Ijaye, and failed. His successor, Consul Hand, planned armed intervention against the Fon to protect the Egba flank, but could not raise the necessary forces. It was left to Henry Grant Foote, during his few months as consul, to break the circle by taking a gunboat to Porto-Novo in February 1861 and bombarding the town in an endeavour to force Sodji to allow the palm-oil canoes a passage down the Ossa. He pressed for official acceptance of his predecessor's plan for sending troops to Abeokuta; and he warned the Foreign Office that the Fon, in alliance with Ibadan, were on the point of invading Egba territory. Within a month of his death in May, orders from Russell to annex Lagos were on their way.[3] The news of the threatened Fon campaign and the action at Porto-Novo, received by the Foreign Office in June, removed the last hesitation.

McCoskry, promoted to the position of acting-consul, neglected to reinforce Abeokuta. Instead, with an eye to trade, he took up the negotiations with the Gun where Foote had left off. Before the receipt

---

[1] N.R.O., Consulate Letter-Book, Campbell to Sodji, 14 June 1856.

[2] Ibid., Campbell to Clarendon, 7 Feb. 1859. In 1859 Victor Régis and two other French firms at Nantes and Le Havre were authorized by the French Government to recruit labour for the Antilles from the West African coast. The contracts ended in 1861, after the British Government offered an alternative source of coolie labour from India. Christian Schefer, *Instructions générales données de 1763 à 1870 aux gouverneurs et ordonnateurs des établissements français en Afrique occidentale* (2 vols. Paris, 1927), ii. 466–8. For the origins of the Ijaye war, see Biobaku, p. 64.

[3] F.O. 84/1141, Foote to Russell, 28 Feb. 1861; Russell to Foote, 22 June 1861; P.P., 1862, lxi (339), 5.

of Russell's dispatch, he obtained a treaty of commerce from Sodji and overawed the chiefs of Badagri into making guarantees on the lines of the traders' agreement with Docemo, drawn up in 1854 and 1859.[1] In return for unrestricted trading rights for British subjects, McCoskry promised that fixed export duties would be paid at Porto-Novo and Badagri. In the case of the latter town, the duties were to be paid through the consul at Lagos, making the Gun authorities stipendiary chiefs of a colony, which had begun to expand before it was constituted.

Russell's dispatch to Foote is usually cited as the complete explanation for the annexation that took place in August 1861. To further suppression of the slave trade, to support 'lawful commerce', and thereby to check the expeditions of the King of Dahomey were the official motives for the reluctant decision of the Foreign Office. In April 1860 Consul Brand had suggested such a course of action for slightly different reasons: lack of stable government, danger to property, and the existence of domestic slavery could only be remedied if the 'feeble, irregular, and irresponsible jurisdiction' exercised from the consulate was superseded by the law and institutions of colonial administration.[2] Russell's were reasons of state; Brand spoke for the consuls who by the end of the decade were unable to solve the problems raised by the changing economic conditions at the Lagos market, and incapable of ensuring by treaty alone the peaceful conditions of trade among the Gun, Awori, Egbado, and Egba necessary to that market. It was fitting that the responsibility for cession fell to a trader and a naval officer. They had no hesitation in browbeating Docemo and the *Idejo* chiefs into accepting the agreement of 6 August 1861 which made over to the Crown the island of Lagos 'with all the rights, profits, territories and appurtenances . . . as well as the profit and revenue' of the port.[3] But it is difficult to see exactly how such a cession would have enabled the Crown to 'prevent the destructive wars so frequently undertaken by Dahomey and others for the capture of slaves' (as the treaty put it), unless the island was to be used as a base for military action in the interior. The cession may be regarded as the 'logical end' of the consular period,[4] if it is remembered that the weakness of the indigenous paramountcy

[1] Treaties, 17 June and 19 July 1861, Hertslet, xi (1864), 37–39.
[2] P.P., 1862, lxi (339), Brand to Russell, 9 Apr. 1860, pp. 2–4.
[3] Ibid., p. 8. See, too, Geary, pp. 38–39; Burns, pp. 135–6; Biobaku, p. 68.
[4] Lloyd, p. 162.

precluded a protectorate with full internal sovereignty as a solution to mis-government and no government. But it could not influence the slave trade at Whydah, unless the expansion of British rule beyond the few square miles of Lagos island was contemplated (which it was not); and control of the port was no assurance against the atrophy of legitimate trade. To convert Lagos into a British fort was to isolate it in a position of economic dependency as surely as the company forts at Whydah had been isolated in the eighteenth century. But this was not understood in 1861, at least not in England; and the Foreign Office which had secured a new settlement in the palm-oil market passed to the Colonial Office the problem of how it was to be administered and paid for.

The price of Lagos was high—£7,000 for the last half of 1862, nearly £17,000 in 1863, rising to about £24,000 annually in 1864 and 1865.[1] Some 60 per cent. of the revenues of the colony between 1862 and 1865 were derived from import duties. The rest came from parliamentary grants, and a small fraction from fines and land transfer fees. On paper the accounts were balanced. But at the end of 1864 there was a debt of £1,800, partly covered by parliamentary grants, resulting from lack of ready cash, which the administration offset by drafts on the agents-general and by borrowing at interest from local merchants.[2] Till 1865 the two dangers to the financial stability of the administration were the prolonged Egba-Ibadan war and the development of markets to the west which threatened to drain off palm products from the Ogun, Addo, Yewa, and Weme routes in return for lower-priced, duty-free goods—particularly spirits, arms, and tobacco which were the staples of Lagos customs returns. There was a danger that the very administration set up to protect the traders would, by raising the retail value of merchandise, create relatively adverse market conditions where it was supposed to encourage them most. And as commitments in recurrent expenditure and necessary

[1] Including parliamentary grants: 1862 (£2,822), 1863 (£704), 1864 (£4,455). *Blue Books*, 1863, 1864; P.P., 1865, xxxvii (287), Appendix No. 26, p. 42. Revenues for the last half of 1862 till the end of 1864 amounted to £46,664, made up of customs duties (61·3%), parliamentary grants (17·3%), court fines (3·9%), land sales and fees (3·0%), and 'miscellaneous', including reserve funds (14·5%).

[2] P.P., 1865, xxxvii (287), Appendix No. 28, p. 43. The 'Total Return of Debts' till 20 Dec. 1864 included the hire of the steamer *Eyo Honesty* (£450); materials from the West Africa Company (£367), goods from William McCoskry (£46), drafts on the agents-general (£2,142), advances from the Treasury Chest (£694), and a sum (£525) from Henry Eales Esq.—'Borrowed for current expenses of the Colony', at 5 per cent. interest.

public works grew, the appetite of administrators for increased customs was insatiable.

The policy of the Colonial Office was clear enough; and Governor Henry Stanhope Freeman, from the date of his appointment, zealously complied with the order to be frugal.[1] His first financial ordinance laid down the customs to be paid at Lagos, Badagri, Palma, and Lekki; and Thomas Tickel who had been vice-consul at Badagri for just over a year was promoted to resident agent and collector on a salary of £100.[2] As from April 1863, merchandise coming to Lagos from Porto-Novo down the Ossa lagoon paid the same tariffs as at the port of Lagos itself.[3] A few months later this regulation was applied to Lekki and Palma, which the Colonial Office accepted with a warning that the need for revenue was not to justify any further expansion along the littoral.[4]

The immediate result of the cession of 1861 was to create the impression among the Gun and later the Egba that the action taken at Lagos was a precedent to be followed elsewhere. There were grounds for this anxiety. Governor Freeman and John Hawley Glover who was sworn in as his Lieutenant-governor in May 1863 blamed the nearest culprits for loss of trade; and impelled by the logic of the 1861 treaty—that the cession of Lagos was to be used to end the slave trade farther west—Freeman urged a full military expedition against the Fon and no less than the annexation of the coast from Lagos to Cape St. Paul.[5] The rumour that such an expansion was imminent reached the ears of Baron Didelot, Rear-Admiral in command of the West Africa Naval Division; and the French Government was warned of the possibility before the British Foreign Office had the chance to reject the idea.[6] At Porto-Novo it required little argument on the part of the agents of Victor Régis to persuade King Sodji, already panicked by the bombardment of 1861, that a British invasion was at hand.[7] In July 1862 Sodji formally offered his town to

---

[1] C.O. 147/1, Newcastle to Freeman, 22 Aug. 1862.

[2] *Blue Book*, 1862, pp. 60–61.

[3] N.R.O., Governor's Letter-Book, Freeman to Tickel, 6 Apr. 1862.

[4] N.R.O., Dispatches, 2, Freeman to Newcastle, 1 July 1862; C.O. 147/1, Newcastle to Freeman, 5 Sept. 1862.

[5] N.R.O., Dispatches, 2, Freeman to Russell, 1 July 1862.

[6] M.A.É., Afrique/51, Didelot to Chasseloup-Laubat, 2 May 1862, encl. in Chasseloup-Laubat to Thouvenel, 2 July 1862; F.O. 84/1187, F.O. to C.O., 21 Aug. 1862. Didelot had picked up the rumour through Capt. Garraud of the *Estaing* who had it from Marius Daumas, agent of Régis at Lagos.

[7] M.A.É., Afrique/51, Régis to Thouvenel, 7 July 1862.

Napoleon III, promising to end the slave trade and to allow French colonists to settle on his lands.[1]

In Paris neither the Ministry for the Navy nor the French Foreign Office was seriously disturbed. Between the survey carried out by Lieutenant Bouët in the 1840's and the brief experiment in labour recruitment in the late 1850's, French official interest in the coast of Africa concentrated on the rich groundnut colonies north of the Gold Coast. A treaty of friendship with Ghezo, concluded in 1851, avoided any mention of the slave trade and simply settled the amount of customs to be paid by Régis at Whydah.[2] At most, in 1862, the Minister for the Navy, Chasseloup-Laubat, thought that a consul should be appointed to report on trade in the Bight of Benin; and at the end of the year the French agent of Régis at Lagos, Marius Daumas, was nominated. As a trader, Daumas had a keen appreciation of what the extension of British jurisdiction would entail for his firm. While waiting at Lagos for transport to Porto-Novo, he employed himself in protesting to Freeman and to the Colonial Office against the local customs tariff which hit the bulk of French imports hardest.[3] Once installed by Admiral Didelot at Porto-Novo in January 1863, he took steps to ensure that such customs would not be applied farther west. On behalf of Régis he agreed to pay Sodji an annual grant of $1,600 (£320) instead of duties. On behalf of France he accepted a treaty of friendship; and on 23 February he witnessed a request for French protection, which promised all Porto-Novo customs duties would be made over to the consul. Two days later he signed a protectorate treaty, guaranteeing trading rights and quartering the French colours in King Sodji's flag.[4] Admiral Didelot who was luke-warm in his support for the consul informed the Ministry for the Navy that Régis would have the unique privilege of simply handing over a fixed sum to a French protectorate administration, rather than paying duties. With this in mind, Chasseloup-Laubat looked on the episode as a piece of commercial legermain by Daumas. But, follow-

---

[1] M.A.É., King Sodji to Napoleon III, 5 July 1862, encl. in Régis to Chasseloup-Laubat, 14 Aug. 1862.

[2] Treaty, 1 July 1851, *Études dahoméennes*, ix (1953), 11–12.

[3] M.A.É., Afrique/52, Daumas to Newcastle, 10 Jan., 7 Feb. 1863; Daumas to Freeman, 12 Jan. 1863, copies encl. in Régis to Thouvenel, 21 Mar. 1863.

[4] Ibid., Treaties, 23 and 25 Feb. 1863 (signed Daumas, Didelot, and Sodji), encl. in Didelot to Chasseloup-Laubat, 24 Feb. 1863; Daumas to Drouyn de Lhuys, 8 Mar. 1863; Régis to Drouyn de Lhuys, 21 Mar. 1863. The request for French protection bore the signatures of eight of the principal Brazilian traders at Porto-Novo—including that of the ex-slaver Joachim Manuel de Carvalho.

ing Didelot's suggestion, he advised the French Foreign Office that the protectorate agreement, even if not ratified by France, should not be rejected, since it might yet prove a useful pawn in negotiations with England 'afin d'arriver à établir une sorte de droit international qui garantisse tous les intérêts engagés dans le Golfe de Bénin'.[1] At the Foreign Office this advice and the news of the formal extension of Lagos Colony to Palma and Lekki made the new minister, Drouyn de Lhuys, hesitate to repudiate Daumas's handiwork. At the end of June 1863 a further report from Didelot made it clear that the slave trade was still actively carried on by Carvalho and Domingo Martinez and might yet provide the English with an excuse for the seizure of Whydah.[2] Desiring neither a Brazilian market, nor wishing to see the further extension of English customs, the Paris ministries resigned themselves to cautious inactivity on the subject.

Meanwhile, Daumas consolidated his position. In July he went to Abomey and obtained verbally a vague 'cession' of Cotonou to France for an annual present of 4,000 dollars to King Glele.[3] With more conviction he raised the French flag at Appa and secured from villages between Nokué and Porto-Novo a guarantee of unrestricted passage for trading canoes.[4] He organized labour to open up a track from Appa to the beach, and cleared a creek for canoes from Appa to the Ossa lagoon. In addition to Porto-Novo there was now a second market for French goods opposite the mouth of the Addo river.

Glover wasted little time in arguing dubiously that Appa was the westernmost point of Lagos territory—'the chief of Appa being a chief of the King of Lagos'.[5] With typical initiative he arranged for the immediate cession of Badagri and concluded three protectorate agreements with Addo, Ipokia, and Okeodan to forestall any further manœuvres by Daumas.[6] In return for a promise of help against the

---

[1] Ibid., Chasseloup-Laubat to Drouyn de Lhuys, 20 Apr. 1863.

[2] Ibid., Didelot to Chasseloup-Laubat, 27 Mar. 1863, encl. in Chasseloup-Laubat to Drouyn de Lhuys, 25 June 1863. The steamer *Nordagny* shipped about 4,000 slaves from Whydah to Cuba, 1860–3; and in March, reported Didelot (who merely observed the fact), a brig was waiting to take off 200 slaves at Cotonou.

[3] M.A.É., Afrique/52, Didelot to Chasseloup-Laubat, 5 July 1863, encl. in Chasseloup-Laubat to Drouyn de Lhuys, 1 Sept. 1863.

[4] Ibid., Daumas to Drouyn de Lhuys, 7 Oct. 1863. By agreement with the chiefs of Katanu, dated 30 Sept. 1863.

[5] M.F.O., Gabon vi/1, Glover to Daumas, 18 June 1863; N.R.O., Dispatches, 2, Glover to Russell, 10 June 1863.

[6] Treaties with the chiefs of Addo, Ipokia, and Okeodan, 27 and 29 June, 4 July 1863, and treaty of cession at Badagri, 7 July 1863, in Hertslet, xii (1905), 103–7.

Fon—which had been repeatedly requested—the Awori and Egbado chiefs agreed to suspend the export of slaves to Porto-Novo.
In the case of Badagri, the *Akran* and seven ward chiefs simply
acknowledged a state of dependence that had existed in practice
since 1861 and had their stipends increased for their compliance.
Glover followed this up by ordering Lieutenant-Commander Dolben
to demarcate the area of the new protectorates which he interpreted
generously as all the territory between the Igbessa and Addo rivers
from Badagri in the south nearly to Ketu in the north.[1] In September
1863 Tickel was appointed resident consul to Okeodan. His first duty
was to inform the chiefs of Okeodan, Ipokia, and Addo that all
European merchandise entering the new protectorates by way of
Porto-Novo was to pay duties, collected at the mouth of the Addo
river. Goods coming by way of Lagos or Badagri were allowed to
enter duty-free.[2]

This preoccupation with the financial consequences of French
intervention was evident in Glover's excuse to the Colonial Office for
his unauthorized actions. Since the declaration of the French protectorate in February 1863, he claimed, local traders had landed at
Cotonou and Appa beach goods worth over £6,000 in customs.[3] To
counter this and attract imports back to Lagos, Glover halved the
tariffs on rum and tobacco; but the losses continued. Accordingly, he
had taken steps to turn the whole of the area between the Ogun and
the Addo rivers into a British customs zone and cripple Porto-Novo
and Cotonou trade by turning the export of palm products south-
east instead of south-west.

Neither Daumas nor Didelot permitted this to happen without a
protest. But the French admiral could not argue the British protectorates away; and he and Glover arrived at a partition treaty in
August 1863.[4] It was agreed that Ipokia was neutral ground for the
present. The banks of the Addo divided the French protectorate
from Lagos territory; and in the south the demarcation line running
from the mouth of the Addo to the beach left Appa on the French
side.

[1] N.R.O., Dispatches 2, Glover to Russell, 8 Sept. 1863.
[2] N.R.O., Governor's Letter-Book, Glover to Tickel, 24 Sept. 1863.
[3] N.R.O., Dispatches, 2, Glover to Newcastle, 9 Aug. 1863.
    '1150 Rolls of Tobacco 50 lbs each at 2*d*. per lb.　　　£4,791　13　4
    1400 Pipes of Rum 100 Galls. each at 6*d*. per Gall.　　£1,750　0　0
    　　　　　　　　　　　　　　　　　　　　　　　　　　£6,541　13　4'
[4] Convention 1 Aug. 1863, *Études dahoméennes*, ix (1953), 13–15.

Glover's protectorate agreements were refused by the Colonial Office—though Glover himself continued to look on Okeodan as a dependency of Lagos as late as 1865.[1] He clung obstinately to his first thesis that French traders would cut out palm-oil supplies from the interior; and his point that customs posts in the west were essential to Lagos revenue won grudging approval, if his method of establishing them did not.[2]

Governor Freeman, when he returned from leave in November 1863, was also dissatisfied with the work of his lieutenant, but for different reasons. He thought Glover had been too generous with Didelot; and he made it clear to Didelot's successor, Admiral Laffon de Ladébat, that the only navigable entrance to the mouth of the Addo river 'will be considered as belonging and subject to the English Government', whether it was in a British protectorate or not.[3] Like Glover, he feared that a permanent occupation of Porto-Novo by the French would probably so damage Lagos trade, 'as to render the revenue insufficient for the expenditure of the Colony'.[4] But he disagreed with Glover's ordinance introducing trading licences—a substitute for increased duties—as unlikely to 'bring Porto-Novo trade through Lagos'. Only a few merchants had taken out the new licences; and the Sierra Leonean traders refused in a body to pay £25 a year for the privilege of doing business during a bad season. The licences were abolished; and in February 1864 Freeman imposed new duties on the import of cowries and extended a general *ad valorem* duty of 4 per cent. to all previously free imports.

Gradually the commercial thorn in the western flank of the colony worked loose. The death of King Sodji brought an unco-operative ruler to the Gun throne. King Mikpon clashed with de Ladébat who ordered the royal princes to refrain from seizing hostages from the Yoruba to exchange against slaves who fled to Lagos. But the admiral had no force to uphold his ruling; and on 2 January 1865 (to the disappointment of the Ministry for the Navy) he declared the unratified protectorate at an end.[5] The handful of marines departed; the

[1] C.O. 147/4, Newcastle to Glover, 23 Sept. 1863.
[2] C.O. 147/4, Glover to Newcastle, 6 Apr. 1863, and Minute by Under-Secretary Elliot; Glover to Newcastle, 6 Nov. 1863.
[3] N.R.O., Dispatches, 2, Freeman to de Ladébat, 8 Mar. 1864, encl. in Freeman to Newcastle, 8 Mar. 1864.
[4] Ibid., Freeman to Newcastle, 9 Mar. 1864.
[5] M.A.É., Afrique/52, de Ladébat to Chasseloup-Laubat, 22 Dec. 1864, encl. in Chasseloup-Laubat to Drouyn de Lhuys, 13 Mar. 1865. See, too, Schefer, ii. 510.

consulate was based at Whydah. But a beginning had been made, and the interests of Régis were not forgotten. It had been agreed by Glover towards the end of 1864 that goods imported through Lagos in transit to Porto-Novo would be allowed a customs drawback of 50 per cent. and he promised to keep to this arrangement for the first half of 1865.[1] This compromise obtained by de Ladébat brought some fiscal compensation to the Lagos administration; and it allowed French traders to make use of Lagos port facilities at those periods of the year when the surf was too dangerous for landings at Whydah and Cotonou. But immediately the French withdrew Glover blockaded the coastal ports for a few months to cut off supplies of arms for the Egba. For obvious financial reasons which were admitted in the blockade proclamation of 7 April, he found it necessary 'to disallow the drawback of 50 per cent. hitherto granted on goods exported to Porto-Novo'.[2] At least one French vessel was forced, while the blockade lasted, to unload at Lagos and pay full duties. As de Ladébat complained, the officials of the Lagos Executive Council had need of ready cash: 'et ils déclarent avec une entière franchise qu'ils iront en chercher dans la caisse des négociants étrangers établis à Porto-Novo'. Compensation on behalf of French traders was demanded, but never paid.

The Egba were treated in the same cavalier fashion, for the same reasons. In 1865 the differences and misunderstandings that had been building up between Lagos and Abeokuta came to a head. The nomination of a British consul to the Egba capital had been refused in July 1862: the evidence of how easily consuls grew into governors was still fresh in Yoruba minds. And after the death of the *Alake* Okukenu, in the same year, the *Ologun* war chiefs spoke with stronger voices in Egba councils. The Ogun was closed to trade with Lagos. When in March 1864 the last Fon invasion was beaten off, the Egba were free to deal with Ibadan, and Ibadan's allies and suppliers in Ijebu Remo.

The succession dispute over the *Alafin* title which had occasioned the war was no longer by 1865 the issue at stake between the Yoruba contestants. More vital to the Egba was the destination of the £23,000 worth of arms and powder imported into Lagos between

---

[1] M.F.O., Gabon, vi/1, Glover to de Ladébat, 21 Dec. 1864, encl. in de Ladébat to Chasseloup-Laubat, 16 Apr. 1865.

[2] Ibid., Proclamation, 7 Apr. 1865, signed by H. T. Ussher, Acting-Colonial Secretary, encl. in de Ladébat to Chasseloup-Laubat, 16 Apr. 1865.

July 1862 and the end of 1864. Much of this went to Ibadan through Ijebu middlemen from the market on the Lagos lagoon at Ikorodu. In March 1865 the Egba laid siege to it. Glover, in his role of clumsy peacemaker, first gave permission for its destruction; and then, fearing damage to Lagos farms on the north shore, and wearying of Egba tactics, he delivered an ultimatum to the Egba force to withdraw, which was rejected.[1] Armed intervention took place at once: and on 25 March the Egba were routed with heavy losses.

During the uneasy truce that ensued, it was clear that Glover's primary anxiety was to unlock the supplies of native produce held at Abeokuta and which would have found their way to the western markets, when his blockade of Cotonou and Porto-Novo was raised. In April, Glover summed up the reasons for his prolonged embargo on trade and his hasty action at Ikorodu: for both were closely linked.[2] Strategically, he had aimed at stopping the supply of arms by the Gun to the Egba. Financially, the colony, according to the collector of customs, had saved £1,204 by suspending the drawback paid on goods to Porto-Novo. As for Ikorodu, he had simply tired of waiting for the route to Ibadan to be reopened.

In the short term, Glover was able to claim that his policy produced the results he desired. In May he reported that native traders were 'flocking in' to the markets at Ikorodu and Egerin: one firm alone had purchased 440 tons of palm-oil the previous month.[3] Threatened with suspension of the drawback (and therefore loss of local traders' support), King Mikpon had been induced by Glover to expel Egba entrepreneurs from Porto-Novo. True, the arms traffic continued in the Egbado towns; but the Ogun was open; and for a period in September and November 1865 produce in transit from Abeokuta to Lagos amounted to just over £8,000, and the import of goods by the same route was valued at £4,262.[4] With some justification Glover could prophesy in April that the policy 'whereby we have opened the roads to the interior, causes the commercial horizon of this Settlement to assume a brighter aspect than it has done at any period since Lagos was added to the British Crown'.[5]

The Parliamentary Select Committee which in the same month was questioning the need for any settlements at all, would have been

[1] Biobaku, pp. 76–77.
[2] N.R.O., Dispatches, 2, Glover to Cardwell, 9 Apr. 1865.
[3] Ibid., Glover to Cardwell, 8 May and 9 June 1865.
[4] N.R.O., Dispatches, 3, Glover to Cardwell, 7 Nov. 1865 and 8 Jan. 1866.
[5] N.R.O., Dispatches, 2, Glover to Cardwell, 9 Apr. 1865.

surprised to hear Glover's verdict. It would probably have made little difference to the partiality of their final report and recommendations if they had.[1] Bent on economy and retrenchment, they set their faces against any defence of the annexation or expansion of Lagos Colony. They censured the cession of 1861, finding that 'Docemo was deprived and pensioned off on the ground of incapacity of government and infraction of treaty'; and without this false step the Lagos administration would not have been embroiled in the Yoruba wars or troubled by the problem of domestic slavery.[2] But despite its leading questions, the committee could not prove that trade conditions were better under the consulate than in the early 1860's: so no satisfactory estimate of the commercial value of Lagos, or indeed any of the settlements, was arrived at. Moreover, the financial returns of the West African posts, supplied by Colonel Ord, received only cursory examination; and there was little statistical basis for the committee's conclusion that all future expenditure could be adequately covered by the previous scale of parliamentary grants and customs revenue.[3] Even the recommendation for no new posts and ultimate withdrawal altogether was weakened by the Colonial Secretary's amendment to the draft report. But in the case of Lagos, the committee's directive for the restoration of 'native rule' was unambiguous.[4]

To be fair, not all the witnesses called were of equal value where testimony on Lagos was concerned. They ranged in temperament from the colonial surgeon, Dr. Henry Eales, who declared that the 'thrashing of the Egbas' at Ikorodu would make them amenable, to the gentle missionary C. H. Gollmer who thought 'a kind word' would have been enough.[5] When the content of the committee's minutes is compared with other evidence, the best of the informants on Lagos appears to have been the sharp trader William McCoskry; the most inadequate was the celebrated traveller, writer, and sometime consul, Richard Burton. But the former prejudiced the committee by blaming all the troubles of the consular period on the 'native king' and by ascribing the reason for annexation to 'the non-fulfilment of treaty obligations by King Docemo'.[6] McCoskry had in mind the traders' treaties of 1854 and 1859, not the treaty of 1 January 1852. This

[1] P.P., 1865, v (1), Draft report, x–xvi, and recommendations, 26 June 1865, iii.
[2] Ibid. x, xiv.   [3] Ibid. xiii.
[4] Ibid., para. 56, iii.   [5] P.P., 1865, v (1), Qq. 5931 and 7008.
[6] Ibid., Qq. 1637–41.

confusion was never cleared up; and other witnesses, including the Foreign Office official W. Wylde (who appeared to know nothing of the later treaties), contradicted him.[1] Burton, on the other hand, though only in the area for four years, said exactly what the leading questions of the committee demanded: that the posts at Lagos, Badagri, and Palma should be abandoned for a single consulate protected by a steamer.

William Wylde, superintendent of the Foreign Office Slave Trade Department, like McCoskry, had no hesitation in frankly admitting that Lagos should be kept for its commercial value, having 'such an immense command of all the water communication' behind the littoral. And keeping order in this rising commercial centre, he argued, had required a stronger authority than that of Docemo who 'was merely a puppet' and a more convincing force than 'one small steamer which was almost useless'.[2] The trader, for his part, explained that palm produce came not from Abeokuta alone, but also 'from the banks of the lagoon running behind Badagry and Porto-Novo up towards Abeokuta'—the region between the Ossa and the Addo rivers.[3] Posts on the flanks were both markets and revenue earners: 'and were those posts not held, other merchants, the French particularly, would establish places and land goods free of duty, and bring them into the same market as Lagos goods'. But pressed for his opinion, he was forced to admit that Freeman and Glover had no 'direct authority' to take these posts.[4] The Okeodan treaty, he confessed, was another unauthorised security for commerce and customs; and he defended it with an argument worthy of Glover himself:

Okeodan was on the main road to the interior, and it was pretty well known that the French were trying to get it; in fact they had assumed the protection of Pocrah, which was on the way to it, and it was believed that they would have taken Okeodan, and then they would have had a road direct to Abbeokuta, through which, if they had held Porto-Novo, they might have held the trade to Abbeokuta, instead of its going to Lagos; that was the real object.[5]

Wylde emphasized, too, that revenue was at stake and that foreign competition was not to be tolerated, even though he admitted it was known the French protectorate would not last.[6]

[1] Ibid., Qq. 2804–5.
[2] Ibid., Qq. 2750, 2808–11.
[3] Ibid., Q. 1612.
[4] Ibid., Q. 1697.
[5] P.P., 1865, v (1) Q. 1846.
[6] Ibid., Qq. 2920–1.

[W. E. Forster] You thought it unreasonable that the French should, by simply putting an officer on the coast, open a trade without exacting a revenue, and thereby get an advantage over the trade through our settlement, which required a good deal of expense to keep up?

[Wylde] Exactly.

[W. E. Forster] I suppose that that did not induce our Government to consider whether it would not be possible for a trade to be opened on the coast just in the same way as it was opened by the French, by simply putting officers there?

[Wylde] No, it did not; because we knew very well it could not last long, and that they would have to interfere more, or withdraw altogether; and we were quite right. Their occupation of Porto-Novo was merely for thwarting our policy in Lagos and the lagoon, and affecting the revenue of the colony.

But for the moment the French had withdrawn, the expansionists were silenced, and Lagos, on the recommendation of the committee, was brought under the supervision of the governor-in-chief of the West African settlements, in Sierra Leone. The formal pattern of colonial administration could be altered; the conditions in which it attempted to maintain law and order could not. Admiral Laffon de Ladébat, also writing in 1865, summed up the dilemma of European intervention in terms that applied to Lagos as well as Porto-Novo:

Dès qu'un poste militaire se trouve à côté d'une factorerie, le traitant devient plus arrogant avec les nègres et les menace volontiers des baïonnettes qu'il sent auprès de lui. L'officier qui meurt d'ennui plus encore que de maladie, recherche avec avidité les moyens de sortir de son inaction, et les occasions d'en venir aux mains se présentent en foule, dès que nous voulons entrer dans le détail des opérations commerciales, afin de les mieux protéger.[1]

[1] M.A.É., Afrique/77, de Ladébat to Chasseloup-Laubat, 2 Feb. 1865, encl. in Cloué to Duclerc, 14 Sept. 1882.

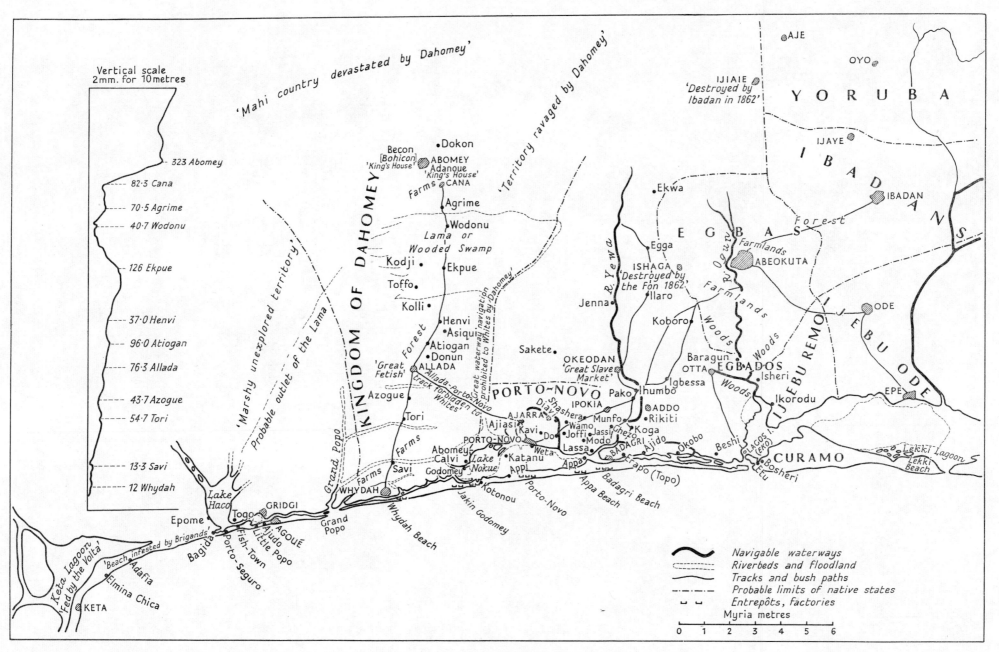

Vertical scale
2 mm. for 10 metres

— 323 Abomey

— 82·3 Cana

— 70·5 Agrime

— 40·7 Wodonu

— 126 Ekpue

— 37·0 Henvi

— 96·0 Atiogan

— 76·3 Allada

— 43·7 Azogue

— 54·7 Tori

— 13·3 Savi

— 12 Whydah

'Mahi country devastated by Dahomey'

'Territory ravaged by Dahomey'

YORUBA

AJE

OYO

IJIAIE
'Destroyed by
Ibadan in 1862'

IJAYE

IBADAN

IBADAN

Becon
[Bohicon]
'King's House'

•Dokon

ABOMEY
Adanoue
'King's House'

Farms •CANA

•Agrime

•Wodonu

Lama or
Wooded Swamp

Kodji• •Ekpue

Toffo•

Kolli•

•Henvi
•Asiqui
•Atiogan
•Donun

'Great
Fetish'

ALLADA

Azogue•

Tori•

'Marshy unexplored territory'

'Probable outlet of the Lama'

KINGDOM OF DAHOMEY

Forest

Allada-Porto-Novo
track forbidden to
Whites

'Great waterway navigation
prohibited to Whites by Dahomey'

Farms

Ekwa•

Egga•

ISHAGA
'Destroyed by
the Fon 1862'

Jenna• Ilaro•

R. Yewa

Koboro•

Sakete•

EGBAS

Forest

Ogun River

Farmlands
ABEOKUTA

Farmlands

Woods

Woods

OKEODAN
'Great Slave
Market'

Baragun

OTTA EGBADOS

Igbessa•

PORTO-NOVO Pako Ihumbo

Shashera
Diavo IPOKIA
Ajiasi• AJARRA
Kavi• Wamo Munfo
Do Jassi Ghezo
Joffi• Modo
Lassa BADAGRI

Abomey-
Calvi• Weta
Lake Katanu
Nokue Appi Appa
Godomey Appa

•ADDO
•Rikiti

Koga
Ajido

ODE

Isheri•

Ikorodu•

IJEBU REMO

Woods

Beshi

LAGOS I.
(LEKO)

CURAMO

EPE

Lekki Lagoon

Lekki
Beach

Bosheri
LEU

Savi

WHYDAH

Farms

Grand Popo

Whydah Beach

Jakin Godomey

Kotonou

Porto-
Novo

Appa Beach

Badagri Beach

Erapo (Topo)

Okobo

Okobo

Lake
Haco

Epome• Togo
Gridgi
Ajudo AGOUÉ
Little Popo

Grand
Popo

Keta Lagoon
'Fed by the Volta'

'Beach infested by Brigands'

Adafia

Elmina Chica

KETA

Bagida
Porto-Seguro
Fish-Town

〰 Navigable waterways
------ Riverbeds and floodland
—— Tracks and bush paths
—·— Probable limits of native states
⊔ ⊔ Entrepôts, factories
      Myria metres

0 1 2 3 4 5 6

FIG. 4. The Slave Coast, 1865, after F. Borghero, Missionary.

CHAPTER IV

The Administration of Lagos Colony and the Western District, 1866–86

THE findings of the 1865 Committee helped to restrain the impetuosity of Glover and his successors. But neither the Colonial Office nor administrators in the field produced any clear definition of the territorial limits of Lagos and its protectorate, during the period they were governed as part of the West African settlements. It was not till 1876, after the colony had become an appendage of the Gold Coast, that an attempt was made to clear up the vagueness of the administrative boundary by substituting legal for geographical or ethnic criteria. According to an Interpretation Ordinance, 'protected territories' under Lagos meant those areas where the Crown had acquired powers of jurisdiction.[1]

This, too, was only a rough and ready rule. In September 1879 the Western District was extended to Katanu at the head of Lake Nokué where no British jurisdiction had ever been exercised; and in March 1884 Appa was brought under British control. No formal Order-in-Council ever ratified this extension westwards. It was enough for the governor of the Gold Coast to acknowledge and approve these measures in September 1885; and for administrative purposes, the new protectorates were placed under Badagri the following year. So far as Badagri itself was concerned, the cession agreement of 1863 was interpreted very liberally: any village between Lagos and the Addo river and within about ten to fifteen miles north of the Ossa lagoon was incorporated in the Western and Northern Districts of the colony. When, in 1886, Governor Moloney asked the town elders and the few remaining signatories of the 1863 treaty to define 'Badagri', they assented to a definition which acknowledged the area administered during the previous two decades, rather than the area of the town and its adjacent farms—some three square miles—which was all that had strictly been ceded.[2]

[1] N.R.O., Dispatches, 11, Interpretation Ordinance, No. 3, 1876, of the Gold Coast Colony, cited in Moloney to Granville, 12 Mar. 1886.
[2] N.R.O., Dispatches, 11, Moloney to Granville, 12 Mar. 1886. The definition

G

So far from withering away and allowing the re-establishment of independent native authorities, the judicial and fiscal powers of the Lagos government were strengthened year by year, as officials ran the courts and the customs posts with a minimum of supervision from above. There was little policy, but much pragmatism. Ordinances laying down rules of conduct were non-existent before Lagos became a separate colony in 1886; and the practical business of running the port and keeping order among the population of the lagoon markets in the 1860's and 1870's was conducted without the political memoranda and copious circulars of later decades.

Indeed, there were few if any senior officials long enough in the colony to acquire the experience necessary for formulating long-term administrative plans. Apart from John Glover whose term of office as administrator lasted six years, there were no less than fifteen acting-administrators, lieutenant-governors or deputy-governors, between 1872 and the end of 1885.[1] Their lines of communication with the Colonial Office were long. They ran via the governor-in-chief in Sierra Leone, or, after 1874, through the governor of the Gold Coast; and these intermediaries, too, were constantly changing.

The primary function of the Lagos officials was to see that conditions of European trade were undisturbed and that the Administration, as far as possible, paid for itself. And the easiest way to become head of the colony after Glover's time was to start as customs-collector: no less than nine of the Lagos administrators-of-passage were promoted directly from this office. Others, like Moloney, were ex-army officers from the Ashanti wars, placed in charge of the native constabulary. A few were simply official oddments—the local surgeon, or the secretary of the Executive Council—filling in a gap till somebody suitable could be found. Their European subordinates were few in numbers before 1875—at most two district commissioners, a chief magistrate, and two customs officers. The establishment relied heavily on literate Sierra Leoneans to fill the score of minor posts as inspectors, clerks, bailiffs, storemen, and 'landing

agreed to by the chiefs was as follows: 'To the Northward or inland and inclusive thereof, Lagbo, Kagga, Ille and a line drawn through these to the Oluge Waters; to the West and Addo River continued to the Sea by a line passing through and inclusive of Quameh; to the Eastward Oluge Waters and a line thence to Okogbo across [the] Lagoon to the Sea; to the Southward the Sea.'

[1] Of these Captain C. C. Lees, C. A. Moloney, and W. Bradford Griffith were in office at Lagos more than once, and Moloney remained on as governor of the colony for periods after 1886.

waiters'. The civil police consisted of Hausa and Yoruba recruits; and the small Hausa militia which replaced the West India Regiment, withdrawn in 1870, had no more than two European officers. But once Lagos became part of the Gold Coast Colony, the establishment proliferated rapidly.[1]

*Lagos Colony and Protectorate**

| | Establishment | | | |
	1866	1870	1875	1880
Europeans and Sierra Leoneans	30	30	49	79
Salaries/Wages . . .	£5,935	£7,545	· £10,029	£13,126
% of total expenditure .	25%	17%	22%	23%

* Excluding two officers of the West India Regiment, Lagos Constabulary, and Hausa Militia.

The increase in salaries between 1866 and 1870 represented a real rise in amounts paid to lower-grade officials. After 1870 salary scales remained stable, though their total amount nearly doubled. It was an increase, however, which the local budget was well able to stand, so long as customs revenues were constantly high.

Both executive and legislative powers remained firmly in the hands of the Administrators, aided by a small council consisting of the chief magistrate, the acting Colonial Secretary and the officer commanding local troops (the West Indians or the Hausas). The two traders, William McCoskry and Edward Le Gros, who were nominated to assist the Legislative Council in 1864 and 1865 were not replaced in Glover's time. After his departure in 1872, Arthur Porter, a clerk of the firm of Banner Brothers, was made unofficial member. But he in no way represented the trading community; and Administrator Fowler recommended two Sierra Leoneans for inclusion in the Legislative Council.[2] In 1874, however, the council ceased to exist; and the colony had no representatives in the Legislative Council of the Gold Coast. It was not revived at Lagos till 1886, when it included the governor, five officials, one European trader, one African trader and an African pastor.[3]

[1] *C.O. Lists*, 1867–81; *Blue Books*, 1866–80. Additional and expanding departments after 1875 were, the Government Printing Office, the Supreme Court, Engineering, Customs, and the Office of the Harbour Master.

[2] C.O. 147/24, Pope Hennessy to Kimberley, 28 Oct. 1872.

[3] C.O. 147/55, Moloney to Granville, 19 Apr. 1886. The unofficial members were, William Hammond, Charles Joseph George, and the Rev. Samuel Johnson.

The population appears to have doubled in size on Lagos island between 1866 and 1881. Some of this increase can probably be accounted for by the thoroughness of the 1881 census, compared with earlier estimates, though there was undoubtedly a slow but steady influx of petty traders and freed slaves into Lagos from neighbouring areas of the mainland.[1]

Population

Lagos Town and Vicinity

			1866	1871	1881
Males	.	.	12,457	16,893	27,059
Females	.	.	12,584	19,030	26,226
Total	.	.	25,041	35,923	53,285

Lagos Colony and Protectorate

			1868	1871	1881
Males	.	.	19,663	27,863	37,665
Females	.	.	21,573	32,358	37,605
Total* .		.	41,236	60,221	75,270

* Including for each year 87, 82, and 117 Europeans respectively.

By 1881 just over 71 per cent. of the whole colony and protectorate was estimated to reside on or near Lagos island. An analysis of the occupational structure of the adult population of the territory indicates that the percentage of those employed in commerce—from European merchants down to petty traders—doubled between 1866 and 1881. A surprisingly small percentage of the population was engaged in agriculture or fishing, compared with the 47·3 per cent. listed as merchants, traders, or artisans, though the latter group certainly included women as well as men. The percentage engaged in agriculture, as might be expected, was larger in the districts than the capital. Nevertheless, it is apparent that the population of the colony, and to a lesser degree, the protectorate, had become increasingly dependent for foodstuffs, as well as produce for export, from areas outside

[1] N.R.O., Dispatches, 9, Pope Hennessy to Kimberley, 28 Oct. 1872; *Blue Books*, 1866–81; *Lagos Times*, 28 Sept. 1881. The 1881 returns may also have been influenced by the innovation of paying the twenty-four 'enumerators' employed, according to the size of their count.

Occupations, 1881*

	Lagos Town	Lagos Vicinity	Western District	Northern District	Eastern District	Total	%
Commerce (clerks, agents, merchants)	11,049	435	1,045	65	39	12,633	32·8
Manufacturers, petty traders, artisans . .	5,173	194	195	..	30	5,592	14·5
Agriculture . .	1,414	3,689	2,099	2,831	1,050	11,073	28·6
Fishermen . .	1,573	2,068	2,003	46	5	5,695·	14·8
'Students'† . .	2,570	30	45	100	19	2,764	7·2
Civil Service‡	292	4	60	8	35	399	1·0
Professions§ .	333	..	2	10	3	348	0·9
Total . .	22,404	6,420	5,449	3,060	1,171	38,504	

* Adapted from *Blue Book*, 1881; *Lagos Times*, 28 Sept. 1881.
† Any child or adolescent in a mission school, or adults paying clerks to learn reading and writing.
‡ Including everybody from European officials down to public works labourers.
§ European and coloured teachers and missionaries, journalists, printers, native doctors, interpreters, and clerks. There were also 2,357 labourers.

the sphere of British control.[1] It is clear, too, that by 1871 the majority of the traders were no longer Sierra Leonean and Brazilian middlemen whose total adult population amounted to only a little over 2,000.[2] In numbers the Yoruba and Gun traders had displaced them.

For Glover and his successors the demographic changes of the 1860's and 1870's brought problems of jurisdiction. The single magistrate's court at Lagos was inadequate to deal with the wave of petty crime and disputes over land that increased the number of cases heard from 537 in 1865 to 985 two years later.[3] Reference to the West African Appeal Court at Freetown was cumbersome and expensive. This rudimentary system was improved by the Supreme Court Ordinance of 1876.[4] A chief justice was appointed to apply local laws in civil cases and sit as a court of assizes for criminal cases. But the provision for a divisional court with the chief magistrate on tour in the districts did not in fact operate. It was left to the district commissioners to exercise jurisdiction in civil cases and a summary criminal jurisdiction with power to imprison for three months or inflict a fine not exceeding £25. Till 1886 appeal was open to the

[1] N.R.O., Dispatches, 9, Griffith to Rowe, 12 Aug. 1881 (report of the lieutenant-governor's tour of market towns).
[2] *Blue Book*, 1881. Sierra Leoneans and Brazilians in 1871 were estimated to number 1,533 and 1,237 respectively.
[3] N.R.O., Dispatches, 3, Glover to Kennedy, 14 Sept. 1868.
[4] See T. Olawale Elias, *Groundwork of Nigerian Law* (London, 1954), pp. 43–44.

administrator and ultimately to the Supreme Court of the Gold Coast. At the same time the Police Magistrate's Court was reconstituted (under the chief justice); and by 1881 it was handling about 1,500 cases a year. By then, too, Lagos had a civil constabulary of 284 and there were small police forces of 12 Hausas at Lekki and 21 at Badagri.

The growth of a European judiciary at Lagos made little difference to the position of the *Idejo* chiefs or to Docemo. The former retained their titles but played no part in the civil administration of the capital; and the latter, living on a pension, was never consulted after the cession of Lagos.[1] In the districts, however, the erosion of the powers of native authorities was a slower process, marked at times by violence. This was particularly true of the Western District where there was a population of about 8,000 to 10,000 Gun and Yoruba under the protection of the commandant or commissioner at Badagri.

The area under the control of officials at Badagri was neatly defined in 1875 according to the number of villages frequently visited for judicial and census purposes (there was no head tax in the colony or the protectorate). There were some forty villages between the Addo river and the Oluge lagoon. A few of the more important of them had small populations of Gun settlers whose lineage founders had come from one of the Badagri wards and whose elders looked towards one of the Badagri chiefs as a final court of resort to settle land and inheritance disputes.

Villages of the Western District 1875*

Under the Akran (Jegba ward)		Under the Jengen (Awhanjigo ward)		Under the Finehnto (Wharako ward)		Under the Wawu (Ahaviko ward)	
Ajara	197	Itohun	118	Meke	172	Topo	197
Itoga	180	Banko	73	Gaingbo	105	Dalli	139
Vreko	160	Mosefejo	56			Doko	40
Aladagun	77	Maba	13				

* N.R.O., Badagry Letter-Book, 1874–7, Tickel to Brown, 25 July 1875. Many of the smaller villages have disappeared as their populations died out or settled within larger units.

Badagri itself had a population of 2,400 in 1875 and was divided into eight wards. It was not the principal market centre for the area. Addo, Porto-Novo, and Lagos were the terminals for canoe-traffic to and from the British sphere and the Yoruba interior. But it was

[1] Docemo died in 1885. His son Oyekan succeeded to the *Eleko* title and was paid a small pension of £150.

important as a customs post, and still more as a court, as the commissioner's house with the police court and jail in its compound rivalled the *Akran*'s ward at the other end of the town, as an administrative centre.

Yoruba Settlements Independent of Badagri*

Ajido	1,018	Agangbemi	87	Vedo	32
Koja Zebe	639	Ganyi	75	Agbomase	25
Wuru	390	Agamadin	74	Ilu Vadumu	28
Vedo	179	Rikiti	69	Epobetu	18
Mowo	163	Ofogun	62	Huntodeko	7
Lado	132	Iragbo	54	Gainko	4
Ebute	109	Iragun	42	Okopadonu	4
Koja Ille	102	Jaron	38	Oko Adangbe	3

* See Fig. 6 below, p. 98.

The official who left his mark on the administration of the Western District was the ubiquitous Thomas Tickel. Originally a European trader from the Gold Coast, he needed no interpreter in his dealing with the Gun or the Yoruba; and for about twenty years, under various official titles, he dispensed justice in civil and criminal cases, strove to limit the authority of local chiefs and fetish priests, and later, as political agent, was instrumental in maintaining the British position against the French on the western creeks.

The Badagri District Court went by various names. Up till 1877 it was known as the Petty Debt Court, or the Police Court, and thereafter, the District Commissioner's Court. The first ten years of the court records bear witness to Tickel's industry and the novelty of entertaining and inexpensive litigation at the price of four shillings costs per suit.[1] Over a hundred debt cases were handled in 1866 alone; and the annual average number of civil disputes before 1874

Badagri District Court

Year	Theft	Assault	Slave-trading	Smuggling	Murder	Fetish practices	Treason	Total
1884	12	9	4	1	1	..	..	27
1885	20	11	5	4	..	2	..	42
1886	16	20	5	3	2	..	1	47
1887	39	28	2	3	2	..	..	74
1888	18	8	2	3	1	..	..	32

[1] N.R.O., Record of Cases in the Petty Debt Court holden at Badagry in the Settlement of Lagos; Civil Commandants' Court Record Book, 1867-77; Gold Coast Commissioners' Civil Court Record Book, 1878-87.

was about sixty. After the Supreme Court Ordinance of that year when the costs for court actions were increased, the annual average dropped to about twenty-five. There are no records of criminal cases before the 1870's, and, indeed, there was no police court in the district before 1874. Five years of the 1880's will serve as an example of the variety of criminal cases heard (see Table, p. 83).

The highest proportion of cases concerned assault and theft. Smuggling was far more widespread than the record of convictions might suggest; but evidence was difficult to obtain. To officials debt-pledging was synonymous with slave-trading, though there were instances of outright sales, particularly to Porto-Novo. The only case of witchcraft in the records occurred in 1878, when the accused was convicted and fined £4 for 'introducing a fetish into a house for the purpose of killing'.[1] The single case of treason in 1886 concerned three inhabitants of Katanu who were charged with taking an oath of allegiance to the King of Porto-Novo and 'intriguing against British rights' over Lake Nokué.[2] The case was reviewed and dismissed by Governor Moloney for lack of evidence. Cases of 'fetish practice' were a feature of the 1870's. For the most part they arose out of instances of trial by ordeal conducted by fetish priests, or from forced recruitment of candidates and novices for fetish houses. At Badagri itself there were no less than thirteen fetish houses, nine of which were listed by Tickel as recruiters of 'fetish-wives'. Their followers petitioned to be allowed some of their old practices, forbidden by Glover in the 1860's. The petition was refused; but, complained Tickel, recruiting was carried on once every year, when Badagri was 'like bedlam let loose', as the fetish followers stormed through the town 'screeching and howling, bedecked with old rotton hats, leaves and rags . . . like mad people'.[3] More serious than these annual outbursts were the bonds between local fetish priests and Porto-Novo which interfered with British jurisdiction and created, in effect, not one but two sets of courts in the protectorate. In February 1876, for example, the fetish priest of Dalli village sent a woman charged with witchcraft to be tried at Porto-Novo where she was found guilty and thrown into prison. The priest was brought before the Badagri District Court by the woman's relatives and fined. Again in 1877 there was a clash of authority between the fetish priests of Ajido and

[1] N.R.O., Badagry Criminal Record Book, 1878–9, entry for 3 Sept. 1878.
[2] Badagry Criminal Record Book, 1884–8, entry for 13 July 1886.
[3] N.R.O., Badagry Letter-Book, 1877–9, Tickel to Brown, 8 Dec. 1877.

the stipendiary chief who prohibited the holding of a fetish trial in the village. The latter was backed up by Tickel, and the priests were sent to Lagos for imprisonment.

But such examples of support for protectorate chiefs seem to have been rare; and the two-way traffic in sacrifices and prisoners between Porto-Novo and Gun settlements in the district was impossible to stop. Tickel's practice was to deny to lineage chiefs their right to levy fines on parties judged in customary courts.[1] He began with the *Akran*'s court at Badagri which was forbidden to meet; and in 1874 he discontinued the stipend of the *Akran* himself. When the chief of Possuko ward died, *Akran* Meje attempted to invest a candidate of his own with the *Possu* title—in return for a share of his stipend. This move was hotly opposed by the late *Possu*'s family, and also by Tickel who was anxious to see an end to the custom of title-investiture. For his pains he was accused by the administrator of Lagos of undue interference in native affairs. In his defence he excused himself by claiming that 'these feudal disturbances before Badagri was ceded to the Crown were always prevalent at the election of a Chief and have generally ended by one or the other being driven out of the town'; and, he claimed, the other ward chiefs threatened to use force if the *Akran* was allowed to have his way.[2] The new *Possu* title-holder was installed, despite Tickel's warning; and the acting-administrator of Lagos was obliged to send a gunboat and a small force of Hausas to keep order.[3] No proceedings were instituted against the *Akran* for opposing the wishes of the majority of the chiefs; but Tickel bided his time and caught him out on a charge of piracy in 1877 and had him removed from Badagri. Two years later, Tickel's campaign against the *Akran* was completed by a petition from seven of the ward chiefs of Badagri to Governor Ussher, rejecting any control of their affairs by a paramount chief and acknowledging no head over them but the British administration.[4] By 1880 only two of these chiefs were still paid stipends. In the neighbouring villages of the Western District seven chiefs were paid small annual sums from £2 to £5; but none of them played any part in the courts held by the district commissioner when on tour. Competition to the judicial prerogatives of the administration was officially discouraged.

[1] N.R.O., Badagry Letter-Book, 1871-4, Tickel to Lewis, 17 Apr. 1874.
[2] Ibid., Tickel to Lewis, 25 Apr. 1874.
[3] N.R.O., Secretarial Letter-Book, 1872-6, Shaw to Berkeley, 4 Aug. 1874.
[4] N.R.O., Badagry Letter-Book, 1879-80, Gardiner to Simpson, 27 Oct. 1879.

The fact was that the outpost of British rule in the Western District was in increasing financial difficulties: it never paid for itself, as originally intended. Revenue from court fees and fines, customs, and canoe licences declined from nearly £1,000 a year in the 1860's to an average of only £60 a year in the following decade. From these revenues were paid the Hausa police force, the stipendiary chiefs, and, with supplements from the Lagos Treasury, the commissioner and his clerk and the expense of general maintenance and supplies. Till 1879 it cost about £60 a month to administer the district. After the establishment of a new customs post at Katanu, this figure rose to about £80 or £90 a month. For example, during 1886, bribes to the chiefs and elders of Katanu to keep them under British control amounted to £437 alone; and the expenses of general administration at Badagri itself were £1,450 for the year.[1] Local revenues for the year covered only a small fraction of this outlay:

	Customs	Licences	Court fines, Fees	Total
1886 . . .	£53. 6s. 6d.	£40	£20. 2s. 6d.	£113. 9s.

The insolvency of the Western District was, by the early 1880's, symptomatic of the colony and protectorate as a whole.

The import and export trade of Lagos on which the revenues of the colony depended suffered two serious crises—one in the early 1870's and the other at the beginning of the 1880's. The first was met by a parliamentary grant of £20,000 which staved off a budgetary deficit. The second was a prelude to more desperate measures designed to remedy foreign competition and the unpredictability of the palm products market.

After a rapid rise in the 1860's, the volume of palm-oil and kernel exports from Lagos maintained a fairly consistent annual average of 7,000 tons and 20,000 tons, respectively, for the next decade. The value of cotton exports fell away to a few thousand pounds by the end of the 1870's; and benniseed, ivory, and shea butter amounted to no more than 1 or 2 per cent. of total export values.[2] The slight increase in the tonnage of palm-products was barely enough to off-set the steady decline in European market prices. Palm-oil dropped from £37 per ton in 1868 to £33 in 1870, and a ton of kernels from £15 to

[1] N.R.O., Badagry Letter-Book, 1885-7, monthly returns in Farber to Lagos Treasury, 14 Feb. 1887.
[2] *Blue Books*, 1866-83; Geary, pp. 54-55, 60.

£13. On the other hand, the local price of palm-products at Lagos, Badagri, Egerin, Ikorodu, and Epe markets tended to remain fairly constant, compared with the 1860's, and did not decline at the same rate as prices in Liverpool or Marseilles. Consequently, by 1881 the margin of profit for a ton of oil bought at Lagos and sold at Liverpool had narrowed to £8 or £9 (compared with about £20 in 1865); and for a ton of kernels the margin between local and European prices was no more than £2 or £3.[1]

This development, together with periods of extended credit and short supplies from the interior, weeded out the weakest of the smaller firms and the commission agents. Of the eleven African merchants consigning to European commission houses in 1886, only two or three had lasted through the two previous decades; the others were new-comers from Sierra Leone and the Gold Coast, or descendants of local families whose lands they mortgaged as credit to the European trading houses, and 'often consigned to one house under a fictitious name and through other persons the produce due to another'.[2] Of the early British firms only Banner Brothers remained in the 1880's. The Company of African Merchants and the West African Company, both at Lagos in the late 1860's, shifted to the Delta. Others—Walsh Brothers, the African Barter Company, and the London and African Trading Company—who had sent agents to the colony either retired or went bankrupt.[3]

The strongest competition to the three or four struggling British firms came from the German traders. In 1869 G. L. Gaiser and John Witt of Hamburg went into partnership and bought out the interests of O'Swald at Lagos and Palma. The partnership broke up in 1876, when Gaiser continued his trading activities and Witt founded the firm of Witt & Büsch. But he stayed in the Lagos market, and two other German enterprises, C. F. Meyer & Co. and Escherich & Co., established themselves in Lagos in 1877.[4] By 1881, out of the 112 Europeans (including officials) in the colony and protectorate, no less than 45 were German agents, clerks, or

---

[1] *Lagos Times*, 23 Mar. 1881; *Colonial Reports Lagos*, No. 58 (1891), pp. 52–53.

[2] *Lagos Times*, 27 July 1881.

[3] N.R.O., Dispatches, 10, Knapp Barrow to Young, 10 Sept. 1884. Firms at Lagos in 1886 were: Lagos Warehouse Ltd., C. McIver & Co., Banner Brothers, Voigt & Co., N. T. B. Shepherd, A. P. Moore, Rothlisberger & Monnier, G. L. Gaiser, C. Fabre & Co., Régis, Santa Anna, G. W. Christie & Co., A. J. Pell, B. Dawudu, and fifteen smaller Yoruba, Brazilian, and Sierra Leonean agents.

[4] Ernst Hieke, *G. L. Gaiser Hamburg — Westafrika 100 Jahre Handel mit Nigeria* (Hamburg, 1949), pp. 34–38.

engineers running the five German steam vessels that plied between Lagos and Porto-Novo.[1] Victor Régis also maintained his agency at Lagos, as well as at Whydah and Porto-Novo; and he was joined in the 1860's by a second French firm, Cyprien Fabre & Co.

All the foreign firms depended, like the British traders, on the Yoruba interior for the bulk of their supplies. But the Germans, and to a certain extent the French, enjoyed a virtual monopoly of the Gun and Fon markets to the west, using Lagos as a transit centre and benefiting from the customs drawback on imports to Porto-Novo. By 1885 the German and the French firms had secured over half of the kernel exports from Lagos and about one-third of palm-oil exports.

Lagos Exports of Palm Products*

	1870		1877		1880		1885	
	Oil	*Kernels*	*Oil*	*Kernels*	*Oil*	*Kernels*	*Oil*	*Kernels*
	('000 tons)							
England .	3·1	10·0	3·0	15·8	2·6	15·1	3·3	14·1
Germany	0·45	2·1	1·3	8·4	0·9	10·8	1·4	13·2
France .	1·8	3·7	5·9	6·4	1·0	3·7	1·2	2·3

* *Blue Books*, 1870, 1877, 1880, 1885; *Statistical Tables Relating to the Colonial and other Possessions of the United Kingdom* (1875), [c. 1038], pt. xiv, pp. 364–6.

Annual import values fluctuated in accordance with the condition of the local export market for palm products. About 50 to 60 per cent. of the goods unloaded at Lagos between 1866 and 1886 were of

Lagos Import Values†

	1864	1870	1886
		(% annual imports)	
Cotton goods .	12·8	41·1	38·6
Wines, spirits .	18·6	7·9	20·0
Tobacco . .	15·7	6·9	8·1
Cowries . .	18·4	5·8	(under 1%)
Guns, powder .	1·7	1·1	(„ „)
Hardware, beads, Admin. Stores, Staves, hoops }	32·8	Hardware, Salt, Haberdashery, Apparel } 37·2	Hardware, Salt, Haberdashery, Building materials } 34·3
Total value .	£120,796	£515,366	£357,831

† *Blue Books*, 1864, 1870, 1886.

[1] The *Gaiser, King Tofa, Tender, Lagos,* and *Oskar,* of between 50 and 240 tons.

British origin; the wine and spirits trade was a French and German monopoly; tobacco came almost exclusively from Brazil, cowries from Zanzibar and Mozambique. The variety of goods imported remained fairly constant; but their proportions, both in bulk and value, changed to yield a more important place to cotton goods and spirits.

Gross customs on imports averaged about £35,000 a year and represented some 75 per cent. of the administration's revenues.[1] £2,000 a year was paid out in drawbacks on goods in transit; and it cost as much again to maintain the customs department itself and pay collectors and clerks. Customs tariffs changed little between 1866 and 1886.[2] But the slight increase in the levy on spirits and tobacco was sufficient to raise the ratio of customs returns to import values from 8 per cent. before 1872 to 18 per cent. in the early 1880's, as the proportion of German spirits imported rose.

It is against this economic background that Lagos relations with the Egba and the Gun must be viewed.

After his defeat of the Egba at Ikorodu in 1865, Administrator Glover resigned himself to obtaining by bluff what could not be obtained by force. The Colonial Office rejected any suggestion that Porto-Novo might be annexed so soon after the findings of the 1865 Committee;[3] and all military or diplomatic expeditions to the interior to settle Yoruba affairs were forbidden by Carnarvon in 1867.[4] As Glover saw the situation, the improved conditions of trade enjoyed by the colony in the late 1860's would not last. The only alternative to territorial expansion was to by-pass the Egba by opening new trade routes either through Ondo territory to the east, or through Ketu to the north-west. The first plan was impracticable without the co-operation of the Ijebu, and they refused to allow unrestricted passage

[1] The rest of the revenues came from court fees and fines, the renting of the government steamer to traders, spirits and trading canoe licences, transfer of deeds and registration of property titles.

[2]	Tobacco (per lb.)	Spirits (per gal.)	Brandy (per gal.)	Guns (each)	Powder (100 lb.)	Salt (ton)	Other goods
1866–72	1d.	4½d.	1s.	1s.	2s.	5s.	4%
1872–86	2d.	6d.	1s.	1s.	2s.	5s.	4%

Spirits in transit to Porto-Novo was allowed a drawback of 4¾d. per gal., tobacco 1½d. per lb., and all other goods in transit 50 per cent. of the *ad valorem* duty.

[3] C.O. 147/11, Cardwell to Blackall, 21 Apr. 1866.

[4] C.O. 147/13, Carnarvon to Blackall, 21 Mar. 1867.

to missionaries or traders. The second, however, had two arguments in its favour: if Porto-Novo could be informally 'protected' and a new route through Egbado country opened, not only would the trade of Lagos be safeguarded, but also the Egba could be blockaded without difficulty and eventually persuaded to keep open the doubtful road from Ikorodu to Ibadan.[1]

The chance to set up a pro-Lagos paramount chief at Porto-Novo presented itself at the end of 1867. Glover took the exiled Prince Dassi (the future King Tofa) with him on the *Investigator* in the hope that the presence of the gunboat would precipitate a court revolution in which King Mikpon would be dethroned and Dassi installed. He did not intend to bombard the town; but he did have in mind the extension of Lagos territory as far as Lake Nokué.[2] The coup was unsuccessful: Mikpon was not intimidated; and Dassi had to wait another five years before the tortuous succession politics of Porto-Novo allowed him to make good his claims to the Gun paramountcy.

The new trade route did not materialize, and Glover was thrown back on his limited patience as a diplomatist to keep the uneasy peace between the Egba and Ibadan. The Egba were not in a mood to receive overtures from Lagos. The defeat at Ikorodu was never forgotten; and it was well known at Abeokuta that Glover had followed this up (as he informed the Colonial Office in 1866) by supplying large quantities of arms to Ibadan and the Ijebu, while denying them to the Egba.[3] The fear persisted that any European encroachment on Egba territory or jurisdiction would be but a prelude to annexation; and worse, the European missionaries who made little progress in their task of making converts were gradually classified as allies of the European traders, certainly enemies of Yoruba religious institutions, and possibly political spies for the Lagos administration.[4] It was this latent hostility and suspicion, rather than any overt or clearly defined policy at the Egba capital that made it impossible for Lagos administrators in the 1860's or 1870's to devise a trade agreement that would be accepted or respected. For there was no single authority or association that could be held responsible for such

[1] N.R.O., Dispatches, 3, Glover to Cardwell, 1 Feb. 1866; Glover to Carnarvon, 20 Jan. 1867.

[2] N.R.O., Dispatches, 3, Glover to Blackall, 4 Feb. 1868. Cf. Akindélé and Aguessy, p. 77.

[3] N.R.O., Dispatches, 3, Glover to Cardwell, 8 Jan. 1866.

[4] Talbot, i. 147; Biobaku, pp. 315–18.

negotiations. Foreign affairs at Abeokuta were military affairs; and the attention of the *Ologun* council of war chiefs was turned to the interior not to the coast. After 1869 when the *Bashorun* Somoye died, there ensued a typical Yoruba dispute over the *Alake* title which was never resolved. On the one hand, a senior lineage chief, Ademola, acted as *de facto Alake* till 1877; on the other, the *Seriki* of the war chiefs pursued a policy of his own, aided by a new organization formed by a few of the literate Sierra Leonean Yoruba who lived and traded in the capital, the Egba United Board of Management.[1] The origins of the board in the 1860's are obscure, but certain features of its functions and claims for itself are reasonably clear. Basically it was a craft guild of returned literati, an association of educated native traders and clerks, under the leadership of George William Johnson, a Yoruba tailor from Sierra Leone. And by reason of its skills in reading and writing, the board assumed the responsibility for conducting diplomatic relations with Europeans in general and the Lagos administration in particular. Johnson undoubtedly intended the board to have powers beyond its function as an advisory body and secretariat to the councils of Egba chiefs. But despite his vision of a 'United Kingdom' of all the Yoruba, his constitutional advice for a central Egba government was not heeded; and his financial policy, designed to raise revenues for running such a government, brought him into conflict with Lagos, and ultimately with the Egba themselves.

In June 1867 the board issued a proclamation signed by Johnson stating that customs posts would be set up by the Egba at various points on the Ogun river to collect duties on the export of palm products to Lagos.[2] Glover's reply to this in July requested that there should be a demarcation of the Egba frontier with Lagos territory first; and to make his point clear he set up posts of armed Hausa at Otta and the village of Isheri, north of Ikorodu.[3] The reaction of the board to what looked like the preliminaries to invasion was to issue a proclamation in September 1867, expelling all Europeans, including the missionaries, from Egba territory. In turn, the war chiefs and the Egba association of trade chiefs (the *Parakoyi*) who viewed the board's customs posts with distaste, expelled Johnson for his meddling.

Though the missionaries were eventually allowed to return after

---

[1] For an account of the conciliar divisions at Abeokuta, see Biobaku, 'The Egba Council 1899–1918', *Odù Journal of Yoruba and Related Studies*, No. 2, (1955), pp. 14–20.

[2] U.C.I., 'Egba Documents', Johnson to Glover, 1 June 1867.

[3] Ibid., Gerard to Johnson, 8 July 1867.

1872, the expulsion ended any hope of a peaceful settlement of outstanding problems of jurisdiction and boundaries between the Egba
and Lagos capitals. When in 1871 the war between Ibadan and
Abeokuta broke out again, Glover turned once more to Porto-Novo
in an effort to offset the sudden decline in trade which plunged the
colony's finances into deficit. Petitions from Lagos traders to justify
annexation of the town were drawn up, and the steamer *Eyo* was
dispatched to Porto-Novo to force King Mikpon to sign away his
market to British control. The Colonial Office remained unconvinced
that possession of Porto-Novo would assist Glover to bring the Egba
to heel by blockading them; and the governor-in-chief of the West
African settlements, Pope Hennessy, whose repeated orders to
withdraw the *Eyo* were ignored, denounced Glover's policy, visited
Lagos in March 1872, and had his impetuous administrator recalled
and sent elsewhere.[1]

Though Glover was removed, there was little alternative to his
intervention policy, so long as the Egba–Ibadan wars continued, and
the greater evil of a military expedition was rejected in favour of the
lesser evil of pushing the boundary of the colony westwards. Administrator Lees, in 1874, advised the Governor of the Gold Coast
that the new King of Porto-Novo, Tofa, might with a little adroit
management be turned into a second Akitoye or Docemo. The best
solution, in his opinion, to end the commercial competition of the
Gun markets, was 'that of the King handing over to the British
Government the fixing and collection of the customs duties, reserving
to himself a commuted allowance in lieu of them . . .'.[2] But, warned
Lees, this would mean providing officials for new posts in the west;
and, more important, the assimilation of Porto-Novo tariffs to those
of Lagos might tend to drive trade away to Whydah, Grand Popo,
and Anecho, unless the whole coast was taken over. This consideration
did not prevent him from going to Porto-Novo the following year,
as Glover had done, and proposing to King Tofa the surrender of all
his rights over customs in return for an annual grant.[3] Commodore
Hewett who accompanied Lees to this palaver to satisfy himself there
was no evidence of slave trading (which could be used as a pretext for

---

[1] C.O. 147/23, Kimberley to Pope Hennessy, 9 Mar. 1872; Pope Hennessy to
Kimberley, 5 Mar. 1872. Glover left in July 1872 and was appointed special com-
missioner at the Gold Coast where he found an outlet for his energies in the
Ashanti campaign. He later became governor of Newfoundland in 1875.

[2] N.R.O., Governor's Letter-Book, 1872–6, Lees to Strahan, 23 Nov. 1874.

[3] P.P., 1876, [c. 1343], Strahan to Carnarvon, 2 Apr. 1875, No. 56, p. 81.

seizing the town) summed up the principal reason for Lees's manœuvre.[1]

I may here remark that the fact of British jurisdiction ending at Badagry, and not extending to Porto-Novo, is highly detrimental to the revenue of Lagos, the duty on rum being as low as $1\frac{1}{4}$d per gallon, in consequence of the facility that is afforded of landing goods at Porto-Novo (the seaport), which renders it necessary to reduce the tax to a minimum in order to ensure this article of trade passing through our customs, instead of being forwarded into the country direct.

Tofa would not agree to Lees's terms. But a considerable amount of evidence was collected by Thomas Tickel to show that the king had been practising sacrificial rites, and this was forwarded to the Colonial Office by the Governor of the Gold Coast to serve as a reason for occupying Porto-Novo. In a postscript to his dispatch Governor Strahan added: 'not only in a revenual point of view, as I have previously pointed out, but in the higher interests of humanity and civilization, it is desirable we should extend our influence to the territory lying between the present limits of the Gold Coast and Lagos Settlements'.[2]

For by 1875 the question of extending British rule westwards from Lagos had assumed a wider significance. The Gold Coast revenue suffered from a similar loss of trade, and therefore customs, on the eastern flank of the colony. But the obstacle to expansion in either case was the fear of the Colonial Office, shared by some of the administrators of the Gold Coast, that action against the Gun of Porto-Novo or the Ewe of the creek ports entailed a risk of conflict with the Fon of Dahomey.[3]

While the Colonial Office and the administrators hesitated, Tofa with a chartered British steamer, the *Renner*, engaged in a minor war of his own, bombarding villages at the mouth of the Weme and around Lake Nokué.[4] In May 1877 he carried this further and installed a tributary chief at Appa. In the same month the Fon destroyed five Weme villages, because, according to Thomas Tickel, the palm products trade of the Weme area 'was gradually getting drawn to Lagos' instead of Whydah.[5] Tofa rounded this off by closing the Weme to Lagos traders.

[1] Ibid., Hewett to Admiralty, 14 Mar. 1875, encl. in No. 60, p. 84.
[2] Ibid., Strahan to Carnarvon, 26 May 1875, No. 72, p. 91.
[3] Ibid., Carnarvon to Strahan, 1 Mar. 1875, No. 28, p. 59; N.R.O., Dispatches, 5, Freeling to Carnarvon, 18 Dec. 1877.
[4] N.R.O., Badagry Letter-Book, 1874–7, Tickel to Lees, 4 Jan. 1875.
[5] Ibid., 1877–9, Tickel to Simpson, 7 May 1877.

Deputy-Governor Ussher brushed aside the timorous objection of his immediate predecessors and took up Glover's old plan of cutting off Porto-Novo traffic with Cotonou in 1879. Acting with the consent of his superior, the governor of the Gold Coast, he visited Porto-Novo in September 1879 and delivered an ultimatum demanding the payment of a fine of £50 for Tofa's embargo on Lagos trade with the Weme area and a guarantee the embargo would be lifted. A blank charge was fired off; and the money was paid at once.[1] Satisfied with this Ussher also took the opportunity to extend the British protectorate to the edge of Lake Nokué. At Badagri a suitably staged deputation of chiefs and elders of the village of Katanu presented a request for protection. They were led by a certain Kojo, brother of a Weme chieftain, and like his relative, an enemy of Tofa. After conferring with Tickel at Badagri, Ussher concluded that Katanu was 'the key to the road between Cotonou and Porto-Novo' and accepted the request. The British flag was hoisted over the creek village, cash and bottles of gin were distributed liberally, and a toll house was set up. No other nation, claimed Ussher, could now gain anything by taking Porto-Novo. 'As to the latter place,' he continued, 'I am of the opinion that by skilful and timely negotiation, a voluntary offer might be made to us by King Toffa to cede his country to Great Britain.'[2] For Porto-Novo was an attractive prize— 'a magnificent town under the misrule of a tyrant'—which would bring to the Lagos administration not less than £200,000 a year in customs duties and make Lagos itself 'the Liverpool of the Coast'.[3]

Ussher's action was disapproved of by the Colonial Office, but because of the possible fiscal advantages for Lagos, the Katanu protectorate was not revoked.[4] The advantages were not immediately apparent, however. In October 1881 Okeodan, in support of Gun princes exiled from Porto-Novo, joined in a campaign against Tofa; and this disruption of trade, together with the prolonged and desultory war in the Yoruba interior, aggravated the economic depression through which the colony was passing. But the western creeks, not Abeokuta, were still looked on as the keys to the interior.[5]

The final westward extension of the protectorate to Appa was sanctioned by the Colonial Office at the beginning of 1884.[6] By then

[1] N.R.O., Dispatches, 5, Ussher to Hicks Beach, 29 Sept. 1879 (No. 1).
[2] Ibid. (No. 2).
[3] Ibid., 7 Oct. 1879.
[4] C.O. 96/140, Hicks Beach to Ussher, 28 Nov. 1879.
[5] C.O. 147/48, Rowe to Derby, 19 May 1882.   [6] See below, p. 108.

a flood of petitions and memorials from Lagos, the Gold Coast, and the Chambers of Commerce of Manchester and Liverpool, complaining of the economic backwardness of the two colonies under joint rule, made formal separation a certainty.[1] But by then, too, the French had returned to Porto-Novo. The wheel had come full circle: it had taken twenty years to return to the position won by Glover in 1864; but the chance of occupying the markets of southern Dahomey had been permanently lost.

[1] P.P., 1884, lvi [c. 4052], Manchester Chamber of Commerce to Derby, 4 Dec. 1883, p. 94; city merchants to Derby, 7 Dec. 1883, p. 95; Rowe to Derby, 19 Feb. 1884, Encl. 1, p. 71.

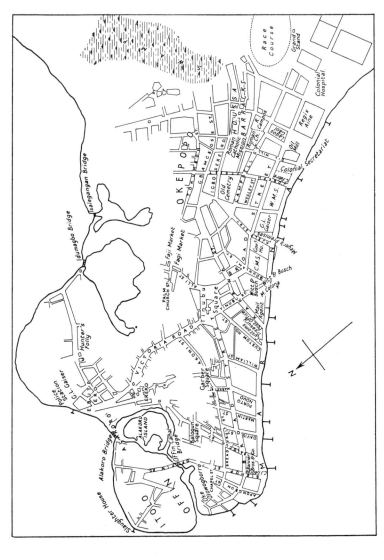

FIG. 5. Sketch Map of the Town of Lagos. After W. G. Lawson, Acting Colonial Surveyor 1884.

CHAPTER V

French and German Interests

WHILE the British enclave at Lagos slowly acquired the features of a Crown colony, the rest of the Western Slave Coast from Badagri to Cape St. Paul remained imperfectly known and, except for the coastal fringe, singularly resistant to European penetration. Climate alone is not a sufficient explanation for the restriction of evangelical or commercial enterprise to the market towns of the creeks. There were missionaries and traders who spent ten to fifteen years at Anecho, Whydah, or Porto-Novo in the 1860's and 1870's without ill effects. But movement into the interior was costly, or prohibited; and the maps of the time reveal how few of the towns of Dahomey, Porto-Novo, or the Gun and Ewe territory to the west were accurately sited.[1] Outside the beaten bush paths on the missionary Borghero's chart of 1865, little was added before the conquest of the 1890's that had not been noted by the Lander brothers or Burton.

The Volta region was something of an exception. There, the missionaries of the *Norddeutsche Missionsgesellschaft* had built stations among the Anlo and Akwamu people as far inland as Peki and Ho by the end of the 1860's.[2] But it was an uneasy and precarious contact, disrupted by wars between the Ewe of Peki and Akan invaders, by an Ashanti invasion in the early 1870's, and by local resistance to the extension of British rule eastward from the Gold Coast. After thirty years of evangelization, the Ewe Church of the Volta and southern Togo had made only about 500 converts by 1886.[3] In southern Dahomey the French Catholics of the *Missions Africaines de Lyon*, which sent out its first fathers in 1861, fared little better at Whydah or Porto-Novo, and till the advent of French rule concentrated on the returned Brazilian populations of Lagos and Agoué.[4]

---

[1] See map, Fig. 4.

[2] Norddeutsche Missionsgesellschaft, Bremen, 1a–17 'Briefe aus Keta'; 35a–41 'Briefe aus Wegbe-Ho'. The first North German Mission pastors, Bultmann, Wolf, Graff, and Flato, arrived at Cape Coast in 1847. See G. Müller, *Geschichte der Ewe-Mission* (Bremen, 1904), pp. 14–143.

[3] M. Schlunk, *Die evangelische Ewe-Kirche in Süd-Togo. Bremer Missions-Schriften*, No. 35 (Bremen, 1912), p. 5. '

[4] Abbé Laffitte, *Le Dahomé: souvenirs de voyage et de mission* (Tours, 1876).

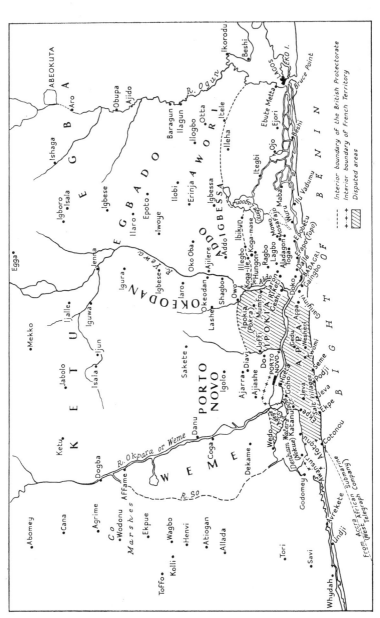

FIG. 6. Western District, Lagos Colony and Neighbouring French Territory, 1888

It was not till 1880 that they ventured into Yoruba country and began a station at Abeokuta. The one solid achievement of the French mission was its farm school and coconut plantation established at Topo near Badagri in 1876 where about eighteen square miles of land were worked by Catholic and pagan families under the seigneurial guidance of Father Bel.

The opening up of the smaller ports west of Whydah to the palm-oil traffic was a relatively late development. French and German firms were encouraged to set up agencies at Grand Popo, Agoué, Anecho, Lomé (Bey Beach), and Keta to escape the tariff policies of the Lagos and Gold Coast administrations in the 1870's. An additional factor which did considerable damage to French trade was a surtax imposed after 1867 on ships breaking bulk at the western ports before entering Lagos.[1] It could be avoided by calling at Lagos first; but the practice of sailing vessels which the French used almost exclusively was to unload part of their cargoes at Whydah and Cotonou before moving down the coast to leeward. To render their position less vulnerable, the French factors, led by the firm of Victor Régis, arranged for the 'cession' of Cotonou itself in a treaty signed in May 1868 by a French naval officer and the *Yovogan* or governor of Whydah.[2] The amount of territory ceded was vaguely described as coterminous with 'la limite naturelle des deux royaumes du Dahomey et de Porto-Novo'; and a clause provided for the payment of customs to the Fon of Abomey. But it was not made clear in the treaty whether customs would still be paid if effective occupation took place; and for this reason the Ministry for Foreign Affairs and the Ministry for the Navy refused to accept it. The expense of occupying some thirty square miles was not justified by the amount of French trade in the area, compared with markets north of Sierra Leone. The free African ports of the Slave Coast furnished an insignificant proportion of French imports from West Africa.[3] By 1868, calculated the French consul at Freetown, imports of West African produce into France amounted to about thirty-six million francs a year.

pp. 47–54; Abbé Pierre Bouche, *Sept ans en Afrique occidentale. La Côte des Esclaves et le Dahomey* (Paris, 1885), pp. 261–7; *Les Missions catholiques*, No. 732 (1883), pp. 281–2.

[1] N.R.O., Dispatches, 3, Berkley to Pope Hennessy, 9 Oct. 1872.

[2] Treaty, 19 May 1868, *Études dahoméennes*, ix (1953), 26–28; M.A.É., Afrique/53, Bonnaud to Moustier, 22 May 1868.

[3] M.A.É., Correspondance Commerciale, Sierra Léone/2, Braouezec to La Valette, 29 Aug. 1869; Angleterre, Freetown/53, Braouezec to Moustier, 17 Aug. 1868. Schefer, ii. 526–8.

Some 75 per cent. consisted of groundnuts, and only 8 per cent. of palm-products—two-thirds of which came through England and Germany. A new post in the Gulf of Guinea, he advised, had little value except as a bargaining point for the consolidation of French possessions north of Sherbro—particularly in the Gambia.

The interest of the Second Empire in the Bight of Benin was at its lowest point in 1865 and 1866, when Chasseloup-Laubat, after the withdrawal of the French post at Porto-Novo, put forward a proposal for an exchange of territory—the Gambia for French posts in Guinea and Mellacourie.[1] The plan was frustrated by the Anglo-Dutch Convention of 1867 which removed the English as neighbours to the French posts at Grand Bassam and Assinie. When the Dutch finally gave up their share of the Gold Coast forts in 1871, French and British posts again competed with each other. The negotiations were reopened in 1875 and 1876. But by then the French attitude towards the West African market had changed.

The change was due as much to the increase in French trade with the Gulf of Guinea, as to fear that the extension of British tariffs to the free ports would make it impossible for any French trade to continue at all. During the early 1870's three French firms, Régis, Cyprien Fabre, and Lasnier Daumas, exported an annual average of 4,500 tons of palm-oil from Porto-Novo and southern Dahomey— a figure which was only slightly under the average exports of oil from Lagos during the same period. The export of palm-kernels averaged 4,000 or 5,000 tons a year (or about one-fifth of Lagos's kernel exports). At European market prices French exports of palm-products from the free ports in 1879 were about half the value of Lagos exports of oil and kernels.[2] By then, claimed a French naval officer, Porto-Novo had more than a fair share of trade from Egba territory.

Les marchandises de traite, pour éviter les droits qu'il faudrait payer si on les débarquait à Lagos ou même les demi-droits exigés pour le transit par la coupée de la grande lagune qui débouche devant la ville, se débar-quent à Kotonou et s'expédient de là par des pirogues. C'est l'unique

---

[1] M.A.É., Afrique/55; J. R. M. Butler, in *The Cambridge History of the British Empire* (Cambridge, 1959), iii. 35, 43. By 1869 Governor Kennedy of Sierra Leone strongly supported the scheme to hand over the Gambia and Earl Granville was also willing, when negotiations were broken off by the Franco-Prussian War. F.O. Confidential Print, 403, 3 Dec. 1869, pp. 48–49.

[2] M.F.O., Sénégal, xx/8, Lieut. Martin, 'Commerce sur la Côte de Guinée', 20 Mar. 1872; M.A.É., Afrique/76, report by Commander de Serval, encl. in Jauréguiberry to de Freycinet, 5 July 1879.

raison de l'établissement de maisons de commerce sur ce point. Presque tout ce qu'on y débarque, l'eau de vie et le tabac notamment, sont destinés à Porto-Novo; la vingtième partie à peine va à Abomey-Calvi, dans le Dahomey.[1]

Farther west the German traders outstripped their French and British rivals. There were five German firms in the early 1880's with agents at Keta, Lomé, Anecho, and Grand Popo.[2] In 1867 the British frontier was pushed eighteen miles east of Keta to Adafia. For the rest of the decade, the profitable smuggling of arms and spirits around the eastern limits of the Gold Coast posts gave a new importance to the markets between Danu and Grand Popo. Lomé which hardly existed before 1881 became an entrepôt for the palm-oil producing area of Agotime and beyond to Salaga on the Hausa caravan route between Kumassi and the Niger. At Bagida there was a still larger oil market with easy communications to interior villages across the Hako lagoon (Lake Togo). The neighbouring market of Porto-Seguro was of little importance except as an off-loading point for steamers. Little Popo (or Anecho) was a transit centre for the interior villages of Wo, Apim, Gbome, and Seva on Lake Togo. Agoué attracted little of this trade. But Grand Popo, situated on the lagoon and at the mouth of the Agomé river, was in a better position, though shut off from Whydah by Fon toll barriers across bush paths and the creeks.

At all these markets English coin and South American dollars were the medium of exchange, whether for the purchase of European goods or palm products. At Lomé, kernels were sold in measures of 13 to 15 lb. for £7 to £8. 10s. per measure. Oil was sold in units of 8 to 10 gallons for about 1s. 6d. per gallon. The exchange rate between sterling and dollars varied: at Bagida a dollar was worth only 4s., and native suppliers took their cash to Anecho to exchange into sterling at the rate of 4s. 6d. per dollar. At Anecho and Grand Popo cowries were still used; and only at these two markets were small export duties paid to local chiefs—a shilling on every ton of kernels or oil.

Some three-quarters of the palm-oil and about half the kernels exported in 1883 went to Germany and the remainder to France.

[1] M.A.É., Afrique/76, de Serval, report, n.d. [1879], encl. in Jauréguiberry to de Freycinet, 5 July 1879.
[2] The firms were J. D. Bode and F. M. Vietor Söhne of Bremen, and Wölber & Brohm, C. Goedelt, H. B. A. Eccarius, Witt & Büsch, and Voigt & Co. of Hamburg. The latter two had their main agencies at Porto-Novo.

Trade at the Coastal Markets 1883*

	Imports				Exports	
	Spirits	*Tobacco*	*Powder*	*Other goods*	*Palm-oil*	*Palm-kernels*
Lome	290,000 gals. £19,000	180,000 kg. £15,000	185 tons £7,500	. . £2,500	166 tons £3,700	550 tons £4,650
Bagida	43,500 gals. £3,250	4,200 kg. £3,500	60 tons £3,500	. . £500	250 tons £5,500	1,000 tons £8,000
Anecho	235,000 gals. £15,750	8,400 kg. £7,000	340 tons £11,500	. . £67,950	1,000 tons £22,500	2,500 tons £23,100
Agoué		(No information)			600 tons £13,500	300 tons £2,700
Grand Popo	200,000 gals. £12,000	. . £6,000	50 tons £1,800	. . £1,800	660 tons £14,500	3,500 tons £31,500

	Total exports	
	Local prices	*European prices*
Palm-oil (2,676 tons) . .	£59,700	£93,660
Palm-kernels (7,850 tons) .	£69,950	£117,750
	Total imports Local prices £168,550	

* M.F.O., French consular reports in Gabon, vi/11; Staatsarchiv, Bremen, J. K. Vietor Papers.

Land purchases by German traders were made as early as the 1860's at Keta where the agent of F. M. Vietor Söhne obtained several blocks near the site of the later British post. The firm worked in close co-operation with the North German Mission, providing transport for the missionaries, and a depot for the palm products which the Akwamu were encouraged to send from the interior. Vietor's agent, Christian Rottmann, by 1880, had made over all his land purchases to the firm. One of the earliest land deeds signed by Rottmann for a block bought from a certain John Tay, a native trader and lineage chief of Jella Koffi (a few miles south of Keta), lists the terms of the contract: 'I paid to the said John Tay for the land a bale containing 100/one hundred pieces of Satin Stripes valued at forty-five pounds Sterling, which goods the said John Tay took and divided among the various Chiefs and Headmen of this country for a witness that the said land had become my property.' And this deed with half a dozen others was formally registered by the district commissioner of Keta between 1877 and 1881.[1]

At Whydah there were no land records; but the perimeters of the old forts seem to have been recognized as European preserves, in return for annual contributions to the King of Dahomey. By the early 1870's Whydah had an estimated population of some 8,000 or 10,000 in five principal wards.[2] Trade duties, as in the previous century, still continued to be levied on visiting ships according to the number of masts of the vessel. The king's agent and resident official were an ex-slave named Kenum and the *Yovogan*, who were also ward chiefs of the Ahwanjigo (or 'French') ward and Zobemi, the market ward. The main customer of the European firms was the Abomey royal house. King Glele was not an easy client to deal with.

'Il achète et ne paye pas', complained the Brazilian trader Dos Santos in 1865. 'A moi seulement il doit le tabac du *Destimodo*, du 1er voyage de l'*Eneantados*, et maintenant celui de la *Maria Rosa*. De même pour les cauries . . . mille pesos que je lui ai prêtés à Porto-Novo pour racheter ses prisonniers et maintenant il ne veut pas me payer.'[3]

When Dos Santos became agent for the British firm of F. and A. Swanzy in 1872 such debts of the royal house were not permitted to continue; and in 1876 an order for cloth was refused Prince Kondo (the future King Behanzin) till outstanding payments had been made. For his presumption, Dos Santos was fined by the Fon authorities at Whydah and his goods were seized. Swanzy's European agent on the Slave Coast, Turnbull, took up the case and was arrested, but not before he had called for naval protection from Commodore Hewett of the Bights Division. Hewett ordered both traders to be freed, fined the King of Dahomey 500 puncheons of palm-oil, and in July 1876 blockaded the coast from Porto-Seguro to Porto-Novo beach till the fine was paid.[4]

Those who suffered most from this disruption of trade were not the Fon, but the French traders. Régis asked why the blockade applied to ports independent of Dahomey, and received no

[1] Staatsarchiv, Bremen, J. K. Vietor Papers, Registration Deeds, 1876–81.

[2] J. A. Skertchly, *Dahomey as it is; Being a Narrative of Eight Months' Residence in that Country, with a Full Account of the Notorious Annual Customs, and the Social and Religious Institutions of the Ffons* (London, 1874), pp. 29, 44–46, 51.

[3] Dos Santos to J. B. Baeta, 19 Jan. 1865, in Verger, No. 104, p. 93.

[4] Dunglas, iii. 12; Paul Barret, *L'Afrique occidentale, la nature et l'homme noir* (Paris, 1888), pp. 170–1.

satisfactory answer before the blockade dragged on for eight months.[1] On the advice of the Admiral of the French Naval Division, and after receiving reports of heavy losses of stored palm products, the French firm offered to pay to the Colonial Office the indemnity demanded from Glele, before (as was feared) an expedition was sent to collect the fine by force.[2]

There was, indeed, talk of such an expedition in the Colonial Office; but the British Foreign Secretary discounted its importance in a communication to the French Foreign Office.[3] On the coast, however, Captain Sullivan could extract no more from Glele than a written apology, addressed to Lord Carnarvon. The Foreign Office agreed to be indulgent, requiring only 'reasonable excuses'. But Sullivan was less complaisant and made remarks to French officers about a march on Abomey which were taken to reflect the views of his superior, Commodore Hewett, if not the British Government. The agents of Régis and Fabre handed over half of the reduced fine of 400 puncheons. The rest was to be supplied by the Fon themselves within a year. A treaty between Sullivan and the *Yovogan* of Whydah was signed in May 1877. It reaffirmed British rights to unrestricted trade (guaranteed in 1852) and rounded off a tedious episode in which Glele had got off scot free and the French firms had in desperation paid to release their deteriorating exports.

The importance of the 1876 blockade was not its partial failure (the rest of the fine was never paid), but the way in which it served to underline the warnings of French traders that the rights acquired during the Second Empire in the Gulf of Guinea provided no lasting guarantees for the interests of the Third Republic there. The commander-in-chief of the French West Africa Squadron, Rear-Admiral Allemand, urged that, at the very least, a treaty similar to the one obtained by Sullivan should be signed, or at most, the 1868 treaty should be revived as a basis for territorial claims to Cotonou.[4]

The French Foreign Office and the Ministry for the Navy agreed with Allemand that only a small territorial concession was necessary

---

[1] M.F.O., Gabon, xiii/2, Régis to Montaignac, 31 May 1876.

[2] M.A.É., Afrique/76, Ribourt to Montaignac, 27 Dec. 1876, encl. in Montaignac to Decazes, 9 Feb. 1877; Régis to Carnarvon, 29 Jan. 1877, encl. in d'Harcourt to Decazes, 5 Feb. 1877.

[3] F.O. 84/1459, C.O. to F.O., 28 Sept. 1876; M.A.É., Afrique/76, d'Harcourt to Decazes, 5 Feb. 1877.

[4] M.A.É., Afrique/76, Allemand, 'Note', 4 June 1877, encl. in Montaignac to Decazes, 12 July 1877.

to ward off the threat of British expansion.[1] A draft treaty was sent to the rear-admiral; and in August 1878 a French officer and the *Yovogan* of Whydah signed an agreement for the cession of fourteen square miles of Cotonou and all customs rights.[2] Whether these terms ever received Glele's consent seems doubtful, particularly in view of the fact that no compensation for the loss of Cotonou customs was offered. In the same year the French consular post, vacant since 1876, was filled by Ardin d'Elteil, formerly vice-consul at Sierra Leone and a keen observer of the results of British customs posts for French trade.

D'Elteil's first report on Cotonou advised the Foreign Ministry to levy a small *ad valorem* duty to pay for a skeleton administration.[3] In February 1879 Cotonou was formally attached to French Gabon and d'Elteil was made resident. But no customs ordinance was ever announced, and Fon officials continued to levy their own duties on imports and exports as in the past. Resident d'Elteil, in any case, had more ambitious plans. Cotonou was useless, he understood, without command of the Gun market at Porto-Novo; and for the next two years he concentrated on improving the French position inland. Together with the agent of Régis, Colonna de Lecca, he persuaded King Tofa to renew the request for protection made by his father in 1863; and when forwarding this to the French Foreign Office he insisted that British annexation of Porto-Novo was imminent.[4] The consequences for French trade were obvious.

L'annexion du Porto-Novo à Lagos c'est l'application immédiate de droits énormes portant plus particulièrement sur toutes nos importations spiritueuses, poudres, armes, tabacs etc. pour en affranchir les tissus et marchandises de provenance anglaise ainsi que cela se passe à Sierra Leone et au Sherbro; c'est frapper à leur sortie de Porto-Novo tous nos produits qui seraient dirigés sur Cotonou de droits tel que notre commerce ne pourrait les supporter; c'est en un mot ruiner ici notre commerce au profit de la Douane anglaise, réduire à néant l'influence que va nous donner dans tout ce pays la prise de possession du territoire de Cotonou, et nous tirer le plus sûr gage qui puisse rester entre nos mains au cas où, dans l'avenir, quelqu'échange de territoire devrait avoir lieu entre les deux gouvernements.

[1] Ibid., Decazes to Montaignac, 15 July 1877.
[2] P.N., Montaignac to Allemand, 29 Sept. 1877; Treaty, 19 Apr. 1878, *Études dahoméennes*, ix (1953), 28–29.
[3] M.A.É., Afrique/76, d'Elteil to Waddington, 29 Nov. 1878.
[4] Ibid., Tofa to d'Elteil, 4 Mar. 1879, encl. in d'Elteil to Waddington, 6 Mar. 1879; *African Times*, 1 Jan. 1879.

This analysis of the commercial and diplomatic position of France on the Western Slave Coast made a great impression on the Ministry for the Navy. But the French Foreign Minister, de Freycinet, treated d'Elteil's report as an exaggeration of British intentions; and on the advice of Rear-Admiral Allemand, d'Elteil's projected renewal of the Porto-Novo protectorate was postponed but not lost from sight.[1] The Minister for the Navy, Jauréguiberry, thought it was futile to leave Cotonou in the care of a vice-consul without adequate funds and a military post to back him up. So far d'Elteil had been little more than a guest of the traders. 'Vis-à-vis les gens du Dahomey, l'action de M. d'Elteil a été nulle, on pourrait même dire moins que nulle.'[2] With this and d'Elteil's report in mind, the French Foreign Office was persuaded that Cotonou, for the moment, was only valuable in the exchange of territories with Great Britain that was under consideration—Matacong and Cotonou for British Gambia.[3] Already towards the end of 1879 the preliminary arrangements for a conference on outstanding difficulties between France and Britain in West Africa were begun, and de Freycinet was inclined to accept Lord Salisbury's proposal that the French should abandon Cotonou, providing the Western Slave Coast remained free from British customs posts.

By March 1880, however, the Paris ministries had made up their minds that the settlement of tariffs and boundaries between Guinea and Sierra Leone would have to be separated from the question of French rights in the Bight of Benin. Cyprien Fabre reported that the Gold Coast Colony had been pushed eastwards to Danu and that the occupation of Bagida, Anecho, and Porto-Seguro was contemplated.[4] Other reports from French naval officers emphasized the effect of the extension of Lagos territory to Katanu where tolls on palm products passing from Porto-Novo to Cotonou had been introduced.[5] Finally, Jauréguiberry's pessimism about the outcome of negotiations with Britain was deepened by the news that the

[1] M.A.É., Afrique/76, Waddington to d'Elteil (draft), 1 May 1879; Allemand, 'Note pour répondre aux propositions de M. d'Elteil', 4 July 1879, encl. in Jauréguiberry to Waddington, 5 July 1879.

[2] Ibid., Jauréguiberry to Waddington, 19 Nov. 1879.

[3] M.A.É., Afrique/77, de Freycinet to Pothuau (Ambassador, London), 14 Feb. 1880.

[4] M.A.É., Afrique/56, Fabre to de Freycinet, 19 Jan. 1880.

[5] Ibid., de Penfenteny to Jauréguiberry, 25 Feb. 1882, encl. in Jauréguiberry to de Freycinet, 11 Apr. 1882; Afrique/77, Villeneuve to Allemand, 7 July 1882, encl. in Jauréguiberry to Duclerc, 14 Sept. 1882.

governor of Sierra Leone (shortly to be governor of the Gold Coast) was active in London—'Sir Rowe, à l'esprit brouillon et au caractère envahissant'—to whom the intransigence of the British Government over the Guinea–Sierra Leone boundary was attributed.[1] Accordingly, it was decided by the French Foreign Office and the Ministry for the Navy in February 1881 to narrow the scope of the Anglo-French conference on West Africa to the Guinea boundary and exclude a discussion of Cotonou in which the French could only argue from a position of weakness.

The Paris Conference of May and June 1881 (after nearly breaking down over customs questions) produced a preliminary convention which was not finally signed till June 1882. During the delay the French Foreign Office cautiously restrained the Ministry for the Navy from taking precipitate action in southern Dahomey. When in September 1881 the French consul at Freetown requested a clarification of the ministry's intentions towards Porto-Novo, he was informed by the Foreign Minister that nothing was to be done which might jeopardize the signing of the Sierra Leone boundary agreement.[2] And when Jauréguiberry and the Minister for Commerce, Rouvier, prepared a draft acceptance of a second request from King Tofa in February 1882, de Freycinet advised them to keep it secret, fearing that a public announcement would provoke 'une assez vive émotion' at Lagos which would have to be taken into account in London.[3] Indeed, the rumour of a second protectorate request reached London in April 1882, and the French Foreign Office was notified of the British Government's 'regret' that any action over Porto-Novo was contemplated.[4]

But Rouvier and Jauréguiberry had their way: the Porto-Novo protectorate decree was signed in April 1882 and not made public till June, though it was agreed between the ministries that the French consul at Freetown might inform Tofa confidentially and accept the offer openly 'dans le cas où vous vous trouveriez en présence de quelque fait ou de quelque indice qui vous paraîtrait de nature à justifier

[1] M.A.É., Afrique/56, Jauréguiberry to de Freycinet, 1 July 1880 (sic, Sir Samuel Rowe). Jauréguiberry refused to accept him as one of the British delegates to the Paris conference in 1881.

[2] M.A.É., Angleterre, Freetown/53, Saint-Hilaire to Bareste, 5 Oct. 1881.

[3] M.A.É., Afrique/77, de Freycinet to Jauréguiberry, 10 Mar. 1882, 5 Apr. 1882.

[4] M.F.O., Afrique, vi/30, Lyons to de Freycinet, 24 Apr. 1882, encl. in de Freycinet to Jauréguiberry, 28 Apr. 1882.

suffisamment les appréhensions exprimées dans votre dernière communication'.[1]

Consul Bareste's 'apprehensions' were that Lieutenant-Governor Moloney of Lagos might move first at Porto-Novo, and Sir Samuel Rowe join up with him from the Gold Coast. After further pressure from Jauréguiberry at the beginning of 1883, the new Minister for Foreign Affairs, Duclerc, agreed to make the protectorate official; and at the beginning of April the trader, Colonna de Lecca, was installed at Cotonou as resident, and the French flag raised over Porto-Novo. At the former post the practice of paying customs to Abomey officials was stopped; at the Gun port, Tofa was allowed 10,000 francs a year as compensation for leaving all customs in French hands.

The steps taken by the French in 1883 left undecided their relations with the Lagos administration which still controlled at Katanu the key customs post between Porto-Novo and the sea. The British administration was not long in appreciating the significance of the re-establishment of the French protectorate.

Out of the 1,436,818 Gallons of Spirits and of the 1,261,622 lbs. of Tobacco imported in 1884, 469,249 Gallons of the former and 599,944 lbs. of Tobacco were absorbed by Porto-Novo while of the £225,112 worth of Cotton goods imported, £19,940 only was absorbed, and, it has been calculated that in the year 1884 £13,453 was lost in duty by goods passing free to Porto-Novo through the Katanu Waters, while £4,165 has been paid in drawbacks; the effect of the Porto-Novo Protectorate under its existing circumstances upon the Revenue of Lagos is easily discernible.[2]

There was little to be done, except to make things difficult for French traders. Katanu territory was interpreted in as wide a sense as possible so as to include Appa and Lake Nokué; and the Foreign Office hinted darkly that the Lagos administration 'might find it impossible, in case of emergency, to suspend all action as regards misconduct on the part of the troublesome chief of Porto-Novo'.[3] The French ministries and Under-Secretary Faure refused to agree to either

[1] M.A.É., Angleterre, Freetown/53, de Freycinet to Bareste, 3 and 12 Apr. 1882.

[2] N.R.O., Dispatches, 11, Evans to Griffith, 14 Aug. 1885.

[3] M.F.O., Afrique, vi/34, Plunkett to Challemel-Lacour, 9 Aug. 1883. Despite this threat the F.O. realized that the situation at Porto-Novo and Appa had come to a stalemate: 'in fact the position is that the French cannot get at Porto-Novo as we stop them at Katanu, and we cannot get at Katanu as they stop us at Porto-Novo; the danger of a collision under such circumstances is obvious'. F.O. Confidential Print, 1883 [4819], *Memorandum by Mr. Anderson on the French Occupation of Porto-Novo, 11 June 1883*, p. 6.

of the British claims to Katanu or Appa, and took steps to meet any threats from Lagos. In July 1884 Colonel Dorat with a small force of Senegalese infantry took over the Cotonou residency with orders to contest British rights to Appa and to determine the exact extent of the Porto-Novo protectorate in the north and west.[1]

Dorat brought an element of decisiveness into the vague and uncertain series of claims and counter-claims exchanged since the middle of 1883, and provided Paris with the first reliable information on the value of Porto-Novo. Undismayed by the small area over which Tofa had effective authority, he prepared, in the words of a French trader, 'de faire rentrer dans l'obéissance tous les peuples qui ne voulant se soumettre à la tyrannie de Tofa, se sont déclarés indépendants'.[2] The colonel began his campaign by arresting Prince Hungbo, a lineage rival of Tofa, who resided at Katanu under British protection and was used by Tickel at Badagri to intrigue against Porto-Novo among the villages around Lake Nokué. He visited Lagos and persuaded Lieutenant-Governor Young not to close the Badagri creek to French canoes. Finally, while diplomacy in Europe turned to the broader issues of the Berlin Conference, Dorat used the delay to bring the Weme under French protection and canvassed Addo, Ipokia, and Okeodan for the same purpose. When negotiations on the Katanu question were resumed between London and Paris in March 1885, the French position had been considerably strengthened. Granville insisted on maintaining the British post at Katanu; Ferry and Admiral Galiber, the new Minister for the Navy, insisted on the boundary agreement made between Didelot and Glover in 1864.[3] Unfortunately, Salisbury in 1879 had assured the French Foreign Office that the Katanu protectorate was to be only a temporary arrangement, and this assurance was now produced and quoted by the French. Equally unfortunately for the French case, however, no copy of the Didelot–Glover agreement could be found in French archives.

When news of Dorat's manœuvres accumulated, it became clear that not merely the creeks but the Yoruba hinterland was at stake. Lieutenant Roget who replaced Dorat continued his work in 1886 by raising the French flag over Ipokia. In Paris the Minister for the

[1] M.A.É., Afrique/80, Faure to Dorat, 28 May 1884, encl. in Faure to Ferry, 29 May 1884.
[2] M.A.É., Afrique/82, Gaillat to Régis, 8 Sept. 1885.
[3] M.F.O., Afrique, vi/45, Granville to Waddington, 23 Apr. 1885, encl. in Ferry to Galiber, 12 May 1885.

Navy and the Under-Secretary for the Colonies, de la Porte, enthusiastically supported a plan put forward by the secretary-general of the *Missions Africaines de Lyon* for annexing Abeokuta.[1] De Freycinet agreed that such an annexation would open a way to the Niger for French traders in southern Dahomey, but argued that it would be easy for the Lagos administration to sever this line of communication.[2] The plan was dropped. But the move to Ipokia was sufficient to alarm British traders (as they put it) 'at the possibility of at least two-fifths of the trade of Lagos being suddenly cut away from us.'[3] Their alarm was increased in June 1887 when French troops occupied Addo; and Governor Moloney, acting on instructions from the Secretary of State, proceeded to salvage what he could. Together with Governor Ballot, he agreed to a *modus vivendi* early in 1888 which left the passes at the head of Lake Nokué open to French canoes, in return for an assurance the French would not penetrate east of the Addo river.[4]

The commercial factors which determined French resistance to British expansion at one end of the Western Slave Coast were also present at the other where German traders, after the British occupation of Danu in 1879, were deprived of one of their principal free markets. Unlike the French, however, they lacked a ministry in Berlin to champion their cause; and the German Government in the 1870's had been antipathetic to requests for the occupation of territory in West and East Africa.[5] It was not till 1881 and 1882 that two pressure groups—the *Westdeutsche Verein* and the *Deutsche Kolonialverein*—were formed to lend strength to older, traditional seats of German trading interests—the Chambers of Commerce of Hamburg and Bremen.[6]

Moreover, where the Germans delayed, the French were active. In the absence of any decisive instructions from Paris, the agent of Cyprien Fabre, with the connivance of the French vice-consul at Freetown, in November 1881 handed out requests for French protection to the chiefs of Anecho, Porto-Seguro, and Grand Popo.

---

[1] M.A.É., Afrique/83, Aube to de Freycinet, 15 Jan. 1886.

[2] Ibid., Daby, 'Note', 24 Jan. 1886; de Freycinet to Aube, 10 Mar. 1886.

[3] Traders' petition, *Lagos Observer*, 9 July 1886.

[4] N.R.O., Dispatches, 12, Moloney to Holland, 9 Dec. 1887, 2 Jan. 1888. Convention, 2 Jan. 1888, *Études dahoméennes*, ix (1953), 76–78.

[5] J. K. Vietor, *Geschichtliche und kulturelle Entwicklung unserer Schutzgebiete* (Bremen, 1913), pp. 18–19.

[6] Both *Vereine* were amalgamated in 1887 into the *Deutsche Kolonialgesellschaft*. See below, p. 151 ff.

Jauréguiberry was keen to accept these requests and take over the coast from Cotonou to Adafia 'pour soutenir le commerce national et lui éviter les taxes anglaises qui le menacent'.[1] After the resumption of the French Protectorate at Porto-Novo, the Foreign Ministry agreed to accept the requests for Grand Popo and a post was set up there in 1883. Over Agoué and points farther west, there was some doubt.

At the beginning of the same year the three German firms with agents in Anecho petitioned the German Foreign Office for occasional visits by a warship.[2] Their motive was not, as yet, the acquisition of territorial rights, but redress against the chiefs of Anecho and Bagida who increased their demands for presents and customs duties from the German traders to bring them into line with those agreed to by French agents. The German Foreign Office, through the Prussian ambassador to the Hansa towns, methodically requested information on the best ways to end such complaints and promote German trade on the coast.[3] In Hamburg the whole question of the protection of national trading interests was debated by a committee of the Chamber of Commerce, after the trading firms had given their views. The committee (with one exception) favoured the acquisition of colonies; the trading firms with interests in the Western Slave Coast favoured only naval patrols.[4] Their joint views were embodied in a report of July 1883. It was forwarded to the Prussian ambassador by the president of the *Senat* of Hamburg, suggesting the annexation of the Cameroons, a naval station at Fernando Po, the neutralization of the Congo, and treaties with chiefs for the protection of German traders on the Slave Coast.[5]

The Bremen Chamber of Commerce was more reserved. It limited its suggestions concerning the Slave Coast to a warship for 'moral effect', and, at the very most, a treaty of trade and friendship.[6]

[1] M.A.É., Afrique/78, Jauréguiberry to Duclerc, 19 Jan. 1883.

[2] Handelskammer, Bremen, Colonisation/19, F. Reimann, H. Randad, H. F. A. Eccarius to Auswärtiges Amt, [3] Feb. 1883.

[3] Handelskammer, Hamburg, 84/A/1/2, Chamber of Commerce to Goedelt & Co., Witt & Büsch, Gaiser, Woermann, Jantzen & Thormählen, Wölber & Brohm, 30 Mar., 1, 3, and 4 Apr. 1883.

[4] Handelskammer, Hamburg, 84/A/1/3, Minutes, 18 June 1883.

[5] Staatsarchiv, Hamburg, CL. vi. 15/6/4, Handelskammer, 'Denkschrift', 6 July 1883, in Senat to Prussian ambassador, 20 July 1883. The Senat supported the suggestion for naval visits and the neutralization of the Congo, but did not favour the idea of a naval base at Fernando Po or the plan for colonizing the Cameroons.

[6] Handelskammer, Bremen, Colonisation/19, 'Kommission für Handelspolitische Fragen', Minutes, 4 July 1883. But the chamber strongly supported claims to South-West Africa.

The initiative passed back to Hamburg, where, by the end of 1883, the chamber was pressing for a full consulate in the Bight of Benin to observe the activities of France whose actions at Porto-Novo and Grand Popo were beginning to arouse as much resentment among the Germans as among British officials at Lagos. But Bismarck and the German Foreign Office had already made up their minds how far they were prepared to go. In December 1883 the Prussian ambassador forwarded to both Chambers of Commerce advice that the government proposed to send a warship to the Slave Coast and appoint a commissioner with powers to negotiate trade treaties.[1] The chambers were asked what kind of provisions they wanted in the treaties. The Bremen chamber declined to make any special requests, preferring to leave the initiative to the commissioner. The Hamburg chamber was more outspoken about the need to forestall England in the Cameroons, but considered naval patrols would suffice for Anecho and Whydah.[2]

Thus at no stage of the preparations for the founding of the German colonial empire in West Africa was the annexation of southern Togo urged or even considered by German trading interests. When Consul-General Nachtigal was appointed commissioner with the task of securing this empire, Bismarck had a final discussion with a small group of merchants in Berlin to determine the commissioner's instructions.[3] The annexation of the Cameroons was definitely decided. The plan for a naval station at Fernando Po was dropped. As far as Togo was concerned, Nachtigal was merely to investigate trader's complaints. He was warned that France might already have treaties with Anecho and Porto-Seguro. If so, they were to be respected, since Bismarck had already given assurance on this point to the French Foreign Office.

He need not have been so punctilious on the question of Anecho. Already in August 1883 the Paris ministries agreed to suspend all

[1] Handelskammer, Bremen, Colonisation/21, Prussian ambassador to Chamber of Commerce, 26 Dec. 1883; Staatsarchiv, Hamburg, CL. vi. 15/6/4, Prussian ambassador to Senat, 26 Dec. 1883.

[2] Handelskammer, Hamburg, 84/A/1/3, Report to Deputation for Trade and Shipping, 12 Feb. 1884.

[3] Staatsarchiv, Hamburg, CL. vi. 15/6/4, Hansa ambassador to Senat, 1 May 1884. Also present were Woermann, Jantzen, Thormählen, and Lüderitz. For the final instructions and Bismarck's minutes to them see Alfred Zimmermann, *Geschichte der deutschen Kolonialpolitik* (Berlin, 1914), pp. 85–87; Staatsarchiv, Hamburg, CL. vi 15/6/5b; Bismarck to Nachtigal, 19 May 1884, in *Togogebiet und Biafra-Bai*, 1884 [117] pp. 29–31.

treaty-making in the area west of Grand Popo. And when in October further objections were received from the British Government the French Under-Secretary for the Colonies definitely renounced all claims.[1] But this was not known in Berlin.

In January 1884 the German warship S.M.S. *Sophie* arrived off Anecho. Captain Stubenrauch found that the chiefs of the Lawson[2] and Kuadjovi lineages who acted as customs collectors for the chief of Gridgi village not only disputed the profits from this function but also the right to represent the new chief of Gridgi who was still a minor. On the one side the Kuadjovi were supported by the German traders. On the other, the Lawsons threatened to call on English support from Lagos. Stubenrauch arranged a treaty with the former group, guaranteeing German trading rights in return for fixed duties on the export of palm produce. The Lawsons refused to co-operate, and four of the Lawson party were carried off by the *Sophie* as hostages.[3] The Kuadjovi, headed by the ex-slave trader Pedro Kuadjo, petitioned the Kaiser for German protection, citing their fear of British intervention from the Gold Coast as a reason.[4]

The hostages were well treated in Germany and returned with Nachtigal on the *Möwe* to Anecho in July 1884. According to the commissioner's report, the German traders insisted that the district officer of the eastern region of the Gold Coast was about to use force to put an end to smuggling across the Volta from Lomé, Bagida, and Porto-Seguro.[5] To forestall this, the *Möwe* moved down the coast to Bagida. There, so Nachtigal claimed, the situation seemed critical: native authorities were about to expel the German agents of

---

[1] M.A.É., Afrique/78, Challemel-Lacour to Peyrou, 17 Aug. 1883; Faure to Ferry, 6 Dec. 1883.

[2] 'King' George Lawson, the elder, died in 1883. He was succeeded by his son G. A. Lawson. Another son, William Lawson, who was an official in the Survey Department at Lagos, arrived in 1883 to act as his adviser and tax-collector.

[3] William Lawson, as a British subject, was landed at Lagos. G. A. Lawson, A. Wilson, and a Brazilian, Gomez, continued the voyage and disembarked at Wilhelmshaven at the end of March 1884. *Deutsche Kolonialzeitung*, i (1884), 204–5.

[4] 'King' Aiaushi of Anecho and Gridgi, Pedro Kuadjo, and eleven chiefs to the Emperor [5 Mar. 1884], in *Togogebiet und Biafra-Bai*, 1884 [117], Appendix III, p. 35. This petition was not accepted because it was presumed that France had prior rights over Gridgi. M.A.É., Afrique/95, Minute, 14 May 1884.

[5] Nachtigal to Bismarck, 9 July 1884, in *Die deutsche Kolonialpolitik: I. Deutschland in Afrika und in der Südsee* (*Togogebiet und Biafra-Bai*), (Leipzig, 1885), pp. 40–49.

Wölber & Brohm and F. M. Vietor Söhne. Dr. Buchner, who accompanied Nachtigal, conferred with the natives and procured a written request for German protection from representatives of the King of Togo village and the chiefs of Bagida. The urgency of the situation, claimed Nachtigal, forced him to exceed his instructions and accept this request.

Auf Grund der dargelegten dringlichen Verhältnisse und einer formellen Bitte der autorisierten Personen um den Schutz des Deutschen Reichs hielt ich es zur Sicherstellung des nicht unbeträchtlichen deutschen Handels in Lome und Bagida für geboten, mit den Vertretern des Königs von Togo und den Häuptlingen der beiden genannten Küstendistrikte einen Vertrag zu vereinbaren, der das Togogebiet unter das Protektorat Seiner Majestät des Kaisers von Deutschland stellt, obgleich Eure Durchlaucht in den mir unter dem 19. Mai v. J. erteilten Hohen Instruktionen eine derartige Sicherstellung vor fremder Besitznahme für irgend ein Gebiet dieses Teils der afrikanischen Westküste nicht in Betracht gezogen hat. . .[1]

In any case, he argued, except for a few agents of the British firm of F. and A. Swanzy, trade was in German hands; and a profitable trade route to the upper Volta and Salaga might be opened. On 6 July the German flag was hoisted and the area around Togo village and Bagida declared protected territory in the name of 'King' Mlapa and the German emperor. Heinrich Randad, agent for Wölber & Brohm, was appointed provisional consul. At Anecho, however, no treaty could be obtained.

It was a curiously vague protectorate, accepted by the German Government in October 1884, when it was clear that France did not object. Randad lost no time in claiming Porto-Seguro and Anecho as well. By the end of 1884 the German and the French consular agents had succeeded in raising both their national flags over the first village. At the second, the Kuadjovi claimed German protection, and the Lawsons, despairing of British intervention, turned to the French for support.[2] Diplomacy lagged far behind these manœuvres. When it caught up, the delimitation of French and German interests turned not on the rights of lineage chiefs to choose their protectors, but, in Europe, on the question of customs tariffs, and locally, on the resourcefulness of French and German officials.

---

[1] Nachtigal to Bismarck, 9 July 1884, ibid.; Treaty, 5 July 1884, Bundesarchiv Koblenz, RI/I/8, ff. 31–33; *Die deutsche Kolonialpolitik*, i. 50. The treaty is often wrongly dated 15 July. For signatures, see below, Appendix II.

[2] M.F.O., Afrique, vi/40, Ferry to Faure, 5 Sept. 1884; and Gabon, vi/11, for correspondence from French and German agents on the coast.

In January 1885 the German Foreign Office made the first suggestion for a customs agreement which Jules Ferry declined. His successor, de Freycinet, approached the question more constructively. While he did not favour a complete customs union between the French and German protectorates (on the advice of the Ministry for Commerce) he was prepared to agree to a fiscal *entente* to avoid differential tariffs on French or German imports into their respective areas.[1] Porto-Seguro he was prepared to give up, against the abandonment of German claims to Dubreka and posts on the Rio Pongo—which the Minister for the Navy, Galiber, would not agree to. Nor would Bismarck. Other suggested compromises were equally unfruitful; and by the end of August 1885 it became clear that both governments had exhausted their list of possible exchanges on the West African Coast. The French Foreign Office made up its mind that Porto-Seguro was lost, but insisted that the Franco-German boundary should be drawn west of Agoué.[2] The debate mattered little. In the fragmented political structure of the coastal society between Grand Popo and Keta all lineage chiefs, admitted the French consular agent, were 'plus ou moins légitimes'.[3] And on receipt of a copy of the Franco-German agreement of 24 December 1885, Colonel Dorat left Anecho and Porto-Seguro to the German commissioner, Falkenthal. The final delimitation was carried out smoothly at the beginning of 1887. For the convenience of the German and French boundary commissioners, a suitable meridian was fixed on and the boundary extended as far as the ninth parallel. True, the farm villages belonging to the Lawsons and the Kuadjovi of Anecho were divided between one side of the border and the other. But Falkenthal could not be dislodged from the residence he had built at Gridgi; and Commissioner Bayol found reason to be satisfied. 'Nous conservons ainsi notre liberté d'action du côté du territoire des Ouatchis et du Dahomey, et il nous sera plus facile d'éviter des annexions allemandes au nord de nos possessions des Popos.'[4]

The customs question was less easily settled and of greater

[1] M.F.O., Afrique, iv/47, de Freycinet to Galiber, 4 May 1885; Galiber to de Freycinet, 19 June 1885; Legrand (Minister for Commerce) to Galiber, 21 July 1885.

[2] Ibid., 'Projet', encl. in de Freycinet to Galiber, 28 Sept. 1885, Galiber to de Freycinet, 2 Dec. 1885. Franco-German Agreement, 24 Dec. 1885, *Deutsche Kolonialzeitung*, iii (1886), 102–3.

[3] M.F.O., Gabon, vi/11, Canteloup to Dorat, 23 Nov. 1885.

[4] *Études dahoméennes*, ix (1953), 69–73; M.F.O., Afrique, vi/61, Minutes of the Boundary Commission, 1 Feb. 1887.

consequence for the German and French administrations and the traders in whose interests the protectorates had been established. In March 1886 the German Foreign Office again proposed a single customs tariff for French and German possessions in the Bight of Benin. In Paris, the Ministry of Commerce agreed in principle, but raised the tariff without consulting the French firms on the coast, and this was accepted by Berlin. It was not accepted by the Marseilles Chamber of Commerce, representing Régis and Cyprien Fabre, who complained that French brandy would be harder hit than German gin.[1] Worse, it was not clear whether the new tariffs would apply to imports through Cotonou. If they did, argued the chamber, French goods would be more heavily taxed than they were at Lagos. On the other hand, the proposed tariffs were lower than those obtaining on the Gold Coast —which satisfied the German traders.

The French Foreign Office was impressed by the force of this argument and agreed to await further information from the French administration at Porto-Novo before making a final decision. The Chamber of Commerce used the interval to refine its arguments against the tariff and suggested, as an alternative, a moderate export duty on palm produce and no import duties at all. This, the chamber claimed, would provide enough revenue for the German administration of Togo. This suggestion was promptly rejected in Berlin. The French ambassador advised the French Foreign Office to accept the principle of a common tariff, lower the duty on rum, and add cloths to the list of dutiable items. This was as far as the German chambers would go.[2] The Foreign Office agreed, with the provision insisted on by the Ministry for the Navy that the tariff in southern Dahomey would only apply to goods imported through ports west of Whydah. The final customs agreement was signed in May 1887, and was in force for a period of two years.

There were now from Cape St. Paul to Lagos not two, but four customs zones. Duties were highest at the Gold Coast ports of entry and lowest at Cotonou and Porto-Novo. The Franco-German tariff zone was a compromise which on the whole applied lower duties than Togo's western neighbour and ensured that the French protectorate at Grand Popo would not for the present become a base

[1] M.F.O., Afrique, vi/61, Chamber of Commerce to Ministry of Commerce, 13 Feb. 1887.
[2] Ibid., Herbette, 'Note sur le régime douanier de la Côte des Esclaves', 3 Apr. 1887.

for smuggling cheap spirits, tobacco, or powder into the German traders' markets. But, as yet, not all southern Dahomey was in French hands. Whydah was still an independent Fon port; French possession of Cotonou was insecure; and no duties could be levied at Porto-Novo at higher tariffs than those obtaining at Lagos. The

Customs Duties 1887*

Goods	Unit	Gold Coast (Keta District)	Togo and Southern Dahomey (English currency)	Lagos	Drawback on Transit for Porto-Novo
Gin . .	per case	2s. 5d.–4s. 3d.	0s. 3·84d.–9·60d.	0s. 10½d.–1s.	4¾d. per gal.
Rum . .	per litre	3·42d.–6·17d.	0s. 0·19d.–0·48d.	0s. 1·5d.– 0s. 1·75d.	,, ,, ,,
Powder .	100 lb.	£2. 10s.	2s. 6d.	2s.	1s. per lb.
Tobacco .	per kilo	1s. 1d.	0s. 1·20d.	0s. 4·25d.	1¾d. per lb.
Guns . .	each	2s.	0s. 6d.	1s.	6d.
Brandy .	per gal.	2s. 6d.	Nil	1s.	6d. per gal.
Other spirits	,,	2s. 6d.	Nil	1s.	6d. ,, ,,
Cowries .	per cwt.	4% ad val.	Nil	1s.	6d. per cwt.
Salt . .	per ton	4% ad val.	Nil	5s.	2s. 6d. per cwt.
Other goods .		4% ad val.	Nil	4% ad val.	¼ of full duty.

* Colonial Reports. Lagos. Report on the Blue Book for 1887, 1889 [C. 5620], pp. 5–14.

first customs agreement of 1887 between France and Germany for Dahomey and Togo expired at the end of July 1889. As it had worked out, French firms imported more spirits in bulk through Grand Popo than German gin which paid double duty, but which, when watered down, sold more cheaply. Governor Ballot and the German commissioner, Puttkamer, wanted a single tariff for all spirits. The French firms, backed by the Ministry for Commerce and the Colonies, were opposed to this. But the French Foreign Ministry, after receiving advice from the French ambassador in Berlin that the German administration needed more customs revenue, proposed to double the 1887 tariff, levy 10 francs per ton on imports of salt, and a general ad valorem of 4 per cent.[1] With the agreement of a committee of French and German traders which met at Anecho, presided over by the German commissioner, a new customs convention was mutually enforced till the end of 1890:[2] duties on powder, arms, and tobacco

[1] M.F.O., Afrique, vi/75, Herbette to Spuller, 24 Oct. 1889, encl. in Spuller to Étienne, 31 Oct. 1889.

[2] Ibid., 'Procès-verbal d'une réunion de tous les Agents des maisons euro-péennes de Petit-Popo appelés le 12 août 1889, à délibérer, sous la Présidence du Commissaire Impérial Allemand, sur un projet de Tarif douanier proposé par le Gouvernement Français', encl. in Fabre to Ministry of Commerce and Colonies, 21 Nov. 1889.

were doubled; and the differential between French rum and German gin was retained. The German customs and the French traders were satisfied.

But this system applied only to the Togo ports and the French protectorate at Grand Popo. The consolidation of the French position at Cotonou and Porto-Novo in 1890 complicated the issue. Goods entering the protectorate through Grand Popo were not permitted to enter French territory to the east. Governor Ballot explained why: 'La zone douanière franco-allemande engloberait donc tous les Établissements du Bénin, jusqu'à la crique d'Adjarra, au détriment des intérêts financiers de la Colonie.'[1] By this he meant that duties on the French side would have been higher than those at Lagos, and smuggling along the frontier would have been rampant. And if new tariffs at Lagos permitted the French administration to raise theirs (as Ballot hoped), it would be tedious to refer to Berlin every time the French colony needed more revenue from its customs.

The artificiality of the international boundary was now fully apparent. The Gun, divided between the German and the French coastal ports, were a single market unit. As Ballot pointed out with some irony, French customs posts would soon be needed between Grand Popo and Whydah to replace the Fon posts which the Germans and French had dismantled in 1886 and 1887 to facilitate European trade. To maintain two distinct customs zones in Dahomey was ridiculous. Ballot insisted that Régis, Fabre, and others would have to change their methods in order to meet the rivalry of small Sierra Leone and Brazilian traders who, like their counterparts in Togo and Lagos Colony, had begun to prefer specie and cotton goods, rather than spirits and tobacco 'et font une concurrence facile à nos factoreries françaises qui continuent à opérer avec des articles importés de Marseille'.[2] And as the expensive operations against the Fon increased the burden on the budget for the protectorate and the annexed territory, customs at Porto-Novo and Cotonou were raised in April 1890 to very nearly the Lagos tariffs.

In point of fact, the French firms, and in particular Régis, no longer depended on spirits of French origin for the bulk of their trade. An inventory of the Whydah factory of Régis in 1890 valued the whole concern at just over half a million francs (or about £27,000).

[1] M.F.O., Dahomey, vi/3 Ballot to Étienne, 30 July 1890.
[2] Ibid., Ballot to Ballay, 1 Oct. 1890, encl. in Ballay to Étienne, 21 Jan. 1891.

Goods of all kinds for trade were valued at 472,724 francs and were made up as follows:

Régis Factory Whydah, 1890*

Trade cloths, cottons	152,688† francs
Spirits	109,782 ,,
Casks and puncheons	95,599 ,,
Specie and palm products	64,401 ,,
Hardware	16,325 ,,
Provisions	11,189 ,,
[French cloths	8,204 ,,]
Containers	4,877 ,,
Tobacco	4,102 ,,
Clothing, hats, shoes	3,974 ,,
Building materials	2,190 ,,
Powder, guns	1,436 ,,
Cutlery	1,041 ,,
Perfumes	1,040 ,,
Miscellaneous	4,091 ,,
	472,724 francs

* M.F.O., Dahomey, xv/2.   † Including French cloths.

Cloth and spirits made up about half the value of trade goods in the Whydah factory. The rest was a varied assortment of provisions, hardware, clothing, and, a valuable item, casks and puncheons sold to native suppliers. Sundry debts to Régis for goods sold on credit amounted to 39,792 francs (about £1,500). The factory also had some small debts—£60 borrowed from a Brazilian trader for ready cash, and the wages of its employees, paid in cowries and English coin.

Farther to the west the necessity to offset the fiscal consequences of the advent of the German enclave also divided the Gold Coast into two customs zones in which appreciably lower duties were levied at posts near the Volta estuary than at other ports of entry in the British colony. The treasurer of the Gold Coast explained the motive and results of this measure to the African Trade Section of the Liverpool Chamber of Commerce in 1894.

In 1890 it was found that the trade of the Kitta District was being ruined owing to the formidable competition exercised by the contiguous German protectorate of Togoland, where the duty on spirits only amounted to 1½d. per gallon, while the tax on our territory was half-a-crown a gallon. Smuggling over the border was carried on to such an extent that the pre-ventive service proved insufficient to cope with it. Our Government then made a special tariff for Kitta, lowering the duty on rum to almost the same rate as that levied in Togoland. The result of this move made itself immediately apparent. The trade of Kitta rose at a bound, and, owing to the preference always evinced by the natives for trading under the British Government rather than with the Germans, the Togoland revenues decreased in the same proportion as those of Kitta multiplied. The Germans, however, not to be beaten, simply transferred their factories to Kitta, and they now trade and barter under English Government with more advantage and facility than they would enjoy under their own paternal rule. So successful are they at Kitta that out of the ten most important factories established in that district eight are German, two French, and one English [sic].

The single district of Kitta now imports half as much spirits as the whole of the other districts of the colony put together; and it is not altogether pleasing to reflect that this very remarkable and rapid increase of trade should, in a British colony, turn only to the profit of foreign traders, who use foreign capital, employ foreign clerks, import foreign goods, and give freight to foreign ships.[1]

At Lagos where no such arrangement could be made with Dahomey, the commercial prophets saw nothing but disaster in the mild French tariff of 1891. The opinion of the Lagos merchants was that the colony would 'lose revenue from spirits and will have to increase the duty on cloth, whilst French Benin will add to its revenue from spirits, and thus be able to admit cloth free, the total result being decadence in the trade of Lagos'.[2]

In fact this did not come to pass, but it was symptomatic of a contemporary view that traders paying for national protection had a right to special treatment on their own section of the coast. The tariff structure of all four colonies in the late 1880's and early 1890's was fluid, and the zones of occupation no more than a dozen miles in depth. The first power that turned the flank of its neighbours to command the interior sources of supply would render the other shallow enclaves economically meaningless. This possibility had been foreseen as early as 1883 by an official of the British Foreign Office; commenting on the return of the French to the Slave Coast, he wrote:

Protectorates are unwelcome burdens, but in this case it is, if my view is correct, a question between British Protectorates, which would be unwelcome, and French Protectorates, which would be fatal. Protectorates, of one sort or another, are the inevitable outcome of the situation. In our case, if Consul Hewett and Captain Moloney are to be trusted (and they do not speak impulsively), they could be imposed almost without an effort on

---

[1] Hesketh J. Bell, 'The History, Trade, Resources, and Present Condition of the Gold Coast Settlement', *African Trade Section Report* (Liverpool, 1895), p. 27.

[2] *The African Trade Section of the Incorporated Chamber of Commerce of Liverpool. Trade in Spirits with West Africa* (Liverpool, 1895), p. 10.

the majority of the Chiefs; they would not be difficult of management, for one gun-boat in the Bights would suffice, under ordinary circumstances, to keep the protégés in order, and they would not be burdensome to the Treasury, for expenses could be managed by manipulating the traders.[1]

Thus the stage was set for that complex realignment of territorial boundaries that marked the course of the 'scramble' for the Ewe, Gun, Fon, and Yoruba interior. The cost of such ventures could not be borne by indirect taxes on the scale of the 1887 tariffs, and the game of 'manipulating the traders' was played by all four administrations as their responsibilities increased. But first, for the French, there was a fifth competitor to be reckoned with—the Abomey kingdom which had been 'manipulating' European traders at the coast for nearly two centuries and was not easily dislodged.

[1] F.O. Confidential Print, 1883 [4819], *Memorandum by Mr. Anderson on the French Occupation of Porto-Novo, 11 June 1883*, p. 9.

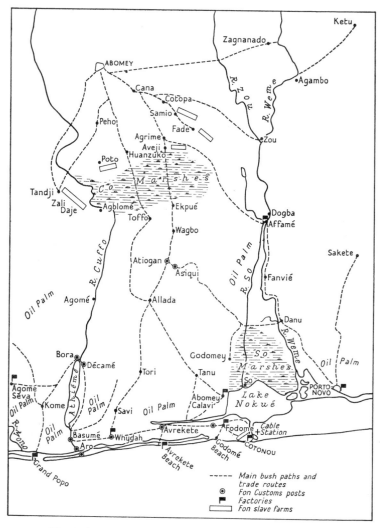

FIG. 7. Southern Dahomey. Trade routes and factories, 1888.

CHAPTER VI

The Establishment of the Fon and Yoruba Protectorates

THE most immediate and important result of the return of the French to Porto-Novo in 1883 was to encourage the transfer of European factories to markets nearer Cotonou and the Weme river. The presence of French officials and a small garrison of coloured troops was a token of security and the promise of a colony. This promise, together with the extension of Fon customs posts west and east of Whydah and the disruption of trade by slave raids along the Mono and Cuffo rivers towards the end of the 1880's, led to a pronounced movement away from the sphere of Abomey control to the Gun kingdom under the French flag. The events of 1889–94 prohibited traffic in palm oil altogether in the Athiémé, Allada, Grand Popo, and Whydah region; but between Porto-Novo and Cotonou, even in these years of crisis, the export trade continued to expand. This general tendency can be observed by comparing the export returns for the firm of Régis which maintained factories in the Fon customs area with the return of palm products exports for southern Dahomey as a whole.

*Export of Palm Products**

	Régis factories (Whydah, Godomey, Avrekete) Abomey-Calavi		All factories Southern Dahomey	
	Oil	Kernels	Oil	Kernels
	(000 tons)			
1887	0·9	2·2	4·0	20·2
1888	0·9	2·3	10·1	19·7
1889	0·4	1·6	7·2	16·1
1890	0·1	0·3	4·3	10·0
1891	0·5	1·2	6·6	16·3
1892	0·2	0·2	5·0 ·	15·6
1893	0·08	0·02	7·5	20·8
1894	Nil	Nil	8·3	24·1
1895	0·2	0·6	12·4	21·2

* M.F.O., Dahomey, xv/2; *Dahomey. Rapport d'ensemble*, 1895, 1898.

The German factories at Whydah persevered rather longer than their French rivals, profiting from the traffic in arms that preceded the outbreak of the Dahomey war. But they, too, after 1888 moved to Porto-Novo, attracted by low import duties, easy communications with Lagos, and the advantages of the cable station built by the French on the sand spit at the mouth of Lake Nokué. By 1892 there were three German, four French, six Brazilian, and two Portuguese firms with agencies in the Gun capital which had an estimated population of about 20,000.[1] Imports into the town were valued at £150,000 to £200,000 a year—80 per cent. of which consisted of spirits and tobacco. Roughly a third of these imports came by way of Lagos, and the rest through Cotonou, as shipments to Whydah beach declined.

Imports, Southern Dahomey*

						Total value	Via Lagos	% total imports
						(£000)		
1886	.	.	.	.	.	106·5	37·9	35·7
1887	.	.	.	.	.	159·6	52·5	32·8
1888	.	.	.	.	.	163·7	45·8	27·9
1889	.	.	.	.	.	148·6	51·5	28·9
1890	.	.	.	.	.	139·6	47·6	34·1
1891	.	.	.	.	.	231·5	83·7	36·1
1892	.	.	.	.	.	257·3	118·9	46·2
1893	.	.	.	.	.	418·0	115·6	27·6
1894	.	.	.	.	.	430·8	128·1	29·7
1895	.	.	.	.	.	421·7	108·7	25·7
1896	.	.	.	.	.	389·2	54·9	14·1

* P.N., Documents du Protectorat II; Ehrmann to Ballay, 31 Dec. 1890; *Dahomey. Rapport d'ensemble*, 1895, 1898, 1900.

The sharp increase in the transit traffic from Lagos in 1892 is accounted for by the need to provision French forces during the campaign against the Fon. The decline in this traffic, relative to total imports, after 1892 resulted from the construction of a wharf at Cotonou which enabled traders to use the port throughout the year and avoid the high freight charges on goods transported by the Lagos–Porto-Novo lagoon. Nevertheless, the future of Porto-Novo as the commercial centre for Dahomey was assured, whatever the route used; and the link with Lagos was strengthened by the considerable proportion of Dahomey palm products exported to the

[1] A. L. d'Albéca, *Les Établissements français du Golfe de Bénin* (Paris, 1889), pp. 64–76; Édouard Foà, *Le Dahomey* (Paris, 1895), pp. 307, 313–17; L. Brunet and L. Giethlen, *Dahomey et dépendances* (Paris, 1900).

British colony and which helped to swell Lagos trade returns till the end of the century. Just how much Lagos benefited from the development of Porto-Novo is rarely indicated in the *Blue Books* of the colony. But it is evident from French returns of trade that the annual export of oil and kernels to Lagos up till 1900 represented, in volume, about one-third to one-half of the total export of palm products from Dahomey, and about a quarter to a third of Lagos exports of the same products.

*Dahomey Export of Palm Products to Lagos**

	Volume (tons)	% of Dahomey palm products exports	% of Lagos palm products exports
1888			
Kernels . . .	7,516	38·1	17·2
Oil	3,885	38·3	47·6
1898			
Kernels . . .	10,437	58·2	24·4
Oil	2,574	42·4	40·8
1900			
Kernels . . .	16,828	76·5	34·6
Oil	1,652	18·5	16·6

* P.N., Documents du Protectorat II; *Lagos. Annual Reports for the Year 1904* [Cd. 2238], p. 158; *The West African Year-Book* (1901), pp. 72–73; *Southern Nigeria Handbook* (1912).

For the development of this transit trade with Lagos the German firms of G. L. Gaiser and Witt & Büsch were responsible. And one observer noted in 1888 that the Ossa lagoon was 'constamment sillonnée par des steamers de 200 à 150 tonnes venant de Lagos par Badagri, le *Gaiser*, le *King-Toffa*, l'*Albert*'.[1] The bulk of Porto-Novo exports, however, was canoed across Lake Nokué to Cotonou. From this port the regular shipping lines ran not to France but to Hamburg and Liverpool before 1900 when the Fraissinet steamship company began to send vessels there.[2] On the other hand, freight charges were considerably higher for trans-shipment to Lagos— 5 or 8 francs per ton for oil and kernels compared with 2 francs per ton across Lake Nokué. And at the ports themselves, freight charges for the same products from Lagos to Europe were about 80 francs

[1] D'Albéca, p. 60.
[2] The two principal steamer lines to the Bight in the 1890's were The British and African Steam Navigation Company (Liverpool) and the Afrikanische Dampfschiffs-Actien-Gesellschaft Woermann Linie (Hamburg).

per ton, while from the Dahomey ports to Marseilles, the rate was only half this sum by sailing vessel.

The growing importance of Cotonou and the demise of Whydah in the 1880's accounts for the unwillingness of the Fon kingdom to see the port pass into European hands, whatever cession agreement had been signed in 1878. For a period there were two customs authorities, one responsible to the court at Abomey, the other to the French resident at Porto-Novo; and traders were obliged to pay duties to both. The Fon officials under the *Agorigan* of Cotonou levied 2 francs 50 centimes on every puncheon of rum and 15 centimes on a case of gin—which was considerably lower than French duties, but which represented an additional charge. Furthermore, they had a monopoly of porters and boatmen whose services could be withdrawn, and complete command of the neighbouring markets on which traders depended for foodstuffs for factory personnel.

The administrators sent to protect trading interests were numerous but ineffective during the first five years of the Residency. From 1884 till the outbreak of war with Abomey in 1889 there were seven naval or military officers burdened with the task of maintaining good relations with Tofa, Glele, the British, Germans, and Portuguese, and with no regular budget till the protectorate and annexed territory were officially attached to the Senegal administration in 1887.[1] By then the two posts cost a little over 200,000 francs a year (about £8,000), half of which was spent on fortifying the Cotonou perimeter. In the same year the settlement of trade disputes between Europeans and natives in the protectorate was taken out of the hands of Tofa whose decisions were apt to be given, complained an official, 'selon l'importance des cadeaux qu'il reçoit'.[2] No attempt was as yet made to introduce European jurisdiction into the annexed territory. Inevitably, too, the expansion of local trade at Porto-Novo and Cotonou raised the question how far indigenous authorities were to be allowed to compete with the French administration for a share of revenues from import and export duties. In Tofa's case the matter was fairly quickly decided. After Colonel Dorat had taken the lower Weme under French protection, the king's claims to tolls on market canoes coming to Porto-Novo were refused. He was allowed

[1] The first drafts received by the Under-Secretary for Colonies in 1883 from the French Resident listed large quantities of spirits 'distribués aux Cabécères et au peuple à l'occasion de la fête nationale du 14 juillet'. M.A.É., Afrique/78, Faure to Challemel-Lacour, 24 Oct. 1883.

[2] M.A.É., Afrique/78, Bories to Peyrou, 12 Aug. 1883.

to retain, however, the right to levy a duty of 5 francs per ton on all exports of palm products from the protectorate which netted him about £5,000 a year.

This generosity contrasted sharply with the policy of the Residents towards Cotonou where French claims were based on a strict interpretation of the terms of the treaty of 1878. But the French were not the only competitors for this section of the coast. In 1885 the Portuguese laid claim to Whydah and Cotonou, as a cover for slave trading from Dahomey to San Thomé.[1] While this complication was being settled by laborious diplomacy, Resident Roget urged that the only way to keep rivals at bay was to enforce the 1878 treaty by military occupation, not only of Cotonou but also of Whydah. The French Foreign Office, however, resisted all suggestions that France acquire areas in Dahomey outside the ceded territory, and de Freycinet, as Minister for Foreign Affairs, laid down the general policy which was adhered to till 1889.

Nos agents ne doivent pas oublier en effet que, si nous proposons à affirmer notre situation à Kotonou en y effaçant les dernières traces d'une souveraineté antérieure à celle de la France, il n'entre nullement dans nos vues de poursuivre en ce moment du côté de Dahomey de nouveaux agrandissements coloniaux (sic).[2]

But to remove 'prior sovereignty' was difficult enough, and de Freycinet does not appear to have seen that this step alone would entail a trial of strength with the Fon. Resident Roget did; and he was strongly supported by the Ministry for the Navy which pressed for permission to send more troops to Cotonou, not only for defence, but also to satisfy the condition of 'effective occupation' required by the Berlin Conference.[3] But for the moment no extra credits for colonial expeditions could be won from the French Parliament; and Roget was powerless to prevent Fon troops from closing a passage between Lake Nokué and the sea, after floods had conveniently pierced a channel which enabled traders to avoid the Fon customs post at Cotonou market.

Information on which to base an account of Fon policy at this period is limited. Seen through European eyes the kingdom was described as an admirably organized despotism. But there are some indications that court politics at Abomey in Glele's last years

---

[1] M.A.É., Afrique/72; *Études dahoméennes*, ix (1953), 58–66.
[2] M.A.É., Afrique/81, de Freycinet to Galiber, 26 May 1885.
[3] M.A.É., Afrique/82, Galiber to de Freycinet, 25 Sept. 1885.

inhibited the king's ministers from taking dangerous and irrevocable decisions for which they would have to account to his successor. At Whydah and Cotonou throughout the last five years of Fon control there was similar evidence of indecision which made it difficult to conduct negotiations. Above all there was the growing certainty both at Abomey and on the coast that the continued presence of European administration entailed the financial attrition of the kingdom, while lesser courts like Tofa's enjoyed an undeserved and spectacular prosperity. Since the decline of the slave trade in the 1860's, the Fon dynasty was hard pressed to find economic compensation in legitimate trade which, in the main, was based on the export of produce from the Weme and Mono basins through ports outside its control. The final decline of the Whydah market and the threatened loss of Cotonou aggravated this condition; and the last years of Glele's reign were marked by a series of victorious but profitless campaigns against Ketu and against the Egbado which contributed little towards the solution of Fon difficulties on the coast. The invitation to the governor of San Thomé to occupy Whydah and Cotonou was no more than a temporary trade agreement. In the same category of half-formed alliances to hold the French at bay was an offer made in 1888 to Governor Moloney to cede the whole of southern Dahomey to the British. This gesture came not from Glele but from Prince Fasinu—a mere boy of fourteen, and son of Prince Kondo who was designated to succeed Glele.[1] Again, in 1888 and 1889 there were rumours that the Fon had negotiated a treaty with the German administration in Togo. But this overture, too, was no more than an attempt to obtain money and arms on credit.

The problem of how to come to terms with the French over Cotonou without sacrificing its fiscal advantages remained unsolved. Relations were further strained in 1888 by a dispute between Glele and Tofa. Glele raided a number of Weme villages for slaves; Tofa, shielded by his new European protectors—'se croyant tout permis'—claimed the villages as part of his own kingdom, and sent insulting messages to the Fon capital.[2] In April the following year the French post at

[1] N.R.O., Confidential Dispatches, 1881–8, Moloney to Knutsford, 14 Dec. 1888. Moloney took the offer seriously and informed the Colonial Office he would occupy Whydah if there was any sign of the French withdrawing from Porto-Novo.

[2] Missions Africaines de Lyon, Dahomey Préfecture, 12/80200, Pied to Planques, 4 Apr. 1889. For the 'official' Fon version of the quarrel with Tofa see J. Melville and Frances S. Herskovits, *Dahomean Narrative* (Northwestern University Press, 1958), pp. 381–4.

Cotonou was reinforced; and two months later, through his Brazilian interpreters, Glele dispatched a formal protest to the President of the French Republic. The treaty of 1878, Glele claimed, was no longer valid: it had never been signed by the king himself, and the Whydah officials who had agreed to it had been executed or had poisoned themselves in disgrace.[1]

In reply, Under-Secretary Faure ordered the lieutenant-governor of Guinea, Dr. Jean Bayol, to improve the defences of Cotonou by annexing Avrekete and Godomey. He was further instructed to deport Tofa to the French Congo, if he provoked the Fon. Finally, he was to conduct an embassy to Glele to settle the treaty dispute by offering to Abomey a fixed share of customs duties collected at the port.[2]

Bayol went to the Fon capital at the end of 1889.[3] His report and a document left by his interpreter, Xavier Béraud, throw some light on court politics and the attitude of the dynasty to the French administration at Porto-Novo at this period. The offer of part of Cotonou customs revenues and compensation of 20,000 francs was refused. Prince Kondo who conducted negotiations during his father's illness flatly rejected all previous agreements with the French, 'disant que ces traités avaient été signés par des chefs n'ayant aucune qualité pour cela et que d'ailleurs ces deux chefs avaient été punis pour s'être permis cela'.[4] Furthermore, reported Béraud later, Glele poisoned himself on 28 November, while the Bayol mission was still at Abomey, rather than face the economic ruin of the kingdom and ridicule by its enemies. Whatever the truth of this, Kondo was enthroned at the end of December and took the 'strong name' of Behanzin. One of his first acts was to put down a palace revolt on the part of some of the princes, seconded by officials at Whydah, who were over-willing to come to terms with the French.

After this failure more troops were sent to Cotonou, and, on Bayol's suggestion, Fon customs officials there were arrested in February

---

[1] M.A.É., Angleterre, Sierra Léone/82, Glele to the French President, n.d., copy encl. in Bontempts to Maillet, 2 June 1889.

[2] M.A.É., Afrique/125, Faure to Bayol, 12 Aug. 1889.

[3] Ibid., Bayol to Étienne, 1 Jan. and 16 Jan. 1890; Kondo to 'les Chefs Français', 27 Dec. 1889. There is an excellent and amusing account of the Bayol mission, based partly on oral evidence, in Dunglas, iii, 16–20.

[4] P.N., Documents du Protectorat II, 'Rapport dressé par l'Interprète X. Béraud', 12 Mar. 1891; see C. W. Newbury, 'A Note on the Abomey Protectorate', *Africa*, xxix, No. 2 (1959), pp. 147–8.

1890. In March a series of attacks on the port were beaten off; all trade at Whydah ceased; and eight Europeans were taken to Abomey as hostages, where Behanzin carefully explained to them that any further occupation of Fon territory on the coast would mean a protracted war.[1] But no expedition against Abomey was, as yet, contemplated in Paris. The impetuous Bayol was recalled; prisoners were exchanged; and in October 1890 a truce was arranged with the *Yovogan* of Whydah which renewed the offer of 20,000 francs a year in return for the recognition of French rights.[2]

It is doubtful whether this compensation was ever paid; and it seems clear from the reports of military officers that there were those in the local administration who were anxious for a pretext to distinguish themselves in a march on Abomey.[3] Unfortunately such pretexts were not lacking. In return for supplies of German arms, villages along the lower Mono were raided for slaves towards the end of 1891, and a number of shipments were made to the Cameroons and the Congo.[4] In a letter to the French resident, Behanzin made it clear that slave-raiding would continue in southern Dahomey wherever the Fon pleased, and that French claims to Cotonou and the region between Abomey territory and the German border were still in doubt.[5]

---

[1] The hostages were well treated and exchanged for Fon officials seized at Cotonou. Dunglas, iii. 29–32.

[2] Agreement, 3 Oct. 1890, *Études dahoméennes*, ix (1953), 101–2.

[3] P.N., Documents du Protectorat II, Captain Decœur, 'Défense du Bénin', encl. in Chef de Bataillon Audéoud to Ballay, 8 June 1891. Audéoud added in his 'Appréciations du Commandant des Troupes': 'La meilleure manière d'éviter les constructions prévues par le Directeur d'Artillerie [fortifications at Cotonou] serait de faire la guerre au Dahomey et de le supprimer, ce qui serait bien facile et ne coûterait pas beaucoup plus cher.' The French missionary, Father Pied, was no less anxious for outright annexation and expansion into the interior. Missions Africaines de Lyon, Dahomey Préfecture, 12/80200, Pied to Planques, 24 Apr., 7 May 1889.

[4] From German and French sources, it appears the following shipments were made from Whydah.
May, 1889, 185 slaves on the *Oscar* for the Congo.
Nov. 1890, 200 slaves on the *Cidade de Bahia* for San Thomé.
Sept. 1891, 300 slaves on the *Pollux* for the Cameroons.
Oct. 1891, 300 slaves on the *Professor Woermann* for the Congo.
Nov. 1891, 380 slaves on the *Daphne Woermann* for the Cameroons.
M.F.O., Afrique, vi/100, Herbette to Ribot, 29 July 1892; Ribot to Jamais, 25 Apr. and 8 Aug. 1892; Herbette to Ribot, 17 Nov. 1892; 'A Note on the Abomey Protectorate', p. 148 and n.

[5] P.N., Documents du Protectorat II; *Études dahoméennes*, ix (1953), 154–6.

Abomey le 2 janvier 1892.
Illustrissime et Excellentissime Monsieur Ehrmann,
Résident de France
Porto-Novo.

J'accuse réception de la lettre de Votre Excellence datée du 10 Décembre de l'année dernière.[1]

Obligé de vous demander une explication sur ce qu'on parle là et qui vous a obligé de m'écrire une semblable lettre.

Alors, je suis le Roi de tous les noirs, et si quelconque de cette nation m'offense et que je veuille le punir, serait-il nécessaire que je donne satisfaction aux blancs?

Si quelqu'un fait du commerce avec Votre Excellence et si cette personne même doit des comptes à une autre personne, est-ce que le créancier n'a pas droit de réclamer sa dette?

Voulez-vous alors Votre Excellence regarder dans notre traité, vous verrez seulement noté Porto-Novo et le territoire de Béta (environs de Porto-Novo) et rien de plus; par conséquent si quelque des territoires de Hueimey, etc. etc. etc. m'offense j'enverrai les punir!

Il y a quelque temps passé j'envoyais punir ceux de Huachicomey[2] pour m'avoir offensé et par cela on a parlé beaucoup que je veux piller Grand Popo: au contraire, parceque Grand Popo est mon pays et il n'y a pas de motifs pour que je puisse envoyer les punir.[3] Je suis la personne qui nomme les Cabécères de là, on peut bien voir que ce qu'on parle est tout à fait faux.

L'autre jour j'envoyai ma canne à Votre Excellence et vous n'avez pas voulu la recevoir ce que j'ai pris pour une insulte! Alors je dois noter à Votre Excellence que je ne suis pas de votre égalité pour me faire une semblable insulte; je pourrais l'accepter de quelque Roi d'Europe, pour être de la même égalité.

Encore plus: Votre Excellence avez envoyé défendre mon cabécère Zodohoncon[4] de n'envoyer plus personne au côté que Votre Excellence occupe! J'espère alors de m'envoyer dire avec beaucoup de brièveté (le plus tôt possible) si le territoire de Kotonou appartient au Dahomey ou la France?

Je trouve mieux Votre Excellence rester à Porto-Novo tranquille et faire votre commerce et de me laisser et me déranger plus; car si ce n'était

[1] Resident Ehrmann had protested to Abomey about Fon raids on villages along the Upper Weme and among the Watyi to the north of Grand Popo, taken under the French protection in Dec. 1885.

[2] Watyicome, or Kome, was an important market town of about 8,000, a few miles west of Lake Athiémé.

[3] An extraordinary claim. There is no evidence that the Gun and Mina of Grand Popo were under Fon rule. The Fon customs boundary on the lagoon was about halfway between Grand Popo and Whydah.

[4] Zodohoncon was appointed *Yovogan* at Cotonou (where there had been none since 1889) and arrived there in May 1891. Ehrmann refused to recognize him as 'Chief of the Whites' within the annexed territory.

pas pour la considération aux Français j'aurais envoyé il y a longtemps piller Porto-Novo pour les insultes que Toffa m'a faites!

Tout ce qui se passe là-bas, Xavier Béraud me l'envoie communiquer, alors Votre Excellence, ne savez-vous pas que ce jeune homme est mon fils?[1] Je ne fais pas des injures à personne.

J'ai su comme Votre Excellence veut envoyer des troupes au Décimère d'Aho ce que j'estimerais beaucoup si cela avait eu lieu.[2] Si c'est vrai ou non, c'est seulement Votre Excellence qui peut savoir: si je le savais, c'est par Xavier Béraud m'avoir envoyé prévenir. Aussi ce que Xavier Béraud m'envoyait dire n'était pas vrai ce que vous m'avez communiqué au sujet des 200 hommes de Grand Popo que l'on dit avoir été pris par les Dahoméens, et si Votre Excellence avez envoyé dire c'est seulement pour constater. Je crois bien au dire de Xavier à ce sujet parce que mes soldats n'ont pas fait aucun prisonnier des gens de Grand Popo.

La mère de Xavier Béraud aussi m'envoie informer beaucoup de choses qui là-bas se passent.

Signé: El Rei Behenazin, Ahy Géré.

le Résident de France	Pour traduction littérale
Ehrmann.	l'interprète principal,
	X. Béraud

In March 1892 Lieutenant-Governor Ballot while exploring the Weme in the gunboat *Topaze* was fired on by Fon troops. The evidence of the arms traffic and the *Topaze* affair persuaded reluctant ministers in Paris that military intervention was inevitable, and funds for the expedition were voted by the French Parliament in April 1892. The following month Colonel Dodds arrived. With 800 men at the beginning of the campaign and 1,200 towards the end, it took him six months to fight his way to Abomey against 8,000 to 10,000 Fon troops and a handful of European mercenaries. Dodds still thought it possible, as late as the end of 1893, to retain Behanzin as a protected ruler. But the king refused any such compromise; and the campaign was not completed till his surrender on 25 January 1894 when he was sent into exile.

Before the return of Governor Ballot as civil administrator in August 1894, it was left to Dodds to lay down the main lines of French policy towards the Fon. The old Abomey kingdom was carved up into two protectorates. One, with the town of Abomey as its centre, was roughly demarcated in the west by the River Cuffo, in the east by the Weme, and by protectorates over the Mahi and

---

[1] i.e. his confidant and client.
[2] Aho or Aroh, the Fon customs post at the mouth of the River Aroh. Ehrmann threatened to occupy the post if raids in the Athiémé area continued.

Ketu in the north and north-east. To the south the reduced kingdom was divided from the Allada protectorate by the Co marshes. At the same time the royal houses of Abomey and Allada were constituted as mutually independent paramountcies under rulers chosen from their royal lineages by the princes and approved by the French. After the collapse of the Fon as a military power, Dodds counted on a 'dislocation rapide' of the provinces conquered and administered since the eighteenth century.[1] But he preferred, in the absence of qualified personnel, to leave Allada, Abomey, Grand Popo, Mahi, and Ketu to themselves with their village administration intact: 'il convient de ne pas trop marcher dans ce pays afin de ne pas être obligé de se mêler trop près à sa vie quotidienne, afin d'avoir aussi des chefs responsables et suffisamment puissants pour exercer une véritable action sur la population'. In short, French administration was to be as 'indirect' as possible.

For Abomey and Allada, the choice of paramount rulers was limited. Since most of the court had fallen into French hands, it was possible to obtain information about the most suitable candidates—those who had opposed Kondo at the time of his succession to Glele. The princes, claimed Dodds, unanimously supported Goutchili, one of Glele's sons, who was proclaimed king with the name of Agoli-Agbo on 15 January 1894. At Allada, a descendant of the *Alladahonu* royal lineage was chosen and installed with the name of Gli-Gla.

In the south the area around Whydah between Lake Athiémé and Lake Nokué was simply annexed at the beginning of the campaign and provisionally administered by two military officers. The families of Fon officials were permitted to remain in the area, but were forbidden any positions of responsibility as ward chiefs or customs officers. Brazilian creoles who served as their advisers and clerks had their properties confiscated along with those of the two German firms that had been prominent in supplying the Fon with arms.

The agreement between the Lagos and Porto-Novo administrations in 1887 and the tension between the French and the Fon which ended in the conquest of Dahomey threw into relief the limitations to British control of the Yoruba interior. As long as the Egbado, Egba, and Awori towns lay outside Lagos Colony, the risk of a commercial and political outflanking movement towards the Niger on the part of the French could not be discounted. But the idea of a formal

[1] P.N., Dodds to Delcassé, 'Rapport d'ensemble', 10 Feb. 1894.

protectorate over the interior tribes was slow to evolve; and when the protectorate treaties were finally made between 1888 and 1893 they were neither uniform in content, nor did they provide a clear guide to the responsibilities of the colony in the Yoruba interior, particularly in the matter of jurisdiction over European and native traders. Indeed, the administration was discouraged from defining too closely the powers of the Lagos Supreme Court in the coastal territory itself; and it was uncertain, as late as 1888, for example, whether the Spirits Licence Ordinance, proclaimed in 1876, could be enforced in the towns of the Western or Eastern Districts.[1]

Consequently, the first treaties to be made with the independent tribes since Glover's day were tentative in character. In May and July 1888 Governor Moloney concluded a series of agreements with the exiled chiefs and elders of Ketu, and the chiefs of Ilaro, Igbessa, Oyo, and Ife, in which the Yoruba signatories promised not to cede their territories to any other European power. Igbessa, as the nearest neighbour to Lagos, was to be considered as part of the colony; Ketu and Ilaro were to be the subjects of 'future agreements'.[2] The motives for this sudden bout of vague treaty-making were, on the one hand, fear of the Fon who had twice sacked Ketu and destroyed Okeodan, and on the other, fear of French expansion, after the example set by the French explorer Viard at Abeokuta.

Viard's exploits in 1888 embarrassed the French as much as they alarmed British traders and Lagos officials. Heedless of the instructions of Governor Ballot, he visited Ilaro and Abeokuta in April, allegedly to carry out an economic survey of markets and trade routes between southern Dahomey and the Niger. With the help of Catholic missionaries he obtained a treaty of trade and friendship from the Egba.[3] His overtures for a similar treaty with the chiefs and elders of Ilaro were rejected; and running out of presents and supplies the would-be explorer returned to Porto-Novo at the end of April, bringing with him three Egba envoys who were given a cool reception by Tofa, but whose presence lent substance to the wild rumours of French annexations in Yorubaland. The worst fears of Governor Ballot were realized: the goodwill carefully built up between himself and Moloney in order to preserve the *modus-vivendi*

[1] N.R.O., Dispatches, 12, Moloney to Holland, 17 Aug. 1887; Moloney to Knutsford, 12 July 1888.

[2] Treaties in Hertslet, i (1894), 425–30.

[3] M.A.É., Afrique/128, Treaty, 11 Apr. 1888, encl. in Viard to Goblet, 17 May 1888.

of 1887 was destroyed in a fury of anti-French petitions from Lagos merchants and the Liverpool Chamber of Commerce, as the press in France and England either boasted of a new colony or protested at a trespass in a British 'sphere of influence'.[1]

The French Foreign Office, however, had no illusions about the worth of Viard's treaty or about the role of the mission at Abeokuta in building up a myth to excite public patriotism and government support for a venture backed by the Marseilles Chamber of Commerce.[2] When the treaty was examined and no clauses of political significance were discovered, the question of an Egba protectorate was officially closed. There were delicate negotiations with England at stake.

The capitulation of French commercial interests in the Niger Delta and the vague and unsatisfactory *ad hoc* agreements with England concerning the partition of the African coast moved the French Under-Secretary for the Colonies, Eugène Etienne, to put forward a proposal for an Anglo-French conference for the purpose of examining 'toutes les contestations auxquelles a donné lieu, sur la côte occidentale d'Afrique, le contact des colonies françaises et anglaises et d'arriver par un ensemble de concessions réciproques à les résoudre d'une façon définitive'.[3] And after a change of ministers and pressure from Salisbury to settle the Gambia boundaries at the end of 1888, the principle of joint discussions was accepted by the French Foreign Office.[4] Pending these discussions, the Colonial Office neither ratified nor rejected Moloney's treaties of May and June. Further responsibilities in the Yoruba interior were not thought desirable; but the possibility that France might in some way benefit from the Viard affair kept the agreements with Ketu, Ilaro, and Igbessa in suspense, till the Paris talks on general questions had begun.[5] While Moloney waited, the British ambassador, Egerton, and the Colonial Office representative, Hemming, agreed with their French counterparts on where to draw the boundaries of the Senegambia

[1] *Lagos Observer*, 9 July and 1 Sept. 1888; Ballot in *Études dahoméennes*, ix (1953), 86–87; M.A.E., Afrique/128, Viard to Krantz, 15 July 1888 (protesting against press exaggerations in France and England).

[2] M.A.É., Afrique/128, Planques (Missions Africaines de Lyon) to Goblet, 14 June 1888; Marseilles Chamber of Commerce to Goblet, 11 July 1888, and Minute, 16 July.

[3] M.A.É., Afrique/86, Étienne to Flourens, 10 Dec. 1887.

[4] Ibid., Minute (Sous-Direction des Protectorats), 18 Dec. 1888.

[5] C.O. 806/299, Knutsford to Moloney, 18 Oct. 1888; N.R.O., Dispatches, 13, Moloney to Knutsford, 5 Jan. 1889.

region, the western sector of the Gold Coast, and the Slave Coast.[1] The solution arrived at for the latter area was simply to leave Ipokia to Lagos, return Katanu and Appa to the French protectorate, and adopt as a common frontier a convenient meridian running from the mouth of the Ajarra creek northwards to the ninth parallel.[2] The boundary agreement was approved by both governments in November 1888, and Moloney took Ipokia under British protection in 1890.

The French administration at Porto-Novo immediately anchored a customs hulk at the mouth of Ajarra creek to discourage Lagos trade with Egbado territory. The Lagos authorities were slow to retaliate. For, till the end of 1889, the Colonial Office was still opposed to anything more than commercial agreements with the Yoruba interior; and it had been decided in Paris at the conference that the area between the Ajarra and the Addo was to remain neutral 'from a Customs point of view', pending a tariff convention between the two colonies.[3] But by the end of 1891, despite repeated protests, it was clear that neither the French administration nor the Paris ministries had any intention of sacrificing the advantages derived from the low scale of duties paid on spirits imports into southern Dahomey.[4] The Colonial Office threatened to set up British posts along the border to prevent trade with Porto-Novo. But this threat made little impression, since the French Under-Secretary for the Colonies was aware that Yoruba territory north of Badagri was still independent.[5] The situation for Lagos traders worsened when customs duties at the British port were increased in 1893: the duty paid on 100 gallons of spirits at Cotonou was only £7. 12s., compared with £16. 16s. 6d. on the British side; and transit duties on goods passing between Lagos and Porto-Novo had to be lowered at the request of the Lagos Chamber of Commerce, in order to allow British traders to compete with the French in the Weme palm products market.[6] Finally, as it became certain that the kingdom of Abomey would fall

[1] M.A.É., Afrique/128, 'Mémento des séances', July–Aug. 1889; 'projet d'entente', Aug. 1889. The French delegates were Nisard and d'Estournelles from the French Foreign Office, and Jean Bayol, lieutenant-governor of Senegal.

[2] P.P., 1890, li [C. 5905], Agreement, 10 Aug. 1889, Art. IV.

[3] C.O. 806/307, C.O. to F.O., 21 Dec. 1889.

[4] M.A.É., Afrique/129, Étienne to Ribot, 2 Nov. 1891.

[5] P.N., Correspondance du Commandant Supérieur, Dodds to Carter, 23 Jan. 1893.

[6] *Lagos Standard*, 5 Oct. 1895.

to French arms and open a route to the Niger, a more positive policy towards the Yoruba interior was called for.

The strongest voice came from the African section of the Liverpool Chamber of Commerce. Champion of British traders against France in the area north of Sierra Leone and sponsor of the Oil Rivers protectorate, the chamber in April 1891 petitioned the Colonial Office to take steps to safeguard the interior for Lagos: '*first*, by making an amicable arrangement with the tribes respecting their roads and tolls, commuting the latter, if possible, by an annual subsidy; and, *secondly*, by mediating between the Chiefs of the Ilorins, Ibadans, &c., and engaging them to abandon their wars'.[1] At the Colonial Office Lord Knutsford replied in the same month that orders had been sent to Governor Carter to put these proposals into effect.

Meanwhile, Acting-Governor Denton took steps on his own initiative to complete the work begun by Moloney in 1888. In his view, the possession of the Egbado town of Ilaro was essential to prevent 'the gravitation of Egba trade towards Porto-Novo which the French hope they will bring about in time'.[2] He toured the area personally early in 1891, visiting Ipokia and Ajilete, where, in return for a British flag, he tried to interest the chiefs in clearing the Addo river. Denton judged that Porto-Novo still had a monopoly of trade with the Egbado towns. Customs posts—as Moloney had urged—might help; but the essential, he thought, was to devise closer administrative ties between the Egbado and Badagri, and between the Egba and Lagos. This plan was strongly supported by District Commissioner Peel whose report on the markets of the Western District Denton forwarded to the Colonial Office in July 1891 together with his comments.[3] Among these was one which called attention to the fact that Badagri was useless as a customs post and that the duties collected there were 'not a hundredth part of the import of spirits into the Protectorate through Porto-Novo from which we derive no benefit'. Addo and Ilaro, he concluded, were to be taken under British jurisdiction at once to drain off Egbado trade southwards and eastwards to Lagos.

[1] Coke to Knutsford, 6 Apr. 1891, in *Report of the Committee of the African Trade Section* (Liverpool, 1892), p. 7.

[2] N.R.O., 'Papers Relating to the Opening Up of Lagos Protectorate', 1890–1906, Denton to Knutsford, 13 Sept. 1890. For French plans to expand towards the Niger, see C. W. Newbury, 'The Development of French Policy on the Lower and Upper Niger, 1880–98', *The Journal of Modern History*, xxxi (1959), 24–26.

[3] N.R.O., Dispatches, 14, Denton to Knutsford, 18 July 1891.

In August and September 1891 the acting-governor went on tour again to give effect to his recommendations.[1] His route took him through Igbessa, where the British flag was raised, to the head of the Addo river, with only a short visit to Badagri in passing—a significant example of the way in which future trade routes were to skirt the capital of the Western District. The flag was raised at Addo and at Owo. On the way to Ilaro, Denton passed through Isalu (whose chiefs claimed British protection since the days of Glover), and thence to Ajilete where he admired rich maize and cassava farms. Ilaro, too, was added to Denton's list without trouble. He then canoed down the trade route from Ajilete to Shagbo and Addo and crossed to Ipokia and the mouth of Ajarra creek whose trade, he noted with regret, still went to the French side.

Denton's tours marked the turning point in British relations with western Yorubaland. The Egba, who claimed tribute from Ilaro, closed the Ogun once more as a protest against the extension of Lagos jurisdiction and demanded a commission of inquiry into the rights of the chiefs of Abeokuta in Egbado.[2] Governor Carter ignored their complaints; and at the end of 1891 he investigated prospects for improved road and water communications in the west and had land cleared for the quarters of the travelling commissioner near Ilaro.

But these developments did not settle relations with the Egba; and the Ogun remained closed. While in England the Liverpool and Manchester Chambers of Commerce pressed the Colonial Office for action, at Lagos an expedition to Ijebu in May 1892 and the subsequent pacification of the north shore of Lagos lagoon by posts of Hausa constabulary warned the chiefs at Abeokuta that diplomacy was better than continued obstinacy. In September, when Carter again toured the Western District, and deposed the *Bale* of Addo for hearing court cases and collecting fines on his own behalf, the Egba opened the Ogun. In the same month, for the first time in the history of Lagos, they invited the governor to Abeokuta.[3]

Carter's embassy to the Yoruba towns at the beginning of 1893 was many-sided: along with Hausa troops and a maxim gun, he took a surveyor, made a detailed analysis of trade routes and local products, and obtained treaties at Abeokuta, Oyo, and Ilorin. It was an

---

[1] N.R.O., Dispatches, 14, Denton to Knutsford, 1 Sept. 1891.
[2] Ibid., Carter to Ripon, 28 Sept. 1892.
[3] Ibid., Carter to Ripon, 31 Oct. 1892.

expedition that looked back to the example of Ijebu with its threat of force, and forward to the building of a railway to the Niger and the promise of new markets. At Abeokuta Carter treated with the *Nlado*, as head of the *Ogboni* council of chiefs, the *Jaguna*, head of the war chiefs, and the influential *Magaji*, descendant of the *Bashorun* Somoye. The latter was the most important: 'the secret of his power', reported Carter, 'lay in the fact that he was rich, and moreover, was possessed of considerable ability and diplomatic talent'.[1]

It was a talent that could argue and refuse. The *Magaji* politely rejected Carter's explanation of Egba difficulties with Lagos and offered one of his own: the seizure of Ilaro, and consequent loss of tribute and slaves who fled there to obtain their freedom under British protection. He refused the sections of Carter's draft treaty providing for the posting of a resident at Abeokuta and the building of a railway. Privately, he conceded that a railway might bring wealth and trade to the Egba. But the chiefs as a whole rejected any form of protectorate which entailed referring disputes to Lagos for judgement, or any clauses defining obligations of hospitality towards traders and missionaries, which they looked on as the thin edge of a colonial wedge. In return for a treaty of trade and friendship, which was all Carter could obtain, they demanded a clause guaranteeing the independence of the Egba. And Carter finally agreed.[2]

By 1894 the shape of the three German, British, and French colonies had been settled below the ninth parallel. The impulse to extend European rule over the interior had come, in the main, from local traders, supported by commercial and shipping interests in Europe. The course of partition, however, revealed some marked contrasts in methods and results. The hegemony of the Fon over the coastal market at Whydah, won in the eighteenth century, was of little fiscal value after the establishment of the French protectorate at Porto-Novo. In the contest for the jointly owned port of Cotonou there is an air of desperation and futility about the spectacle of an African kingdom attempting to stave off the challenge of late nineteenth-century imperialism by reviving the slave raids and export of slaves that had been the basis of its earlier power. This power collapsed after a short and bitter struggle which destroyed the independence of the dynasty.

For the Egba, the example of Ijebu was sufficient warning; and what might have been so easily lost by conservative obstinacy was

---

[1] P.P., 1893 lxii [C. 7227], 4.   [2] Ibid., Treaty, 18 Jan. 1893, Appendix I.

preserved by able diplomacy. One of Carter's principal objects in the negotiations—land concessions for a railway through Egba territory to Ibadan—was not conceded. But Carter himself in 1893 was optimistic about the eventual outcome.[1] Like Dodds he had implicit faith in the economic value of a 'European peace' for the West African interior; but unlike Dodds he was spared the difficult task of appointing his own indigenous rulers to help preserve that peace.

For the German commissioners the Ewe and the Gun of southern Togo presented no such problems; and it was with a mixture of admiration and envy that the French resident wrote of his colonial neighbours in 1891:

> Il est impossible de ne pas être frappé de l'activité déployé par les Allemands pour le développement de leur petite colonie. Je n'ai certes pas l'intention de représenter l'Administration allemande comme le modèle des Administrations coloniales; il est évident qu'un pays comme le Togo, qui n'a jamais de complications politiques, est bien plus facile à administrer qu'une colonie morcelée comme la nôtre dont les chefs sont perpétuellement et en tout à compter avec cette épée de Damoclès qui s'appelle le Dahomey.[2]

The patrol reports from southern Togo, on the whole, bear out the assertion that the German colony enjoyed an absence of 'political complications'. But in any case the ambitions of its administrators were strictly limited in the 1880's and early 1890's to securing a link with the middle Volta, and not, as in Dahomey or Nigeria, linking the coast with the upper Niger. In 1886 Commissioner Falkenthal and his secretary Grode secured possession of a trade route through Tove, Keve, and Agotime as far as the southern outcrop of the Togo mountains. The following year a series of protectorate agreements were negotiated with the sub-tribes of Buem and Kpandu, and in 1890 the first interior station was opened at Misahöhe which provided both a bridgehead for new posts established in Kete-Krachi after 1894 and protection for traffic passing from the coast up the Volta to the Salaga market. There the first phase of German expansion halted. The boundary agreement with Great Britain which was confirmed in 1888 arbitrarily relegated to Togo, the left bank of the Volta from Kete-Kratchi to Kpandu but kept the estuary of the river and the important port of Keta for the Gold Coast.

[1] Carter, in *Reports of Proceedings at a Banquet given by the Chamber* (Liverpool, 1893), p. 11. Carter attributed his success to the Ijebu expedition 'which I do not hesitate to say has done more for the Colony of Lagos than any event in its history since the cession to the British Crown'.

[2] Ehrmann to Ballay, 8 May 1891, in *Études dahoméennes*, ix (1953), 142.

CHAPTER VII

Trade, Agriculture, and Colonial Finance

THE expansion of the three European powers beyond their coastal bases which had begun in the early 1890's was not completed till the end of the nineteenth century. The course of this expansion north of the forest belt and the international partition of the savannah peoples of Northern Nigeria, Dahomey, and Togo is beyond the scope of this study; but it is necessary to bear in mind that the strategic pre-occupation of German, French, and British administrators with the hinterland outweighed the attention given to the political organization of the south-western Yoruba, Gun, and Ewe, until the northern frontier had been settled and a skeleton of road and rail communications was constructed by about 1908. And as the three colonies were rough-hewn and took on their present shape, the future of contiguous ethnic groups between the Volta and the Ogun was increasingly determined by their incorporation in larger economic and political units. This process was taken a stage further in 1902, when Dahomey became part of the French West African Federation. It was completed in the sphere of British influence by the amalgamation of Lagos and Southern Nigeria in 1906 and in 1914 by the union of the Southern and Northern Provinces. After the First World War it was arbitrarily revised in the case of German Togo by splintering the colony into two separate mandates.

The frontiers of southern Togo, Dahomey, and Yorubaland were less important as rigid dividing lines than the economic and administrative links forged between the three colonial capitals and their respective 'protectorates'. European rule at the earliest phase of consolidation up till 1914 was less like 'a great steel grid over the amorphous cellular tissue of tribal Africa'[1] than a series of tenuous but ever-strengthening threads which linked regions of social and political diversity, binding the markets of the interior to the coast. Around the threads of interior trade, woven by engineers and road-builders, the colonies crystallized. The evolution of three distinct

---

[1] Margery Perham, cited in James S. Coleman, *Nigeria Background to Nationalism* (Berkeley and Los Angeles, 1958), p. 45.

colonial entities with contrasting financial and native policies took two decades. And the development of the three capitals during this period is symptomatic of the process of creating a common administrative centre for the heterogeneous components resulting from arbitrary partition. At the beginning of the 1890's it was still possible to describe Lagos as 'only a trading station for the native producer'.[1] By the end of the century it was the terminus for the railway, already constructed as far as Ibadan, and about to be extended to the Niger. Similarly, Porto-Novo and Lome acquired an economic and administrative importance as capitals and markets that produced a minor demographic revolution in the towns themselves and their immediate environs.

Coloured Population

Lagos Town	Porto-Novo	Lome
32,508 (1891)*	16,229 (1899)§	1,518 (1891)‖
76,000 (1911)†	20,000 (1908)	7,090 (1911)

Lagos Island and Colony‡	Porto-Novo District	Lome District
85,607 (1891)	138,215 (1899)	75,000 (1905)
166,000 (1911)	191,846 (1908)	119,000 (1911)

* *Lagos Annual Report for 1891*, No. 58, p. 42.
† Including Ebute Metta. *Blue Book*, 1917, R. 4.
‡ Central, Western, and Eastern Districts.
§ Government-General, Dakar, 22 G 19–20.
‖ Robert R. Kuczynski, *The Cameroons and Togoland. A Demographic Study* (London, 1939), pp. 336, 337.

Though the strict accuracy of the statistics is questionable, the heavy increase in urban population in the space of two decades for Lagos and Lome, and in a decade for Porto-Novo is clear enough. The same is true of Lome District and Lagos Colony. Some of the increase in Porto-Novo District during the short space of nine years can be accounted for by a considerable Yoruba migration from Egbado territory across the Ajarra creek to the area between the towns of Ajarra and Ajohon—the latter, a market second only to Porto-Novo itself by 1914.[2] By that time the only other centres that could

[1] *Lagos Annual Report for 1891*, No. 58, p. 51.
[2] P.N., Braucher, 'Rapport politique, 1914, Cercle de Porto-Novo', f. 7. There was a general increase in the number of Yoruba in Dahomey from 83,979 in 1904 to some 98,000 by 1914. Ethnic groups in the Porto-Novo District in 1908 were Gun (104,431), Yoruba (47,931), Mina (1,425), Hausa (542), others (115).

rival these in any of the three colonies were Abeokuta (51,000), Ibadan (175,000), and Badagri (7,000).

Fundamental to these demographic changes was the construction of 'vertical' systems of communication, both road and rail, which opened up new secondary markets in the palm-oil belt, particularly in southern Dahomey and Togo, and replaced the lagoons and navigable rivers as the main avenues of transportation. In south-western Nigeria the railway was begun in 1895 as a government project, and completed as far as Abeokuta and Ibadan by the end of 1900. It was financed and continued eastwards into the interior from an initial loan of £2,500,000 at 3½ per cent. interest.[1] The total cost of the first section to Ibadan (excluding the construction of Carter and Denton bridges) was £882,961. By contrast the Dahomey and Togo railway systems were in two cases constructed and run by private companies, assisted in the initial stages by government loans. The initiative for the central Dahomey railway from Cotonou to Parakou came originally from Governor Ballot as a strategic plan to link the coast with the Niger, after preliminary surveys made in 1897. The basic work was undertaken by the colony, and the laying of the track was left to the Dahomey Railway Company, formed in 1901 by the Marseilles firm of Mantes Frères and Borelli de Régis, with a capital of £320,000. By 1914 the line was constructed via Abomey as far as Save on a series of interest-free loans to the Colony from Dakar. A small branch line from Porto-Novo was built at the same time; and by 1908 a third line connected Porto-Novo with Sakete and Savalou along the eastern frontier, constructed and managed solely by the Colony.[2] In Togo the development of the two railways to the interior complimented the construction of a landing pier at Lome in 1904. The Lome–Anecho line was contracted to the *Aktiengesellschaft Augsburg-Nürnberg*, opened to traffic in 1905, and its management entrusted to another private company—*Gesellschaft m. b. H. Lenz & Co.* Inland, the railway from Lome to Palime was planned by the *Kolonialwirtschaftliches Komitee* and capital in the form of a government loan of M. 7,800,000 at 3½ per cent. interest was provided in 1904. Construction was carried out by Lenz & Co., completed in 1907, and the running of the railway leased for twelve years to the *Deutsche Kolonialeisenbahn Bau- und Betriebs-Gesellschaft* for a minimum

[1] P.P., 1905, [Cd. 2325], 19; F. Baltzer, *Die Kolonialbahnen* (Berlin, 1916), pp. 164–5. Cf. McPhee, pp. 111–12.

[2] Baltzer, pp. 215–16.

annual rent of M. 306,500. The second railway, Lome–Atakpame, was built by the latter company between 1908 and 1913 and in 1911 incorporated in the lease, when the minimum annual rent was raised to M. 523,000.

The initial costs of the five main lines varied considerably.[1]

	Line section	Miles	Construction (£)	Cost per mile (£)
South-west Nigeria	Lagos–Ibadan 1895–1900	125	882,961	7,064
Dahomey	Cotonou–Save 1900–12	162	840,000	5,185
	Porto-Novo–Sakete 1905–13	23	83,692	3,638
Togo	Lome–Palime 1902–7	63	390,000	6,190
	Lome–Atakpame 1908–13	102	560,000	3,456

On the whole, lines laid by private companies were cheaper, though it should be remembered that the construction of the Lagos–Ibadan line was seriously interrupted between 1897 and 1898 by scarcity of labourers who were commandeered as carriers during military operations in north-western Nigeria. There is no evidence that the scale of wages differed greatly in the three colonies; but there was certainly a considerable amount of forced labour to supplement voluntary labour (both paid), particularly in Togo and Dahomey.[2]

Great changes were expected in the internal markets of Lagos Colony and the protectorate from the advent of the railway. In 1901 it was confidently predicted that Lagos would supplant Ikorodu and Ejinrin as a collecting point for native palm-products suppliers.

Ikrodo market depends mainly upon the supply of native produce from the Egba country, the Ijebu Remo country, and the Ibadan country, and the corresponding demand in those territories for articles of European manufacture or preparation.

[1] P.P., 1905, [Cd. 2325], 20; *Bulletin de renseignements sur la situation économique et politique de l'Afrique occidentale française, Année 1920* (1921), p. 64.

[2] In Lagos Colony the daily wage for labour in 1898 was 9*d.* to 1*s.* (and 3*d.* extra if employed outside the colony). Servants were paid 15*s.* to £2. 10*s.* a month. In Togo at the same period the rates were: males, 30–75 pf. a day, women and children 15–25 pf. Carriers were paid M. 1·25–M. 1·50 per day, for loads of 50–60 lb. Skilled labour earned M. 2–M. 3 per day. Plantation labour was paid M. 20 per month. In Dahomey wages ranged from 60 centimes for carriers to 5 francs a day for servants. *Colonial Report Lagos, 1899,* No. 284, [Cd.3–7], p. 19; *Deutsches Kolonialblatt,* ix (1898), 204-8, and xii (1901), 281; *Dahomey. Rapport d'ensemble* (1902), p. 27.

The railway taps the Egba and Ibadan countries directly and it is certain that so soon as native producers have acquired confidence in the line the effect will be that Ikorodu market will become nothing but a large local (Ijebu) market for Remo only. Attendance at this market has been known to average anything from 10,000 to 15,000 persons. To bring produce from Ibadan to Ikorodu by foot takes three days; from the north of the Remo two days; and from the Egba country from one to two days. An extra day must be added for the journey to Lagos. The railway halves these times at least, and instead of a native producer in Ibadan having to wait from six to eight days for the price of his produce he can now have it in about three days. So soon as the native producer appreciates this it is reasonable to expect that every ton of produce that used to be sent to Ikorodu from Egba and Ibadan territories will be sent direct to Lagos via the railway.[1]

Five years later it was by no means certain that these predictions had come true. The tonnage of palm products and other domestic produce carried by the railway was relatively small compared with the volume of Lagos exports; and the greatest increase in tonnage came not from public merchandise but from stores carried for government departments and from railway materials for further construction. Cotton bales were carried free, to assist the work of the British Cotton-Growing Association. It had been learned that a railway by itself into the interior was not a striking economic asset without considerable development of feeder roads, and these were totally non-existent. Moreover, relying for revenue solely from the transport of merchandise did not pay. A report for 1905 summed it up:

The freight and passenger rates have been fixed at rates that are un-remunerative on the present volume of traffic and much lower than is customary on West African lines, which have proved exceptionally costly to construct and require a highly-paid European staff one third in excess of requirements in order to provide for the frequent absences on leave necessary to Europeans in this climate. The Government, while anxious to see the railway paying maintenance, interest, and sinking fund charges, is unwilling to increase the rates to accelerate the attainment of this desirable result, and looks more to the indirect revenue receipts owing to the development of the country by means of the railway than to direct railway receipts.[2]

In Dahomey the railway company which ran the Cotonou–Save line made a deficit till 1913 and had to be assisted by an annual grant from the colony. The administration, on the other hand, squeezed a small profit out of the line from Porto-Novo to Sakete. The fact

[1] *Lagos. Report for 1900–1901*, No. 348, pp. 6–7.
[2] *Southern Nigeria (Lagos). Report for 1905*, No. 507, [Cd. 2684], p. 45.

was that local traders were extremely slow to follow the railway into the interior; and for the palm-products which remained the staple of Dahomey exports, the River Weme provided the cheapest and most direct route to the Porto-Novo market for native suppliers. The principal interest of the administration in the line remained strategic; but the ambition to extend it farther towards Borgu, as planned in 1910 when it was suspected that the Lagos administration would begin a branch line towards Bussa, was never fulfilled.[1]

There are no financial statistics to indicate the progress of the company railways in Togo. The administration was content to receive its fixed annual rent which together with small receipts from the Lome landing pier provided a modest annual sum—but comparable in proportion to the gross transport revenues from Southern Nigeria.[2]

	Togo		Southern Nigeria		Dahomey	
	Gross rev. £(000) Railway and pier	% rev.	Gross rev. £(000) Railway	% rev.	Gross rev. £(000) Railway and wharf	% rev.
1908	15·3	11·6	145	10·4	4·0	
1909	16	10·1	194	14·2	5·1	less than 5%
1910	20	16·3	266	13·7	6·5	
1911	31	13·0	308	15·8	9·4	
1912	27·6	17·5	387	17·3	11·0	
1913	29·5	14·6	545	23·7	10·9	

Politically the railways were enormously influential in binding together into an administrative unity the disparate areas of different jurisdiction. Commenting on the completion of the line in eastern Dahomey in 1913, Lieutenant-Governor Noufflard wrote:

Nous savons quel admirable instrument de pacification ce chemin de fer a été pour la région de Sakété, cela nous permet de préjuger de son action sur la région Holli; pour juger de sa valeur économique il suffira de constater, que le matériel malgré le service intensif auquel il est soumis n'a jamais été suffisant.[3]

But this demand for transport came from administrators as much as

[1] Government-General, Dakar, Conseil de Gouvernement, 5 E 23–5, Minutes, June 1910.

[2] Colonial Reports. Southern Nigeria, 1909–14; Die deutschen Schutzgebiete in Afrika und der Südsee, 1910/11, Appendix C, pp. 253–4, and 1912, p. 324; P.N., 'Rapports d'ensemble', 1901–14; Government-General, Dakar, 'Affaires Financières', T 30.

[3] P.N., Noufflard, 'Rapport annuel, 1913', f. 16.

the peasantry; and rail transport did not mean (as originally sur-
mised) that a smaller number of officials could administer more
economically. It is doubtful, moreover, in the case of Togo and
Dahomey, whether the staple domestic exports increased greatly
after construction.

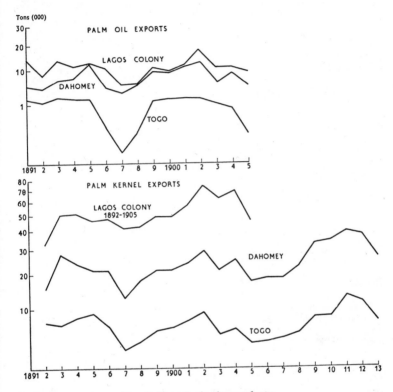

FIG. 8. Export of palm products.

   The staple exports, despite experiments with other crops, remained
palm oil and palm kernels. The annual fluctuations in the volume of
these domestic products paralleled each other closely in Togo, Dahomey and Lagos Colony, according to climatic factors, except
during the Dahomey war (when Lagos exports also declined, as the
transit trade from Porto-Novo fell away). After 1905 the statistics are
not strictly comparable, given the addition of the Delta trade to the
exports for Southern Nigeria. Even so the periods of palm products

'depression' and 'peak' are consistent till the First World War. Where there are gradual changes these are in the relative positions of the palm oil and kernels staples, as percentages of the total export values for each colony.

*Palm Oil and Kernel Exports**

	Select years		
	Togo	Dahomey	Lagos Colony
1895:			
Palm oil (000 tons) . .	2·5	12·4	12·8
Kernels (000 tons) . .	9·0	21·2	46·5
Value	£62,853	£390,600	£525,987
% total exports . . .	89%	92%	53%
1897:			
Palm oil (000 tons) . .	0·3	4·1	6·2
Kernels (000 tons) . .	9·0	21·2	46·5
Value	£25,618	£190,000	£404,425
% total exports . . .	66%	85%	49%
1902:			
Palm oil (000 tons) . .	2·9	12·7	17·5
Kernels (000 tons) . .	9·4	29·8	75·4
Value	£137,630	£510,728	£1,153·891
% total exports . . .	63%	93%	91·2%
			Southern Nigeria
1905:			
Palm oil (000 tons) . .	0·4	5·6	50·5
Kernels (000 tons) . .	3·2	17·5	108·8
Value	£37,848	£253,148	£1,947·904
% total exports . . .	19%	83%	76%
1911:			
Palm oil (000 tons) . .	4·0	15·6	79·4
Kernels (000 tons) . .	13·3	39·3	176·4
Value	£263,342	£826·624	£4,271·280
% total exports . . .	52%	94%	79%

* *Annual Reports* (Lagos and Southern Nigeria), 1890–1914; *Dahomey. Rapport d'ensemble*, 1899–1914; *Die deutschen Schutzgebiete*, 1901/02–1914; *Report on the British Mandated Sphere of Togoland for 1920–1921*, [Cmd. 1698], p. 36. Values have been calculated at the rate of £ Sterling = M. 20 = Fr. 25.

It is noticeable that throughout this period palm products dominated the export trade of Dahomey to a much greater extent than in the other two colonies, even after the union of Lagos Colony with the Delta region. Between 1904 and 1908 Dahomey furnished 73 per cent. of the kernels and 59 per cent. of all the palm oil produced in the French West African colonies. By contrast the domestic exports from Lagos Colony in the late 1890's and during the first five years of the following decade contained a much smaller amount of palm produce than is generally realized. It was the period of an important boom in local rubber, with relatively high prices and uncontrolled exploitation, when from 1895 till 1899 the value of rubber exported from Lagos accounted for no less than 28 per cent. of total export values. After 1900 the rubber industry, like the export of local timber, suffered for want of scientific management.

In this industry, as in the timber trade [lamented the Colonial Secretary] labour has been wasted which might have been put to profitable use in collecting and exploiting palm oil and palm kernels. . . . Labour diverted from working palm oil and kernels to the industry of cutting down, hauling, and floating to Lagos immature and unsaleable logs, and to hunting through the forest to collect a few cupfuls of rubber from a small remnant of undersized and overtapped Iré rubber trees, is waste of labour in the worst possible degree.[1]

Finally, the palm produce statistics for Togo indicate that the German colony depended less and less on oil and kernels as staples of domestic exports. By 1913 the effort of the local administration to encourage and diversify the variety of agricultural products, particularly in southern Togo, compares favourably with exports from the immensely richer colony of Nigeria and differed strikingly from the intense monoculture practised in Dahomey.

Domestic Exports, Nigeria, Togo, Dahomey

		1913 Select Commodities							
	Total export Values*	Kernels	Oil	Rubber	Cocoa	Cotton	Ground nuts	Maize	Tin
	(£)				% total exports £				
Nigeria	6,779,000	45·9 | 29·3		1·3	2·3	0·9	2·6	..	8·4
		75·2							
Togo	236,457	54·0 | 10·9		7·6	7·0	12·6	..	6·0	..
		64·9							
Dahomey	655,080	61·6 | 23·7		..	..	1·8	..	8·2	..
		85·3							

* Excluding specie.

While it was to be expected that so vast a region as Nigeria would find markets for subsidiary products, the case of Togo and Dahomey

[1] C. H. Harley Moseley, in *Lagos. Report for 1900–1901*, [Cd. 788], p. 5. For the 'rubber-rush' at Lagos, see *Lagos Standard*, 1 May, 4 Sept. 1895. The value of local rubber exports for the financial years 1895–9 was just over £1¼ million. By 1905 the value of exported rubber had dropped away to £22,656. McPhee, p. 57.

merits closer examination, since the former colony offers a contrast to German plantation and concession policy elsewhere, and the latter was run by an administration singularly impervious to arguments for improving local agriculture.

As early as 1888 detailed reports on the suitability of Togo for large plantations were prepared by Dr. Henrici and Commissioner Falkenthal and forwarded to the *Deutsche Kolonialgesellschaft*.[1] And these reports received sympathetic support in 1891 from the *Kolonialrat* which formulated a number of plans for concessions to cotton companies, subsidized by the State and with labour guaranteed by the local administration.[2] Nothing came of these plans; and the initiative for the introduction of coffee, cocoa, coconuts, and cotton came not from the metropolitan merchants, but from local creole traders and farmers and the German trader J. K. Vietor, on small leaseholds around Anecho and Bagida. The first evidence of active

Plantations, 1900[*]

	Area (hectares)	Coffee trees	Coconut palms	Rubber trees	Labour
Lome District:					
Octaviano Olympio	57	..	6,000	..	54
Anecho District:					
J. K. Vietor	120	25 ha.	10 ha.	5 ha.	5
Catholic Mission	15	3 ha.	2 ha.	..	1
Kpeme Plantation Co.	886	..	190,000	..	71
Creppi	5	..	..	..	?
d'Almeida Bros.	(unregistered)	30,000	5,000	6,000	11
Paul	,,	7,000	..	6,000	2
Joseph Ayavon	,,	4,000	2,631	10,515	?
Antonio and Chico d'Almeida	,,	1,303	4,749	1,600	?
		Cocoa trees	*Kola trees*		
Misahöhe District:					
Agu Plantation	42	1,500	620	400	50
Neuwerk Plantation	270	10,000	1,000	1,000	36

[*] *Jahresbericht*, 1901/02, p. 183.

[1] *Deutsche Kolonialzeitung*, 1888, No. 1, pp. 82, 95.

[2] Ibid, 1891, No. 4, p. 121. The *Kolonialrat* was founded by Imperial decree, 10 Oct. 1890, and held its first meeting in June 1891. See Mary Evelyn Townsend, *The Rise and Fall of Germany's Colonial Empire 1884–1918* (New York, 1930), p. 158.

participation of the Administration in these experiments is the effort
of Dr. Gruner at Misahöhe station to superintend native cocoa
cultivation in 1892. When he became *Bezirksamtmann* of Misahöhe
District in 1899 he extended his experiments to a block of government plantation land near Agome-Palime, cleared primarily for
cocoa growing.[1]

The situation of the various small plantations in 1900 was as
shown in the table on p. 150. The last two concession plantations—
Agu and *Neuwerk*—were in reality the foundation of what might
well have become an enormous agricultural and land monopoly. In
1897 and 1898 a mission led by Freidrich Hupfeld, an Austrian
geologist and ex-Togo official, financed by the *Deutsche Kolonialgesellschaft*, explored the hinterland of Togo in the guise of a scientific
expedition. A second expedition the following year was entrusted
with the task of obtaining land for plantations and examining existing
enterprises—with a view to buying them out.[2] Hupfeld, as the guiding
hand, appears to have negotiated in 1899 for the outright purchase
of no less than 85,000 hectares in the Agu hills and the Buem sector
of Misahöhe, for the ridiculously low price of M. 440.[3] Governor
Köhler, however, delayed the ratification of the deed for about fifteen
months till he received instructions from the Colonial Department
of the German Foreign Office (*Kolonialabteilung*). This delay and the
unwillingness of the German Government to face a storm of criticism
by admitting the truth of the Togo concession rumour prevented
Hupfeld and his backers from exploiting to the full their advantage and initiating a plantation policy of the Cameroons type.
Nevertheless, two small plantations were set up in the area of the
concession; and in 1902 the pre-emptive rights obtained by Hupfeld served as the basis for the constitution of the *Deutsche Togogesellschaft*.

The certainty that Hupfeld's new company claimed such rights
in a potential cotton-growing area was a major factor behind the
formation of the rival Association of West African Traders (*Verein*

[1] *Jahresbericht*, 1898/99, p. 33.

[2] *Deutsches Kolonialblatt*, x (1899), 313. Hupfeld had been *Stationsleiter* in
Bassari, Northern Togo. Jacob, p. 234.

[3] For a general discussion of concession policy and the changing attitude of
the German Government towards colonial questions, 1899–1905, Otto Diehn,
'Kaufmannschaft und deutsche Eingeborenenpolitik in Togo und Kamerun.
Von der Jahrhundertwende bis zum Ausbruch des Weltkrieges' (unpub. doctoral
thesis, Hamburg, 1956), pp. 44–46.

Westafrikanischer Kaufleute) in the same year, uniting great and small Bremen and Hamburg firms with interests on the coast.[1] At one of the first meetings of the Association in 1903 a petition from the Togo traders, sponsored by J. K. Vietor and based on information from the North German Mission, attacked the Hupfeld concession. A modified form of the petition was sent in protest to the Colonial Department (which neither affirmed nor denied the charge). According to Vietor, Togo could only be developed by leaving the land in the hands of the native peasantry and avoiding the pernicious social and economic problems that would arise if the Ewe farmers were reduced to the status of wage labourers on their expropriated farms. Underneath this humanitarian argument also lay the fear of the smaller exporters that an agricultural and shipping monopoly in southern Togo would ruin the free market on which their supplies of palm products and (they hoped) native cotton, coffee, and cocoa depended.

The battle was never satisfactorily resolved for either side. Many of the members of the Association itself were small-scale planters, as well as exporters, and their objection to the *Deutsche Togogesellschaft* was directed against its pre-emptive rights to an area it would never fully develop, and not against the existence of European plantations. Moreover, the Hupfeld–Vietor debate was outweighed in importance before it had really begun by the necessity to find for German industry alternative sources of cotton in East and West Africa during the 'famine' at the beginning of the century. In 1901 the Economic Committee (*Kolonialwirtschaftliches Komitee*)[2] of the *Deutsche Kolonialgesellschaft* had already sent out an expedition of four coloured American planters from Alabama who reported that the Tove area in Misahöhe was suitable for cotton-growing and who, with the help of the political officer, began to distribute cotton seed and instruct native growers—this within the area of the Hupfeld concession.[3] The British Cotton-Growing Association attached sufficient importance to the Togo experiment to request detailed information; and this the Economic Committee was pleased to supply in

---

[1] The Association was founded 5 June 1902. Handelskammer, Hamburg, Protokolle des Vorstandes des Vereins Westafrikanischer Kaufleute, I, 1902–13.

[2] This influential body was founded in 1896 to stimulate interest in the German colonies. By 1914 it represented 1,100 economic and scientific institutes, industrial corporations, trading firms, and chambers of commerce.

[3] The Americans were James Calloway, Allen Burke, Shepherd Harris, and John Robinson, *Deutsches Kolonialblatt*, xii (1901), 244, 287, 717, 832.

1902, indicating that the money for continued research under its auspices was made available by cotton interests in Germany.[1] From these interests the *Togogesellschaft* undoubtedly received enough encouragement to withstand the attacks of the Association. By the end of 1902 two-thirds of its capital of M. 750,000 had been subscribed; its two small plantations near Tove in the Agu hills were amalgamated; and it had bought out, in September 1902, a short-lived plantation company with property on the coast at Agome-Tongbe.[2] Its acquisitions and rights were formally recognized by the local administration in March 1903.[3] By 1914 the *Togogesellschaft* and four affiliated companies under Hupfeld's chairmanship had registered about 6,000 or 7,000 hectares, though not all of this land was under cultivation, and the parent company itself was engaged primarily in purchasing produce, ginning cotton, and financing

Companies*	Founded	Land regis-tered (hectares)	Capital assets (M.)	Net profit 1913–14	Direc-tors and over-seers	Labour from Coast	Labour from In-terior
Deutsche Togogesellschaft	1902	(85,000)	1,124,021	110,582	..	..	..
Pflanzungs-gesellschaft, Kpeme . .	1904	1,700	..	25,087	6	25	85
Agu-Pflanzungs-gesellschaft .	1907	1,000	..	15,338	11	..	150
Togo-Pflanzungs-Aktiengesellschaft	1910	970	..	511	13	..	440
Gadja-Pflanzungs-Aktiengesellschaft	1914	1,900	..	..	1	..	55

* *Der Tropenpflanzer* (1915), No. 11, pp. 609–20. Properties sequestrated and sold in 1920 in the mandates included the factories of F. M. Vietor Söhne, the *Deutsche Togogesellschaft*, Kulenkampff, Oloff, Martin-Paul, Wolbrecht, Kallweit, J. K. Vietor, Goedelt, Luther & Seyfert, Bödecker & Meyer, the Togo *Palmölwerkgesellschaft*, the Togo *Baumwollgesellschaft*. Plantations are all listed as belonging to the *Togogesellschaft*, not its subsidiaries. *Rapport annuel du gouvernement français sur l'administration sous mandat des territoires du Togo pour l'année 1924* (1925), pp. 43, 48; *Report . . . on the Administration under Mandate of British Togoland for the Year 1924* (1925), [Colonial No. 14], p. 82.

[1] Stark to Newton, 23 Aug. 1902, in *British Cotton Growing Association* (Oldham, 1902), pp. 37–38; *Kolonialwirtschaftliches Komitee* to Newton, 3 Sept. 1902, ibid., p. 39. The British Cotton Growing Association was founded 7 May 1902 by the Oldham and Manchester Chambers of Commerce. See J. A. Hutton, *The Work of the British Cotton Growing Association* (Manchester, 1904), pp. 17–19.

[2] The *Togo-Handels- und Plantagengesellschaft*, founded in Aug. 1901 to grow cocoa and rubber. *Deutsches Kolonialblatt*, xiii (1902), 493.

[3] *Deutsches Kolonialblatt*, xiv (1903), 196.

subsidiaries. Apart from the land registered, no attempt was made to dispossess the Ewe peasantry of the remaining 75,000 hectares originally claimed.

It was not till after 1905 that the effects of limited plantation concessions began to be appreciable in the value of exports of cotton, cocoa, coffee, and rubber which, together with the export of maize amounted to 28 per cent. of total export values between 1907 and 1913. To protect themselves against the long-threatened monopoly of Togo agricultural produce, the small traders, led by J. K. Vietor, formed themselves in 1908 into the Togo Cotton Company (*Togo-Baumwollgesellschaft*).[1] The company was essentially a purchasing not a planting organization; but the local market was too small to allow the traders to compete with the Hupfeld concern without coming to terms. Accordingly, in 1912 the Cotton Company, the *Deutsche Togogesellschaft*, and the *Pflanzungsgesellschaft*, Kpeme, entered into a contract whereby the Cotton Company, as a buyer of native cotton, obtained ginning rights at its rivals' factories. The price was fixed at M. 35 per bale, M. 15 of which went to one of the two ginneries, and the rest into a joint account to be distributed between the three organizations at the end of every year.[2] The Cotton Company was not very successful. In 1911 it made a loss of M. 39,213 (£1,960) and had captured only about 40 per cent. of the total cotton production of the districts in southern Togo. The rest was being handled by the Hupfeld consortium. Towards the end of 1911 the fall in world cotton prices—and consequently the local price—resulted in large numbers of native growers refusing to pick their crop. The administration appealed to the *Kolonialwirtschaftliches Komitee* for a subsidy towards a guaranteed price to enable both native planters, companies and exporters to withstand the trade depression till a better season. Governor Herzog zu Mecklenburg also suggested to the German Colonial Office a subsidy to buyers to help pay for freight charges from the interior.[3] It was too late, however, to remedy the finances of the Cotton Company which insisted on keeping its buying price at 15 pfennig per kilo. The native planters preferred to hold back 'weil sie als kluge Kaufleute auf höhere Preise spekulieren,

---

[1] Formed by the trading firms C. Goedelt, *Bremer Kolonial-Handelsgesellschaft*, Luther & Seyfert, Knoop & Sohn, Bödecker & Meyer, J. K. Vietor, F. M. Vietor Söhne.

[2] Bremen, J. K. Vietor Papers, contract 10 June 1912.

[3] Ibid. Herzog zu Mecklenburg to Togo Cotton Company, 9 Oct. 1912.

eine Spekulation, die für die weder mit Zinsverlust noch mit Lagerspesen rechnenden Eingeborenen sich vielleicht als gar nicht ungeschickt herausstellen wird'.[1] For the Cotton Company the year 1912 closed with a deficit of M. 25,000—a loss from which it never recovered.

In Dahomey there were no parallels to the Togo concessions, though there was no lack of demand from small speculators in 1894 when the Ministry for the Colonies received a score of applications for land grants in the new colony.[2] Governor Ballot's policy, however, was to refuse land for European settlers, and to encourage instead the return of former Gun, Mina, Mahi, and Yoruba slaves from the Americas and from San Thomé. The object was not purely philanthropic: like Moloney in the 1880's, the Dahomey administrator calculated on receiving a supply of skilled and semi-skilled immigrant labour for public works. But there is no record of Africans returning to the colony from Brazil at this date; and neither Ballot nor Governor Liotard succeeded in convincing the Portuguese authorities at San Thomé that French Dahomey had any claim to slaves or descendants of slaves shipped from the Fon ports—even if these could be discovered and classified.[3] Plans for large-scale agricultural enterprises were officially discouraged. In 1899 the acting-governor reported that the palm belt of southern Dahomey was too densely populated for alienation of land to be considered; from the coast as far north as Zagnanado, there were not more than 10,000 hectares of land unclaimed by peasant farmers, and these lots were unsuitable for cotton, coffee, or cocoa.[4] A short-lived agricultural company at Allada leased 364 hectares and set up a palm-oil press, but for lack of a cadastral survey it encountered continual difficulties from local maize and cassava growers who encroached relentlessly on the company's preserves. The only other attempt to monopolize large areas in Dahomey was made by the Railway Company which claimed nearly 300,000 hectares as part of its contract with the colony in 1904, but was forced to renounce the claim in the face of hostile opposition from traders and peasants alike.[5]

---

[1] Ibid., Togo Cotton Company to Herzog zu Mecklenburg, 6 Dec. 1912.
[2] M.F.O., Dahomey, xv/1, Lebon to Ballot, 21 July 1894.
[3] M.F.O., Dahomey, xv/2, Liotard to Decrais, 23 Apr. 1900.
[4] P.N., Correspondances, 1899–1901, Pascal to Decrais, 2 Dec. 1899. There seems to have been a concession of 136,000 hectares made to a certain *Compagnie de l'Ouemé* in Sept. 1899; but the company was liquidated in 1903, and there is no record of its activities in the colony nor any evidence its claims were registered. Edgar Maguet, *Concessions domaniales dans les colonies françaises* (Paris, 1930), p. 93 n.   [5] Maguet, p. 93 n.

In the Western District of Lagos Colony there had been experiments to diversify agricultural production since Moloney's governorship and two botanical stations at Olokemeji and Ebute Metta were distribution centres for plants and seeds. Cotton seed was imported in bulk by Elder Dempster in 1901; and the British Cotton-Growing Association set up a steam ginning plant in 1904. But the principal cotton-growing centres in the south were Oke Ho and Iganna about 120 miles from Lagos and at least three or four days from the railway; and much of the production was absorbed (as it always had been) into the manufacture of country cloths. Official encouragement to cotton-growing by offering the Association free rail transport did something to boost exports from the north. But there was no organization to compare with the German agricultural and cotton school at Nuatja, founded in 1904 by the *Kolonialwirtschaftliches Komitee* and taken over by the Togo government in 1908.

Exports of Ginned Cotton, 1903–8[1]

Togo	South-West Nigeria	Dahomey
	(lb.)	
2,575,129	1,060,000	718,441
	Southern and Northern Nigeria.	
	5,523,840	

Whatever the efforts of the British and German administrations to encourage the cultivation of crops other than palm produce, it is clear that the destination of domestic exports was not necessarily to the metropolis of the administering power. After 1897 a decreasing percentage of the exports (excluding specie) of Lagos Colony were sent to the United Kingdom; and in the last year before the amalgamation with Southern Nigeria, about £700,000 of domestic products were destined for other European ports, compared with £262,000 of exports for the United Kingdom.[2] This is mainly accounted for by the capture of the palm-kernel trade by German firms, until, by 1913, over three-quarters of the kernel exports from Nigeria were destined for German ports. The same is true of Dahomey. Between 1898 and 1902, for example, export of kernels to Germany increased in bulk six times, while exports of the same commodity to France decreased. Exports of palm oil to Germany quadrupled, at the same rate as the

---

[1] *Colonial Reports for Southern Nigeria*, 1906–9; *Kolonialwirtschaftliches Komitee. Deutsch-Koloniale Baumwoll-Unternehmungen*, xii (1910), 15–16.
[2] *Southern Nigeria (Lagos). Report for 1905*. No. 507, [Cd. 2648], Appendix V

volume of oil exported to France.[1] On the other hand, in Togo, no more than one English firm had an agency at Lome, and French firms kept to their own side of the border at Grand Popo. But it is noticeable in Togo export statistics that while just over 60 per cent. of the colony's products went to Germany, a further 30 per cent. during the period from 1900 to 1914 is listed as passing to neighbouring African territories. A small proportion of this was simply transit traffic (cattle and hides) from the Sudan which crossed northern Dahomey on the caravan route to Salaga and Kumassi. The bulk of the 'African' export trade was maize—an important cash crop valued at as much as £102,000 in 1908—most of which went to Dahomey.[2] The Secretary of State for the German Colonies, Dr. Solf, noted with pleasure during his tour in 1913, that native silos in the Anecho District held bumper crops. He was informed by the local political officer 'daß der Mais nach Dahomey ginge, ebenso die Palmkerne, da die Franzosen in der Lage seien, höhere Preise zu bezahlen'.[3] The influx of domestic foodstuffs from one colony to another was not, of course, limited to the Togo-Dahomey frontier; but in view of the fact that the Porto-Novo area had been, as late as the 1880's, the granary of Lagos, and an exporter of palm products to Togo in the 1890's, it is interesting to find the French colony had become a heavy importer of maize not only from Togo, but also from the border villages of Southern Nigeria after 1908. The reason lay not in the inability of the Dahomey population to produce food, but in the high prices obtaining in the French territory where production concentrated on palm oil and where, in exchange for maize in the local markets, spirits could be bought more cheaply than in Togo or Nigeria.

The boundaries took several decades to 'harden' as economic and political realities. And while the flow of native traders from one colony to another (and with them the flow of specie and goods) was impossible to control with the limited personnel at the disposal of the French, German, or British administrators, it was no easier to reconcile the demands of European traders for fiscal advantage from their own colonial governments with the constant necessity to tax imports in order to pay for those governments. The impression left

[1] *Dahomey. Rapports d'ensemble*, 1899–1903. Not including produce in transit from Porto-Novo to Lagos handled by Witt & Busch and G. L. Gaiser.

[2] *Die deutschen Schutzgebiete in Afrika* (1909–10), p. 105; *Report on the British Mandated Sphere of Togoland for 1920–1921* (1922), [Cmd. 1698], Appendix I.

[3] Dr. W. H. Solf, 'Mittelafrikanisches Reisetagebuch', C Togo, entry 5 Oct. 1913.

by the records during the last quarter of the nineteenth century and the first decade of the twentieth is that of erratic and ill-co-ordinated endeavours to preserve the non-differential tariff structure on spirits at the coastal ports while extracting from it, in the name of the Brussels Conventions and the local budgets, as high a duty as possible. Those who imported French spirits (dearer than German or Dutch gin) claimed they were penalized. But on the whole German and Dutch spirits and British cotton goods were imported by all nationalities alike. None of the three administrations introduced preferential tariffs to favour national products (indeed, the ease with which smuggling was carried on would have made any such tariff void, if the article surtaxed was in high demand). Instead, customs at all ports were based on a general *ad valorem* duty with special duties on arms and spirits. But while all three administrations raised the *ad valorem* and special duties between 1890 and 1914, they did not do so at the same pace; and attempts to bring order to the customs zones east of the Volta by international agreement broke down either because of French traders' insistance on protection, or because the unreality of the boundaries made such agreements difficult to enforce. All that finally resulted was the negative convention of 1898 which prohibited differential tariffs on goods crossing the boundaries of the three colonies.[1]

Trade for the French firms was badly disrupted by the events of 1890–2. But their German competitors who sold arms to the Fon and a few of the smaller Brazilian traders who collaborated with Behanzin had their goods confiscated and their stores closed. The Franco-German customs *entente* of 1887–90 never recovered from the evidence of arms traffic from Togo to Abomey brought forward by the French administration. A single customs tariff was decreed for the whole of the French colony in 1891; and when in March 1892 the German Government suggested a tripartite agreement between the Gold Coast, Togo, and Dahomey, both the French Government and the Marseilles Chamber of Commerce rejected the proposal. Tariffs on both sides of the frontier continued to rise in the 1890's. But while the average duty on spirits in Togo was about 22*s.* for 100 litres by 1895, in southern Dahomey it was only 12*s.* Duty on powder, too, by that date was higher in Togo than Dahomey; and the Minister for the Colonies, André Lebon, refused to remedy German complaints of smuggling across the frontier.

[1] Convention, 14 June 1898, Art. IX.

Si les poudres de commerce étaient frappées au Dahomey de droits aussi élevés que ceux de Togo, des importations frauduleuses ne manqueraient pas de se produire sur notre territoire par la frontière de Lagos, vu cette marchandise ne paie qu'une taxe très faible. Or le préjudice causé serait d'autant plus appréciable que les poudres de traite introduites jusqu'ici au Dahomey sont d'origine française.[1]

In the west a customs agreement between the Gold Coast and Togo in 1894 fixed a common tariff of 9d. per gallon on spirits imported into the German ports and the Volta estuary—which was less than the tariff for the rest of the British colony. The traders who had flocked to Keta in 1890 moved back to Lome. But subsequent boundary agreements ensured that the Volta trade in salt passed through British and not German territory to Keta-Kratschi and the north, and the Ewe block between the Volta, Ho, and Danu was not allowed to pass into German hands.[2]

After the break-down of Franco-German customs agreements it was expected by Régis and Fabre that preferential treatment would follow. But nowhere is the irony of European administration better illustrated than in Dahomey: the original motive for protectorate and annexation—to secure the position of French firms against foreign competitors and the exactions of native rulers alike—was lost sight of in a mass of legislation on trading licences and constantly revised tariffs that came in the wake of the new rulers. If some of the German traders complained they suffered unjust fines at the hands of customs-collectors,[3] their voice was mild compared with the angry correspondence addressed to the Ministry for the Colonies by Régis and Fabre till the end of the century. Slowly it became clear that the French were more exacting than the Fon.

Both of the French firms waged a long legal battle to win compensation for losses suffered during the Dahomey war, carrying the case to the Council of State—where it was finally rejected in 1905.[4] Meanwhile, they pressed for a special export duty on the German transit trade to Lagos, lower import duties, and, above all, a tax on English specie imported into the colony. Fabre, whose local agents had paid half the total customs duties for Dahomey in 1894, informed

[1] M.F.O., Afrique, vi/144, Lebon to Bourgeois, (draft) 4 Aug. 1897.

[2] *Koloniales Jahrbuch*, iv (1891), 230, 237–8; Solf, 'Mittelafrikanisches Reisetagebuch', C Togo, entry 8 Oct. 1913.

[3] Handelskammer, Bremen, Oloff to Auswärtiges Amt, 28 Nov. 1895; Vietor to Handelskammer, 27 Nov. 1895.

[4] M.F.O., Dahomey, xv/2, and ix/6. The amount of the claim was 605,960 francs.

the Ministry for the Colonies that the question of foreign currency was the most serious obstacle preventing moderate duties.

Au total, en 1894, Porto-Novo a reçu environ deux millions de francs en livres sterling représentant un mouvement entrées et sorties réunies de 4 millions de francs, soit presque la moitié du mouvement annuel de Porto-Novo qui est d'environ 9 ou 10 millions, et tout ce mouvement, nous le répétons, n'a pas contribué pour un centime aux charges de la Colonie qui pèsent presque toutes sur le Commerce français.[1]

Additional grievances were lack of representation on the local Administrative Council, and the cancellation of Régis's land concessions at Cotonou where this desirable real estate—originally the excuse for French annexation—was expropriated by the administration.[2] Bleak comparisons with the commercial progress at Lagos and the work done by a handful of officials in Togo usually rounded off the correspondence.

All these charges were answered by Ballot himself in 1897. The currency problem, he confessed, was insoluble; but the French firms were free to pay their duties in French notes and coin, instead of using foreign specie themselves. Lome and Lagos, too, had high duties; and if payment was demanded at Cotonou without delay, he had heard no complaint from German traders on this score. Then, going to the heart of the matter, he continued:

En réalité MM. Fabre n'ont pu jusqu'à présent s'habituer à la concurrence des autres maisons et ils voudraient être protégés contre les nouveaux établissements créés au Dahomey, de manière que le monopole qu'ils partageaient autrefois avec la maison Régis, soit rétabli à leur profit. MM. Fabre, de même que MM. Mante & Borelli de Régis Aîné, ne veulent pas admettre qu'il est impossible, à une administration française libérale et impartiale, de prendre à leur égard des mesures semblables à celles qu'employaient, avant la conquête, les autorités indigènes du Dahomey pour leur assurer la totalité des transactions commerciales dans la Colonie.[2]

If the two French firms were reluctant to invest in the interior, it was no argument (as they claimed) that Lagos traders confined their activities to the coast. Ballot easily countered this by producing a copy of the spirits licence list in the *Lagos Gazette* to show the amount of business done in the market towns of southern Yorubaland. To what end had Dahomey been taken, he asked, if trade did not expand inland?

[1] M.F.O., Dahomey, xv/2, C. F. Fabre, 'Notes sur le Dahomey à Monsieur le Ministre des Colonies', 9 Mar. 1895.

[2] M.F.O., Dahomey, xv/8, Ballot to Lebon, 22 July 1897.

When it did, after the completion of the railroads; Régis had withdrawn from the colony, and Cyprien Fabre had diverted their attention to shipping lines in West Africa, though retaining one agency at Porto-Novo.[1]

By 1914 all three colonies had a 10 per cent. *ad valorem* duty, though the Lagos duties on spirits remained consistently higher than at Cotonou or Lome. While in Togo the actual volume of spirits imported increased very little throughout the period between 1903 and 1914, in Southern Nigeria it rose by about 25 per cent.

Imports of Spirits, Select Years

	Lagos Colony and Southern Nigeria		Dahomey		Togo	
	Gals.	% imps.	Gals.	% imps.	Gals.	% imps.
1903 .	2,797,000	10	64,600	15	231,376	18
1906 .	3,322,000	10	45,900	11	108,300	9
1912 .	4,450,000	7	87,977	11	237,296	6

By 1913 revenue from spirits imports for Nigeria amounted to £1,140,000, compared with £619,000 from other imports, although spirits, as a percentage of imports had slowly declined since 1903.

Nowhere do the three colonies present more striking contrasts than in the financial policies of their administrations, applied according to European assessment of revenue-producing capacities of the coastal towns and the populations of the forest belt. Customs on imports, and particularly on spirits, were, of course, in each case, the staples of local budgets. But these duties varied considerably, after the failure of early attempts to synchronize customs tariffs; and for Dahomey indirect taxes of this kind were lost to the government-general of French West Africa after 1904.

Over the whole period from 1896 to the First World War the British colony relied more on indirect taxes than its neighbours, though this dependency on trade revenues decreased slightly as loans for railway construction swelled the budget after 1905.[2] In Dahomey the proportion of customs to other sources of revenue was also consistently

---

[1] Of the twenty-eight companies and small firms with branches in Dahomey in 1914, ten opened between 1900 and 1914. Only three were British—Grace Bros., John Holt, and Swanzy. As in Nigeria, the tendency was to amalgamate the smaller concerns into large emporia like C.F.A.O., *Comptoirs Réunis,* the *Société Commerciale du Dahomey,* &c.

[2] McPhee, pp. 108, 114 and n.

high. Gross customs rose steadily to the point where, from 1907 to 1913 they were in excess of the net annual revenues by as much as 30 to 50 per cent.[1] The Togo budget for a few years had no other source of income; but after the turn of the century the proportion of customs in the annual revenues of the German colony is consistently low, as metropolitan subsidies and loans for public works increased.

Customs Duties as Percentage of Annual Revenues *

	Lagos and Southern Nigeria		Dahomey		Togo	
	£(000)	%	Fr.(000)	%	M.(000)	%
1896 .	163	90	1,552	93	304	100
1897 .	160	90	1,329	69	301	100
1898 .	180	87	1,565	65	315	82
1899 .	176	91	2,318	86	526	61
1900 .	191	91	2,648	78	369	49
1901 .	216	90	3,580	79	891	47
1902 .	286	79	4,427	77	1,016	90
1903 .	260	·78	3,540	67	1,000	44
1904 .	254	75	3,753	68	1,289	24
1905 .	263	69	3,187	..	791	14
	Southern Nigeria					
1906 .	886	81	3,657	..	1,255	44
1907 .	1,178	81	4,489	..	1,221	55
1908 .	1,015	73	3,145	..	1,401	53
1909 .	988	73	4,947	..	1,497	48
1910 .	1,440	75	6,677	..	1,801	73
1911 .	1,439	74	7,183	..	1,506	47
1912 .	1,569	70	7,168	..	1,568	50
1913 .	1,547	66	5,836	..	1,622	40

* *Colonial Reports, Lagos and Southern Nigeria*, 1901–14; *Jahresbericht*, (1901–2), Appendix III, p. 390; *Deutsches Kolonial-Handbuch* (Berlin, 1896), pp. 47–48; A. Zimmermann, *Geschichte der deutschen Kolonialpolitik* (Berlin, 1914), p. 221; *Rapports d'ensemble*, 1896–1914.

Togo was one of the few African colonies that by 1914 'paid for itself'. But this was a late development and exceptional in the financial history of the colony.[2] From 1899 till 1907 subsidies and loans from Germany are continuous and adequate; during some years these made up as much as half of Togo revenues.

Construction of the Lome–Atakpame, the Lome–Anecho, and the Lome–Palime railway lines cost the state budget for the colonies about M. 19,000,000. It was only after 1907 that the railways showed any returns in the receipts of the colony; and the loans were never

[1] See Appendix.   [2] Cf. Townsend, p. 264.

fully paid off, although Togo was required from 1911 onwards to contribute a modest sum (£200) to a central colonial reserve fund.

1899–1907

Gross Revenues M. (000)	Subsidies and loans M. (000)	%
22,619	10,331	45·6

Dahomey was financially handicapped by its membership of the French West African Federation. After 1904 all customs revenues were paid into the budget for the government-general at Dakar; and in return, subsidies and loans for capital investment were made available to the colony. But Dahomey in the years of the flourishing palm products trade was second only to Senegal as a revenue-earner for the federation. Left to itself the territory could have been one of the most prosperous colonies in French West Africa. A general balance sheet of the financial relations between Dahomey and the federal administration indicates that more was contributed by the colony to the government-general than the colony received in return.

Dahomey Finances 1905–14*, Fr. (000).

Dahomey Customs revenues to the Federal Budget	Colonial subsidies from the Federal Budget	Share of Disbursement of loans for A.O.F.
50,183	17,976	12,926

% total customs A.O.F.	% total subsidies A.O.F.	% total loans A.O.F.
26·1	35·5	8·0

* *Compte définitif des recettes et des dépenses du budget des fonds de l'emprunt de 65 millions, 1909–1912* (Dakar, 1914); *Compte définitif des recettes et des dépenses du budget des fonds des emprunts de 65 et 100 millions* (Dakar, 1917).

In addition a small loan of 1,738,000 francs was paid from Dakar to help a private company construct a wharf at Cotonou and start building a railway. The fact has also to be taken into account that certain administrative services—the judiciary and customs personnel —were paid for by Dakar. Nevertheless it is clear that the financial benefits did not equal Dahomey's contribution to the welfare of the federation. When the local administration was severely criticized in 1914 by a colonial inspector for outbreaks of violence in the eastern districts of Dahomey, Lieutenant-Governor Noufflard pointed to excessive head-taxes as the cause, stemming from the financial tutelage exercised by the government-general.[1] Considering all the payments made to Dahomey from the federal budget, the colony had, in Dakar, a balance of some 13½ million francs from its indirect taxes—from which it derived no benefit. In reply, Governor-General Ponty blamed excessive imports of spirits for the high proportion of customs and drew attention to the plight of poorer members of the federation, in particular Upper-Senegal, Niger, which had benefited even less than Dahomey from federal loans, while, on the other hand, Mauretania was supported almost entirely by subsidies.

Given the principle on which the government-general was based—that the rich should pay for the poor—there was little the Dahomey administration could do, except to rely on direct taxes to make up for the parsimony of the Dakar authorities. Head-taxes, introduced in 1899 at the rate of 2 francs 25 centimes for adults and children over

*Dahomey Head-Tax, Fr. (000)**

	1900	1909
Upper Dahomey		
Parakou	..	31·8
Nikki	..	38·0
Djougou	..	69·4
Niger	..	72·2
Total	140·6	211·4
Lower Dahomey		
Porto-Novo . . .	207·4	400·9
Abomey	60·4	172·9
Allada	54·2	155·0
Mono	17·6	115·3
Zagnanado	19·6	56·3
Savalou	21·7	51·2
Whydah	19·2	50·0
Grand Popo . . .	8·2	22·1
Save	..	..
Cotonou	8·4	11·9
	416·7	1,034·6
Total	557·3	1,246·0

* Government-General, Dakar, S 15, Monguillot, Report, June 1914, typescript with appended observations by Noufflard and Governor-General Ponty, 27 June 1914.

[1] *Rapport d'ensemble, 1900*, p. 25; *Dahomey. Comptes définitifs, 1909.*

10 years of age in the southern districts, and at 1 franc 25 centimes for the same categories elsewhere, were a burden, which inevitably fell on Gun, Fon, and Yoruba.

These proportions remained constant till 1914, with an additional burden of commercial licences. Southern Dahomey, with an estimated 69 per cent. of the colony's population, bore 83 per cent. of the head-taxes for 1909. Over 30 per cent. of these taxes came from the Porto-Novo District, with Allada, Abomey, and Mono Districts contributing about 12 per cent. each. Collection was more thorough after 1907 when less was left to chiefs and the districts were more closely supervised by French officials. The net tax returns levelled off to just over one million francs a year. A confidential annual report for 1913 praised the co-operation of the native population with revealing simplicity.

Le coût de la vie a quadruplé en quelques années et il est maintenant supérieur dans les cercles du Bas Dahomey à ce qu'il est à Dakar. L'indigène néanmoins auquel nous demandions des tirailleurs pour le Maroc, des travailleurs pour la Côte d'Ivoire et pour les grands travaux en cours dans l'intérieur de la Colonie a satisfait à toutes nos exigences. Il a versé intégralement l'impôt et les taxes diverses qui le frappent. Pour cela il a dû, il est vrai, se démunir de ses dernières réserves. Il ne possède plus rien et il n'en faut pour preuve que l'affluence dans les caisses du Trésor de la monnaie de billon vert-dé-grisée dernière ressource à laquelle il n'a recours qu'après que toute l'incommode monnaie d'argent est épuisée. La récolte prochaine qui s'annonce meilleure, l'exécution imminente de travaux sur fonds d'emprunt viendront heureusement porter remède à une situation qui ne pourrait durer et feront affluer à nouveau le numéraire devenu trop rare pour les besoins d'une vie commerciale intense.[1]

In Togo, by comparison, there was a liberation of labour tax from September 1907, when the twelve annual days' work demanded from all males could be commuted into cash. As from April 1909 Africans of Lome and Anecho were required to pay a special urban tax. The rate for commuted taxes varies according to different German sources.[2] Only males were entered in the tax-roles of the colony. For the financial year 1912 the general tax returns amounted to M. 695,853 and M. 21,735 for the native head-tax of Lome and Anecho; but this amount included ordinary trading licences, spirits and rubber licences, and returns from a dog-tax, as well as

---

[1] P.N., Noufflard, 'Rapport Annuel, 1913', f. 13.
[2] Graf Zech's Decree of 20 Sept. 1907 is silent on this point. *Deutsches Kolonialblatt*, xviii (1907), 1185; Kuczynski, p. 383 and n.

commuted labour.[1] In German accounts these categories of direct taxes are not broken down. Direct taxes in Togo, as a whole, are roughly comparable in proportion to head-tax alone in Dahomey, which is an indication of the difference in financial policy in two colonies of approximately equal population.

	Togo direct taxes (incl. head-tax)			Dahomey head-tax	
	M. (000)	Fr. (000)* approx.	% rev.	Fr. (000)	% rev.
1899 . . .	38	47·5	4	292	11
1900 . . .	33	41·2	4	589	17
1901 . . .	46	57·5	2	713	16
1902 . . .	56	70·0	5	636	11
1903 . . .	80	100·0	4	664	13
1904 . . .	87	108·7	2	699	13
1905 . . .	95	118·7	2	695	22
1906 . . .	87	108·7	3	781	18
1907 . . .	57	71·2	3	1,067	30
1908 . . .	162	202·5	6	1,105	34
1909 . . .	499	623·7	16	1,217	35
1910 . . .	310	387·5	13	1,257	35
1911 . . .	484	605·0	15	1,281	29
1912 . . .	696	870·0	22	1,265	33
1913 . . .	775	968·7	19	1,299	26

* Calculated at the rate of M. 20 = F. 25.

Gross expenditure of local revenues and money from loans shows a consistent rate of growth in the accounts of Lagos Colony and Southern Nigeria. In Togo expenditure increased by nearly 400 per cent. between 1901 and 1905, as the landing-pier and railways were constructed and the town of Lome enlarged. Expenditure then declined sharply in 1906, but continued to grow during the seven years before the world war at a rate not inferior to the British colony. The position is less clear in Dahomey: some accounts were paid in Dakar, not through the local treasury. But the general picture of a comparatively slow rate of growth between 1901 and 1913 in gross expenditure would not be altered by the inclusion of these federal accounts (salaries of a few government-general officials and technicians).

On the expenditure accounts for Lagos Colony and Protectorate, the main items were marine, police, medical, public works and the Lagos battalion of the West Africa Frontier Force—all of which

[1] Cf. Metzger, p. 29. The same mistake about head-taxes and direct taxes is made in French mandate reports.

required from £100,000 to £200,000 annually, between 1900 and 1905. The most striking increase was for expenditure on the railway, tramway, and bridge-building projects which rose from a mere £4,000 in 1901 to £60,000 by 1905. By 1912, as capital loans increased, Southern Nigeria had a public debt of £8,267,565.

Gross Expenditure

	Rates of growth					
	Lagos Colony*		Dahomey†		Togo	
	£ (000)	(base 1901)	£ (000)	(base 1901)	£ (000)	(base 1901)
1901 .	224·9	100·00	111·4	100·00	71·1	100·00
1902 .	225·5	100·25	193·0	173·28	51·1	71·80
1903 .	310·1	137·86	198·3	178·01	85·1	119·69
1904 .	325·2	144·57	182·2	163·59	235·5	331·15
1905 .	414·6	184·34	118·0	105·98	270·1	379·82
	Southern Nigeria (base 1906)					
1906 .	1,056·3	100·00	173·5	155·78	133·0	187·06
1907 .	1,217·3	115·24	138·5	124·32	103·8	145·92
1908 .	1,357·8	128·59	122·8	101·24	149·0	209·56
1909 .	1,648·7	156·15	138·7	124·51	135·9	191·21
1910 .	1,592·3	150·75	137·4	123·33	122·6	172·36
1911 .	1,717·3	162·59	167·3	150·16	160·8	226·16
1912 .	2,110·5	199·90	116·1	104·19	160·9	226·42
1913 .	2,096·3	198·48	181·7	163·08	210·1	295·43

* Excluding special grants-in-aid. For totals for both Southern and Northern Nigeria, see S. Herbert Frankel, *Capital Investment in Africa its Course and Effects* (Oxford, 1938), table 77, p. 317.
† Including government-general subsidies after 1904.

Lagos (and later the Western Province of Southern Nigeria) also ran separate accounts for the districts and for the Egba United Government. The former were included in the general financial returns, but not the latter, though audited at Lagos. Some idea of the slender resources on which a District was run may be gained from the statement of accounts for the Badagri, or Western District.

The district was hardly more expensive in 1903 than in the days of Thomas Tickel. Customs do not figure on the official financial returns. From the district letter-books it is safe to assume that the hulk at the mouth of Ajarra Creek collected very little; and there was no customs post at Idiroko, on the main road to Dahomey till 1913. Nor are there any official figures for imports and exports into the district.

Revenue and Expenditure, Badagri District 1903*

Revenue	£	s.	d.	Expenditure	£	s.	d.
Spirit licences . .	2,341	0	0	Wages, pensions .	1,361	11	1
Fines . . .	103	9	0	Stipends . . .	466	15	0
Canoe licences . .	70	12	0	Porters . . .	124	13	0
Court fees . .	46	16	0	Canoe transport .	46	8	0
Postage stamps . .	22	0	10	Prisoners' rations .	28	14	6
Launch tickets . .	21	0	6	Travel allowance .	28	13	8
Misc. fees . .	7	17	9	Police marching pay .	14	12	6
Miscellaneous . .	50	6	3	Presents to chiefs .	12	1	9
				House allowance .	9	0	0
				Hammock allowance	8	0	0
				Entertainment of			
				chiefs . . .	4	0	0
				Miscellaneous . .	78	4	3
Total . . .	£2,663	2	4	Total . . .	£2,182	3	9
% Revenue Lagos Colony and Protectorate . . . 0·2				% Expenditure Lagos Colony and Protectorate . . 0·7			

* N.R.O., 'Badagri Political Notes, 1903–1913'.

The populous and independent Egba state was a very different matter. So long as the independence of the Egba Yoruba, guaranteed by the treaty of 1893, continued to be recognized, it was possible for Abeokuta to develop a system of native administration, modelled on the colony of Lagos itself. Despite the opposition of Lagos traders and the Liverpool Chamber of Commerce, the principle that native authorities at Abeokuta and Ibadan had the right to levy customs on goods from the coast and the interior, was conceded in 1903, provided the tolls and the estimates of native government finance were published and accounted for. Most of the revenues went to the chiefs themselves; the rest were used to pay for a rudimentary secretariat, treasury, audit office, and customs collectors. After 1904 resident officials at Ibadan supervised the finances of the *Bale*'s government; at Abeokuta the Egba United Government employed its own educated Africans, though the accounts for the Egba too, were supervised from Lagos. The receipts of the Egba Government for the financial year 1904–5 amounted to £13,210.[1] By 1911, as trade increased with the development of the railway, the revenues of the Egba United Government had risen to £40,978, about six times as much as the revenues of the old Western, Central, and Eastern

[1] See the excellent account in E. Baillaud, *La Politique indigène de l'Angleterre en Afrique occidentale* (Paris, 1912), pp. 217–30, 249.

Districts of the Lagos protectorate put together.[1] In the opinion of the administration, the time had come to acknowledge that the provincial government of Yorubaland which had by then increasingly ceded to the colony judicial aspects of its internal sovereignty, should make over to the government of Southern Nigeria complete responsibility for provincial finances and abolish the internal tolls, while maintaining and systematizing the collection of taxes and licences.[2]

By then, too, the arbitrary boundaries of the adjacent colonies had been finally modified. The increased mobility of populations under European rule made them demographically meaningless. The influx of Yoruba into Dahomey has already been mentioned. In Togo there was by 1910 an equally important annual exodus of wage labourers to the Gold Coast numbering about 7,000 or 8,000, most of whom returned to the German colony. Emigration of this kind was officially discouraged but not stopped. The German administration prohibited the recruitment of Togo labour for the Cameroons; the French administration sent a Fon pioneer corps to Madagascar in 1898 but refused local labour for other French colonies before 1913; the British administration levied a head-tax on labourers sent for service outside the colony and protectorate—which produced the surprisingly large sum of £4,222 in 1902, when Yoruba were engaged for work on the Gold Coast railway.[3]

There were several other population exchanges of an official kind. In 1897 the southern section of the Togo–Dahomey frontier was modified so that the River Mono became the boundary and some 40,000 Watyi passed from French to German rule. Again in 1913, when the boundary was checked by a joint commission, Dahomey lost the towns of Toun, Tado, and Gabolé whose Adja population was added to Atakpame District in Togo. Governor Noufflard, however, was undisturbed by this loss:

Il est intéressant, toutefois, de constater que les populations des centres de Toun et de Tado sont venues s'installer sur notre territoire afin de conserver leur qualité de sujets français avec les avantages qui s'y attachent et que le voisinage de Tado leur rend encore plus sensibles par certains exemples qu'ils ont pu avoir sous les yeux.[4]

[1] N.R.O., 'Administrative Policy in Yoruba States (Western Province) 1912–1913', Young, 19 Oct. 1912.

[2] F. D. Lugard, *Political Memoranda. Revision of Instructions to Political Officers on Subjects chiefly Political and Administrative. 1913–1918* (London, 1919), pp. 176–8, 179.

[3] *Colonial Reports. Lagos 1902*, No. 400, [Cd. 1768–5], p. 10.

[4] P.N., Noufflard, 'Rapport annuel, 1913', f. 17.

In the same year there were some late changes on the Dahomey–Nigeria frontier. It was recognized that the Yoruba villages of Ilara and Iwoye, previously occupied by the French, were in fact within the British sphere. On the other hand, Jabata and Isale were handed over to the French.

The extent to which the Yoruba had been divided was not appreciated at Lagos till this re-delimitation of the boundary. With the exception of Ilorin, Nigeria had lost the whole of the kingdom of Save from Kokoto in the north to Okpa in the south, bounded by the Weme and Okpara rivers. The kingdom of Ketu had been divided in half, extending southwards to Agombo and Ilemon. The eastern sector, without the capital of Ketu itself, from Jabata to Igbo-iro, formed the district of Mekko on the British side. The small chiefdoms of Isale, Ifoyin, Ikolaje, each with an Oba formerly under the *Alafin* of Oyo, were also split up. Isale, according to the British boundary commissioner Partridge was a particularly 'hard case': 'for, while the very reluctant Awba and people live in the village which is just inside Dahomi, nearly all their land, including the large farm of Mojana, is in British territory.'[1] The *Oba* of Ifoyin remained on the Dahomey side, but his jurisdiction extended over a large sector of southern Mekko District; on the other hand, the village inhabited by the *Oba* of Ikolaje was just inside Southern Nigeria, while his tributary villages were in Dahomey. Near the coast the Gun had lost the villages of the eastern sector of the old Appa kingdom which extended as far as Topo.

The encouragement given by the French to new markets at Ifoyin, Gbowojo, and Modogan had an adverse effect on markets on the British side: those at Idofa, Asa, and Ihumbe and at Mekko were 'either deserted and overgrown or considerably dwindled in size'. A new eight-foot road on the Dahomey side of the border was cited by Partridge as the principal reason for the diversion of trade to the Porto-Novo–Ketu–Save routes.

In all border-villages, the guns and powder—in great demand, for all men and boys are hunters, and every death is an occasion for a *fusillade*—have been purchased from the French. At Ihumbe I spoke of this to the Chief, and he said 'But where can I get English guns and powder? There is no good English market near us; we get everything from the French'. In many of the English villages one sees, put to various uses, empty rum-tins,

[1] N.R.O., Government House Archives, C. Partridge to Director of Surveys, 29 Apr. 1913, f. 2.

red in colour, and French. Proceeding along the R. Ajara between Jofin and the hulk 'Sentinel', one notices that the left or English bank is entirely uninhabited and uncultivated, whereas the right or French bank is just the reverse; clearings with huts built and canoes moored alongside, neat stacks of fuel ready for exportation to Porto-Novo, a brick-yard (excellent bricks are made), and cultivated patches of cassada and sweet potato.[1]

As if this attraction of trade westward were not enough, Partridge also found that British coin was unknown in the British border villages as late as 1912, though French centimes were used everywhere.

Finally, there was the humiliating discovery for the Lagos adminis-tration that no less than eight villages in the Ihumbo area were all paying head-taxes to the French.[2]

Besides the above villages [reported Partridge] (all formerly under the Alafin of Oyo), there are also numerous small farm-villages or farmsteads which, established since the suppression of Dahomi, in British territory between Ilashe and Ihumbe, are all taxed through the Oba of Ifoyin, whom they look upon as their ancestral Chief—a Chief formerly subordinate to Oyo.

Partridge recommended a new district commissioner for Mekko with jurisdiction as far south as Ilashe, constant touring, and a frontier road built by labour from the border villages. He also made an im-portant political recommendation:

That Chief Seriki Abassi of Aiyetoro (Badagri District) be given a sort of trade jurisdiction over the whole of Mekko district, and be asked to pay special attention to opening up trade with, and establishing markets wherever profitable in, all the now-neglected border-villages, so as to divert trade from French into English channels. This Chief is a great trader, and a very able, progressive, and far-seeing man. It would be much to his own interest to bring all trade from the border villages to his canoes on the R. Yewa, and thus to the factories at Badagri.[3]

So far as smuggling or free trade across the border was concerned, little could be done except on the creek route at the coast. The Customs Preventive Service, according to Partridge (who had worked for it), was 'more or less, a farce'.

'Carving' colonies out of the Slave Coast was a misnomer for a complex process which by 1914 still left the shape of the three areas of German, French, and British rule vague at the periphery while effecting important changes at the political and cultural centres, where contact with the catalysts of European rule was closer.

[1] Ibid., ff. 3–4.   [2] Ibid., f. 6.
[3] Ibid., f. 9; and below, p. 194.

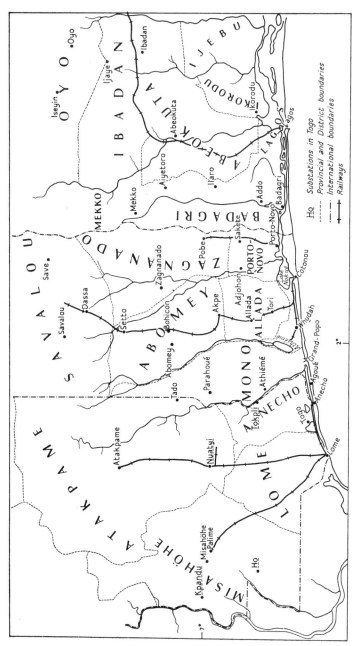

Fig. 9. Railways and boundaries 1912–14

CHAPTER VIII

The Search for Formulas

FUNDAMENTALLY the problem of internal administration in the forest belt of the three colonies was the same: to determine in practice the relationship between indigenous authorities and the centres of colonial government. The initial disparity in status among the Egba, Egbado, Gun, Fon, and Ewe chiefs, as viewed from the coastal capitals, arose from many factors. The functions of chiefs were diverse, ranging from the conciliar role of arbitrator in small isolated communities to the complex ritual and military leadership of the Yoruba and Fon states. Their contact with the status-destroying element inherent in European rule where practised as a rival source of authority was extremely uneven, both in duration and degree. The Egba in the 1890's were in theory a small state within a state, independent, but unable to contract an agreement with any other European power. The Egbado towns, too, were outside the jurisdiction of the colony, but in practice were visited and administered from Badagri which provided a model of thirty years of direct rule. In southern Dahomey, Tofa's kingdom for the first time in its history was headed by a Gun chief whose position was permanently safeguarded by the presence of Europeans; but the fact that Porto-Novo was also the administrative capital for the whole colony made it impossible for Tofa or his heirs to exercise much authority without consulting their protectors. Allada and Abomey were experiments in supervised paramountcies in which only the obligations, but not the privileges of chiefs were made clear. As a highly centralized sacred monarchy, the most conservative of the Fon and Yoruba states suffered the severest blow to the political leadership enjoyed by its royal lineage whose last representative was removed from office in 1900. In Yorubaland, too, there are examples of deposition; but how far the general pattern of lineage leadership was affected by the presence of Europeans is a subject for detailed examination. In Togo, even by 1895, German administration had hardly been felt beyond the coastal towns. There, a few of the mixed Brazilian and Gen lineages were allowed some financial compensation for the loss of tolls on exports, but they were too small and too weak to be considered as effective units of local government.

During the period of road and railway construction, the provision of labour, some voluntary, but more often contracted from villages, was the principal reason for maintaining the position of Allada or Abomey rulers in southern Dahomey. As Acting-Governor Pascal summed it up in 1898: 'nous avons un intérêt considérable a ce que le chef de cette contrée populeuse, autrefois si riche, conserve ou recouvre, sous notre protectorat, le pouvoir dont il a besoin pour nous aider et pour seconder l'œuvre de progrès commercial et de transformation économique'.[1] And everywhere in the coastal sectors of the three colonies the chiefs were enjoined to undertake the responsibility of road building, sanitation, clearing the lagoons and creeks for the passage of canoes and steamers. It was a constant and pressing consequence of the economic development of the three colonies: services once established had to be maintained. One remedy was to adopt a system of annual *corvées*, practised in Togo and Dahomey—twelve days of labour for every male which could be commuted into a money payment. In south-western Nigeria exhortation and occasional threats were the only recourse. An entry in the Badagri district commissioner's diary for 1913 is fairly typical of a recurrent routine.

Monday 24th. November. To Addo, on arrival there found a fair piece of about three miles of new road towards Ajilete completed, but only a few people work daily. Held a meeting and spoke on the following:— (1) Road work and the necessity for having the roads made quickly (2) The obedience of the people to Government orders (3) The advisability of sending carriers to the D.C. when called on to do so (when *21* carriers were ordered on the beginning of the month only *3* were sent down). Told them that refusal to obey Government orders is liable to punishment.[2]

On the whole, however, the Lagos administration was precluded from exploiting the labour resources of the Egbado and Egba, without offering an acceptable price, by reason of the shortage of officials engaged in administering a population which numbered about two million in the Western Province by 1911. 'Indirect rule', where it existed in south-western Nigeria before 1914, was as much the product of a lack of personnel, as of any administrative principle. In 1899 there was an impressive constellation of fourteen administrative

[1] M.F.O., Dahomey, i/18, Pascal to Hanotaux, 23 Jan. 1898.
[2] N.R.O., Badagri, Richardson in 'District Commissioner's Diary', 1913.

departments, in addition to the Secretariat and Supreme Court, located on Lagos Island. At Ibadan there was a resident, first appointed in 1894; and for the rest of Yorubaland there were only ten district commissioners and three travelling commissioners. At Badagri there was still only one commissioner responsible for the whole of his own district and the area north of Mekko; and at Abeokuta there was a railway commissioner after 1900. Out of the total establishment for the colony and protectorate (excluding Hausa militia and Yoruba police), some 250 officials of every grade were stationed in Lagos itself, and over a hundred of these were Europeans.[1] One governor was not impressed by their quality when he arrived in 1897. McCallum complained to the Colonial Office of the 'mountain of inertia' that existed in the numerous departments. Compared with the Malay States, Lagos, in his opinion, was about twenty-five years behind: 'things have been allowed to drift and get along somehow; economy is a matter of secondary consideration and a desire to push the colony there is absolutely none; leave us alone until it is time for our leave and do not worry about the African seems to be the order of the day'.[2]

Deprecation of administrative arrangements immediately after the period of expansion was not confined to Nigeria. In Dahomey Governor Ballot made similar criticisms of the handful of army officers left by Dodds. For the whole colony there were no more than a dozen to fourteen residents and *Commandants de cercle* in the 1890's to run the eight or ten districts. But by 1914 there were at Porto-Novo twenty-two European officials (*Administrateurs* and *Administrateurs-adjoints*) to run eleven departments with a score of native clerks and interpreters. In the office of the lieutenant-governor there were an additional six officials including the secretary-general. Compared with the British colony, the southern districts of Dahomey were well staffed with twenty administrators or assistant administrators for six *cercles* plus an equal number of European personnel from the central departments (Finance, Public Works, Health, Post and Telegraph, Customs, Agriculture) who were discouraged from gravitating to the capital.

Southern Togo as late as 1895 was still a *Landeshauptmannschaft*

---

[1] The rest were literate Africans—mostly second-generation Yoruba from Sierra Leone. The Hausa militia numbered 844 officers and men, and the civil constabulary 382. Both were armed with quick-firing rifles.

[2] N.R.O., Miscellaneous, ADM/91373, McCallum to Antrobus, 12 May 1892; and for similar views, McCallum to Bramston, 20 May 1897.

with fourteen officials in all for a protectorate which did not include Atakpame till two years later and did not have a formally constituted colonial government before 1898, when the capital was moved to Lome. After this date the commissioners took the title of governor. They were assisted by a Colonial Secretary (*Referent*) and, after 1903, by a Legislative Council of officials and three traders.[1] By 1914 the Secretariat, Customs, Public Works, and subsidiary departments employed about thirty Europeans. In the districts there were five *Bezirksämter* for southern Togo and three stations in the north. They stayed in the districts for exceptionally long periods, compared with their neighbours. Dr. Solf, who was not easily impressed by colonial officialdom, on his tour in 1913, noted the consequences of this excellent apprenticeship.

Es ist ein Glück für Togo gewesen, daß seine Bezirksamtmänner jahrelang auf ihren Posten ausgehalten und mit Begeisterung und persönlicher Anhänglichkeit für ihre Distrikte gearbeitet haben. Der ehrende Beiname des Musterländchens hat sich mir bisher bei jedem neuen Bezirk, den ich besichtigt habe, aufgedrängt. Dabei ist mir wiederholt der Gedanke gekommen, ob sich nicht gerade Togo für die Gründung einer Schule zur Ausbildung von Kolonialeleven eignet. Denn gerade in Togo kann man übersichtlich und bequem die mannigfachen Probleme der Kolonialverwaltung und Kolonialwirtschaft studieren.[2]

The question of what was meant by 'protectorate' in Togo (and the colony was never called anything else in the official literature), produced only the vaguest of answers. The treaty with Mlapa was not recognized by German jurists as a valid contract in international law between two equal parties, but rather as a formula by which the native population had voluntarily placed itself under German rule.[3]

---

[1] By Decree, 24 Dec. 1903. The Togo *Gouvernementsrat* replaced an earlier *Verwaltungsrat* (Administrative Council) begun in 1886 which broke down under the strain of permitting every local firm to send a representative to its meetings. In practice it proved impossible to get them to meet at a time suitable for all. Dr. Helfferich, *Zur Reform der kolonialen Verwaltungs-Organisation* (Berlin, 1905), pp. 18–19; A. Full, *Fünfzig Jahre Togo* (Berlin, 1935), p. 62.

[2] Solf, 'Mittelafrikanisches Reisetagebuch', entry for 7 Oct. 1913. There were some outstanding examples of administrative longevity in Togo. Dr. Gruner who had been in the colony since 1892 was political officer at Misahöhe, 1899–1914; Major von Döring had been station officer at Bismarckburg in 1892 and was in charge of Keta-Kratchi and Atakpame, 1894–1913, when he became deputy-governor; Graf Zech rose from the position of station officer at Keta-Kratchi, 1895–1904, to governor of Togo, 1904–10. Solf himself had been governor of German Samoa, 1900–11.

[3] Karl von Stengel, 'Die rechtliche Stellung der Eingeborenen in die deutschen Schutzgebiete', *Deutsche Kolonialzeitung*, iv (1887), 363; Friedrich Schack, *Das*

That it did not apply to any of the interior tribes was immaterial. Other treaties, where they were concluded, were never published; and it was assumed that the whole of the Ewe were governed by their chiefs as a concession from the administrating power.

In practice the administration was not faced by any serious military opposition during its contact with the interior.[1] The small Ewe population, fractioned into over a hundred sub-tribes, had no political organization comparable to the Fon or the Yoruba, and had no urban units larger than 2,000 or 3,000 persons. The only titular chiefs of interest to officials in the Misahöhe District were the *Akpanya* of Buem, the *Dagadu* of Kpandu, the *Plako* of Nyamvo, and the *Hosu* of Ho, who were singled out by the political officer as trustworthy agents for taxation and labour purposes. When two of these chiefs died in 1898 they were succeeded by their brother's sons, and the new title-holders were officially confirmed by the German administration as head chiefs. In the adjacent district of Atakpame which did not come under German rule till 1898, there was only a small town of 2,000 huts, grouped into three wards, two of which were Yoruba, and the third inhabited by Ewe. In the near vicinity of the town there was a mixed population of about 2,000 Ewe and 1,200 Fon living in farming villages along the tributaries of the Mono river. The only head chiefs recognized by the administration were Toigbe of the Ewe ward in Atakpame, and chief Ajaite of Nuatyi—the old Ewe migration centre.

The first reports from German officials in the area concluded that these chieftainships were conferred with the approval of lineage chiefs on candidates from two families in Atakpame and Nuatyi.[2] If there was no suitable candidate from the sons of the deceased chief the title reverted to one of his father's brothers. With these title successions (and there were six during the period of German rule), administrators did not interfere.[3] The political officer of

deutsche Kolonialrecht in seiner Entwicklung bis zum Weltkriege (Hamburg, 1923) 1923), p. 351.

[1] Apart from an uprising at Tove in 1895 and a clash with the Akposso near Agome-Kotukpa (Atakpame) in 1898. Trierenburg, pp. 168, 176; Heinrich Klose, *Togo unter deutscher Flagge* (Berlin, 1899), pp. 46, 162–4. The native constabulary for the whole colony numbered 550 by 1914, 144 of whom were stationed at Lome. There was no *Schutztruppe* in Togo.

[2] *Jahresbericht*, 1897–8, pp. 31–32.

[3] For the election of chiefs in Misahöhe, see Dr. Asmis, 'Die Stammesrechte der Bezirke Misahöhe; Anecho und Lome-Land (Schutzgebiet Togo)', *Zeitschrift für Vergleichende Rechtswissenschaft*, xxvi (1911), 7–8. The elected chief,

Atakpame restricted his official relations with the two head chiefs to an annual conference at district headquarters when they and the chiefs of sub-divisions in the district were informed of new administrative ordinances.

On the coast in the Lome District (*Lome-Land*) there were no headmen of units larger than villages of a few dozen people recognized by the administration; and few of these seem to have had authority outside their own compounds, unless they showed exceptional ability in accumulating wealth from trade or small plantations. The only exception to this pattern of fragmented authority was at Gamme in the northern sector of *Lome-Land*, where half a dozen farming villages acknowledged the headship of the chief of Gamme. To avoid the burden of working continuously through headmen, the Administration after 1898 began to choose and appoint head chiefs over groups of adjacent villages. Occasionally they were village chiefs; more usually they were literate clerks and tax-collectors, trained at mission or government schools, who were given the duty of hearing civil disputes and organizing labour for road-building. They were, in effect, native officials of the German Government, often with no kin ties among the people they administered.[1] In Anecho District, after the end of the century, recognized head chiefs were limited to the lagoon villages of Voga, Vokutime, and Gridgi. The prosperous Lawson lineage took no part in local government; and the Kuadjovi, although signatories to the treaty of 1884, are not mentioned in any of the official reports.

The policy of building up the elements of local native government through village councils and defining the powers of hereditary chiefs was a late development. It was not started until 1907, during the governorship of Graf Zech. Even then it was applied only in the northern Ewe district of Misahöhe and the mixed Yoruba-Ewe district of Atakpame. On the coast the business of tax collection and justice was more easily concentrated in Lome. The head chiefs in Misahöhe and Atakpame were—within certain limits—empowered to punish, and to appoint their own interpreters and policemen (trained by the administration) who were paid from fines and court fees. For the responsibility of collecting taxes, the head chiefs received

after consultation with village elders, paid a sheep, a goat, one crate of gin and M. 24 towards the celebrations that followed. He could also be deposed just as easily.

[1] *Jahresbericht*, 1898–9 ,p. 39; Henrici, p. 151.

5 per cent. of revenues from the villages in their sub-district.[1] Other duties were the isolation of lepers and victims of smallpox and sleeping-sickness, village sanitation, procurement of labour, provision of food and shelter for European travellers (officials or traders). 'On the other hand, the Chief is entitled to expect from both Government officials and. private persons considerate treatment and the avoidance of any degradation of his prestige in front of his people.'[2]

Shortly after this ordinance came into force, 'improvement camps' (*Besserungssiedlungen*) were organized by the political officers of the two Ewe districts to deal with malcontents who disobeyed the rulings of the Native Courts. The experiment was apparently successful and in 1909 was extended to northern Togo.[3]

Till 1908 political officers had a large measure of autonomy in their handling of criminal cases arising in their districts. Only sentences requiring capital punishment or terms of imprisonment of over six months were referred to the governor for sanction. It was realized, however, that officials were too few to act as anything more than a court of appeal for civil disputes settled before councils of elders in the Ewe villages. And in the absence of any thorough studies of customary law among the Ewe, the basis of the colonial civil and criminal code remained the German *Reichsstrafgesetzbuch* and other legal manuals which were inadequate for African conditions. In the late 1890's officials on tour in Misahöhe and Atakpame made an effort to attend and encourage traditional village courts and instruct the chiefs in European methods of presenting evidence. The result was a burdensome increase in the number of cases referred to the political officers, particularly concerning property disputes.[4] To understand such cases better, a number of studies were made for the administration by Dr. Henrici and Dr. Asmis in the early 1900's, and from these studies emerged the basis for the codification of Ewe customary law. But it was felt that the material was inadequate, and it was not fully utilized during the period of German rule.[5]

[1] Graf Zech, 'Denkschrift', 11 Feb. 1907, *Deutsche Kolonialzeitung*, xxiv (1907), 138; Full, p. 101; Trierenburg, pp. 49–50; *Report on the Mandated Sphere of Togoland for 1920–1921* (1922), [Cmd. 1698], Appendixes D and E, pp. 28–31.

[2] *Report on the Mandated Sphere of Togoland for 1920–1921*, p. 13.

[3] One of these camps was located on the Chra river near the Lome–Atakpame road, another in the Sokode–Bassari District. 'Settlers' were allowed to keep the produce they farmed and bring their wives and children. Metzger, p. 107.

[4] *Jahresbericht*, 1897–8, pp. 29.

[5] Codification of Ewe customary law was left to the French mandate administration. For German criticisms of the French Code of 1926, see A. Schlettwein,

The criminal court records are not consistently standardized or completely published; but they indicate, for native cases, a general increase in fines, imprisonment ('improvement camps'), as more of Togoland came under the jurisdiction of German officials, and a decrease in the more ruthless punishments (death penalty and chaining).

District Courts: Criminal Cases*

	Death	Chaining	Prison or 'Improvement Camps'	Lashing/ Birching	Fines (Marks)
Lome, 1898/99	5	64	95	111	98 (2,730)
Lome, 1899/00	..	15	72	70	97 (1,514)
Togo, 1901/02	1	..	514	162	575 (10,138)
Togo, 1907/08	3	..	1,533	434	1,412 (19,168)

* *Jahresbericht*, 1898–9, p. 40; ibid., 1899–1900, p. 31; ibid., 1907–8, p. 54.

No records of the civil cases handled by the Lome court or by political officers are available. But the general policy from the late 1890's was to leave more and more to the village courts, retaining only cases involving Europeans. As the official organ for the German colonies summed up the position in southern Togo: 'Da der Mangel an Einfluß auf Seiten der Häuptlinge eine geregelte Verwaltung sehr erschwert, so wurde eine Hebung ihrer Stellung nach Möglichkeit befördert.'[1] But the formal definition of the status of chiefs as customary judges was not made till 1907 when, as a complimentary measure to the ordinance dealing with their political position, a Chief's Court Ordinance was passed for Misahöhe and Atakpame. All civil cases between Ewe or other natives residing in the district were the responsibility of village chiefs and head chiefs who were authorized to impose fines amounting to M. 50 and M. 100 respectively. Civil cases involving literate natives or Europeans came before the political officer's court. All criminal cases were taken out of the hands of the village courts.[2]

In Dahomey Dodds's policy of reviving the Allada and Abomey

'Kodification des Eingeborenenrechts in Togo', *Zeitschrift für Vergleichende Rechtswissenschaft*, xliii (1927), 248–52.

[1] Ibid., p. 38.

[2] Graf Zech, 'Runderlaß', 11 Feb. 1907, in Metzger, pp. 101–4. The High Court of Appeal (*Kaiserliches Obergericht*) with jurisdiction over European cases in Togo was situated in the Cameroons first at Duala then after 1903 at Buea.

kingdoms under approved rulers was put to the test after the withdrawal of French troops from the colony in July 1894. The Allada experiment never resulted in a successful paramountcy, and more and more of the southern sector of Gli-Gla's 'kingdom' was taken over by administrators at Whydah or Cotonou. There was a minor uprising in 1895 against the 'king' when he assisted the French to recruit labour for a pioneer corps sent to Madagascar.[1] Gli-Gla pardoned the rebels; but his authority never recovered from his association with an unpopular measure. Three years later, when the recruits returned from Madagascar, they refused to recognize him as paramount chief and stirred up a revolt in the villages of the Kpome area which was only suppressed after the death of two *gardes civils*. Thereafter, Gli-Gla played little part in the administration of the 'kingdom'. At his death in 1909 he was succeeded by a nephew who took the 'strong name' of Jihento. The population of the Tori area refused in a body to provide goods and services to celebrate the event; and the Allada protectorate was reduced to insignificance by the inclusion of Tori in the Whydah District.[2]

In the Abomey kingdom Agoli-Agbo began his reign, backed by French arms, and ended it in 1900 under sentence of deportation.[3] In the short space of six years the assumption by Dodds that the Fon court might retain internal independence with only nominal supervision by a French resident proved unfounded. The court was prohibited from the outset from financing its retainers and officials; after 1898 it competed with the French for direct revenues from the Fon population.

Part of the difficulty encountered by Agoli-Agbo lay in the fact that he was encouraged in 1894 to believe that the area between the Zou and Weme rivers was still a tax farm for Abomey. The Yoruba villages there had been left inside the protectorate; but their inhabitants refused to move, as ordered, to the left bank of the Weme, away from a fertile source of palm products and maize which were fetching high prices in the early 1890's at the coastal markets. Some of the villages were placed under the charge of a French official at Sagon, half-way down the eastern boundary of Abomey. The remainder, along the Zou river, were left to Agoli-Agbo, whose authority was enhanced by permission to pronounce the death sentence in July

---

[1] M.F.O., Dahomey, i/18, Loquety to Guieysse, 23 Nov. 1895.
[2] P.N., 'Rapport Politique, Allada', in Mallan to Ponty, 2 May 1909.
[3] 'A Note on the Abomey Protectorate', *Africa*, xxix (1959), No. 2, pp. 149–54.

1894 on three chiefs of Agoni, Cové, and Nahogan, who had been tardy in surrendering to the French. Encouraged by this initial support, the king made claim to tribute from Agoni and from the Mahi which resulted in a general uprising against Abomey officials in the Zou-Weme area in 1895. But this time the new French resident at Abomey arrested six of Agoli-Agbo's ministers and had them imprisoned at Porto-Novo.

The Abomey residents made every effort to work through chiefs opposed to the protected ruler. After the introduction of the head-tax in 1898 it was not difficult to by-pass the king and the court and to encourage village chiefs to act as government collectors for a percentage of the returns. Agoli-Agbo raised such an opposition to this procedure, that at the end of the first year of direct taxation the resident suggested interning him in his palace and recommended that the pretence of 'protected monarchy' should be brought to an end.[1] Acting-Governor Pascal supported this recommendation: the paramountcy was no longer necessary, and indeed was a financial competitor to the French administration.

C'est surtout depuis l'établissement de l'impôt de capitation qu'Agoliagbo fait preuve de sa mauvaise volonté. . . . Les dîmes que prélevait autrefois Agoliagbo sur son peuple étaient environ 150.000 fr. Ces ressources ayant été supprimées et remplacées par des remises dont le maximum a été fixé à 10.000 fr., le roi d'Abomey se trouve dans l'impossibilité de faire face aux dépenses d'entretien des nombreuses personnages de son entourage. Dans ces conditions il est naturel qu'il s'efforce d'entraver l'action de l'administration locale dans son pays et pour obtenir ce résultat il ne reculera pas devant l'emploi des moyens les plus criminels. Ses sujets l'accusent de plusieurs empoisonnements.

Il est évident d'autre part que le maintien de la souveraineté d'Agoliagbo n'a qu'un intérêt historique car la population ne lui obéit plus et toutes les affaires du cercle d'Abomey sont traitées directement par le Résident.[2]

As soon as permission had been received from Paris to depose the king a small force of *gardes civils* removed him without opposition from the palace. He was exiled to the French Congo till 1910, and then allowed to return to reside at Save, coming to Abomey only for occasional ceremonials.

By then, the residency had substituted itself completely as the administrative head of the Abomey *cercle*. But though the title

---

[1] P.N., 'Rapports mensuels, Abomey', Aug. and Nov. 1898.
[2] P.N., Correspondance avec le Ministère des Colonies, Pascal to Decrais, 30 Dec. 1899.

'protectorate' was dropped, little was changed. The formal division of the kingdom into nine cantons in 1900 was based on former village groupings under the monarchy's officials;[1] canton and village chiefs were efficient tax-gatherers and organizers of labour for the railways; and there was little support, except from princes who held no government posts, for the proposal to elect a new king in 1904.

With the advent of Governor Liotard, the policy of Dodds with regard to Allada and Abomey was completely reversed; chiefs descended from the last kings of Abomey were to be kept out of positions of importance in the cantons or the villages. 'De faire accepter aux indigènes des chefs autres que ces personnages dont le prestige subsiste encore', ordered Liotard, 'il me paraît de toute nécessité d'éliminer ces candidatures en usant à cet effet des moyens persuasifs.'[2]

In the annexed territory of Whydah–Cotonou and in Porto-Novo tax collection was kept firmly in European hands after a number of chiefs had been caught keeping back a large part of their receipts in the late 1890's. Tofa would have nothing to do with these unpopular exactions. After 1904 when the colony lost the bulk of its revenues from trade to the government-general and received insufficient subsidies in compensation, trading licences were added to the burden. Their introduction into Porto-Novo provoked a riot which was only quashed by the arrest of some of Tofa's ministers. At Sakete in 1905 there was a more serious outbreak on the part of the Yoruba population which resulted in the death of two French officials. Order was restored by a punitive expedition led by the governor in person.

With some justice the general report on the colony for 1909 claimed that direct taxation was still the 'pierre de touche de la situation politique'.[3] Wherever collection was slow the security of the administration was felt to be in jeopardy. By 1910 the Yoruba of the eastern region of the colony had been pacified, but less by the presence of *gardes civils* than by the prolongation of the railway as far as Sakete which lowered the cost of European imports and provided a steady means of transport for local produce to the Porto-Novo market. The last pocket of serious resistance to the head-tax was in the So area of the lower Weme. A patrol sent there in 1913 to collect

[1] P.N., Abomey, *Arrêté*, 12 Jan. 1900. The nine cantons were the town of Abomey itself, Dona, Oumbigame, Cana, Zobodome, Sinhoué, Tindki, Allahé, and Tandji.

[2] P.N., Correspondance, 1901–4, Liotard to Veissyre, 4 Dec. 1900.

[3] P.N., Mallan, 'Rapport politique', 1909.

tax arrears encountered serious opposition; and a report by Administrator Le Herissé pointed out that the lower Weme population of about 50,000 refused to pay taxes through local chiefs in whose honesty they had no confidence.[1] It was not until a post of twenty *gardes civils* was permanently maintained at Djekin that the area came under effective political control and collection of revenue was carried out without recourse to the chiefs as intermediaries.

At Porto-Novo the protection of Tofa's segment of the royal lineage against the claims of candidates from rival families guaranteed the Gun king the longest reign in the history of the kingdom. The price paid for this feat of dynastic endurance was the gradual surrender of the goods and services and the fees from court hearings which Tofa had expected would continue under the 1883 Protectorate Agreement. The kingdom itself was cut down to about ten square miles; and the claim of Tofa to extend it with the help of the French to the Upper Weme, or eastwards to the Ajarra, was tolerated neither by the Wemenu, Gun, and Yoruba of outlying villages, nor by the French themselves. The remedy to the problem posed by the original territorial definition of the protectorate (claimed in Dorat's time to be under Tofa) was suggested in 1893 by the resident of Porto-Novo: the pseudo-kingdom was to be broken up into smaller units by the administration which would place at their head 'des chefs influents dont le prestige et l'autorité s'augmenteraient encore par l'appui que leur apporterait le Gouvernement local'.[2] And on the whole this policy remained unchanged for the next twenty years, though it raised difficulties of its own which were not properly understood till the end of that period.

In short the prestige which Tofa gained in the early 1890's from being on the side of the victors did not help his political ambitions. By 1905, when his court had been replaced by a new judiciary, his

[1] P.N., Le Herissé, 'Situation dans la Sô', 18 June 1913. Le Herissé, as was his habit, used a Porto-Novo chief, one Zissou Alaba, to supplement his own observations and took him on tour as an informant. 'Il est intéressant de noter que Zissou Alaba donne comme principal motif du désordre dans la région Sô le manque d'Administration: "Les habitants sont livrés à eux-mêmes", dit-il. En ce qui concerne plus spécialement les difficultés de l'impôt, Zissou Alaba critique le mode de perception. Pour lui un indigène n'a jamais confiance dans l'honnêteté de son semblable. Par suite, faire verser le montant des côtes au Chef du village entraîne fatalement contre celui-ci la suspicion de ses administrés qui ne croient jamais, quoiqu'on leur dise, qu'aucune somme n'a été détournée de sa véritable destination.' Against which Lieutenant-Governor Noufflard wrote the curious marginal note: 'C'est le secret de notre autorité.'

[2] P.N., Affaires politiques, 1893–4, Cornilleau to Dodds, 31 Dec. 1893.

prison closed, and his personal militia disbanded, he was compelled
to disassociate himself officially from any manifestation of dis-
content on the part of his subjects. Governor Liotard prohibited him
from settling disputes among the Gun themselves; and his messengers
were accompanied by *gardes civils* when making approved proclama-
tions to the population. At his death in 1908 Lieutenant-Governor
Marshal nominated Tofa's son who took the 'strong name' of
Gbedissin to the position of 'Chief of the French Benin Territories'—
('pour éviter formule de protectorat')—with a stipend of 25,000 francs
a year.[1] His uncle, Sohingbe, after years of exile in Lagos Colony,
lodged a claim to the throne, which was rejected, though he was
permitted to return to Porto-Novo, whence he had been driven by
Tofa. Apart from the stipend, there was little advantage in the
position of official paramount chief: for Gbedissin, in Marshal's
words, was 'un chef supérieur institué par nous n'ayant d'attributions
que celles que le gouvernement jugera utile et opportun de lui
déléguer'.

With the death of Tofa was also removed the last obligation to
allow an independent native tribunal in the colony. The formal
organization of a judiciary in Dahomey was given little attention
till after 1900, when the question was treated as part of the general
policy towards colonial jurisdiction in French West Africa. The
earliest European court in the colony was at Cotonou where a
French administrator acted as justice of the peace for European and
European-native civil cases. At Porto-Novo King Tofa was permitted to run a court of his own for both civil and criminal cases,
assisted after 1901 by a French official whenever Europeans were
involved. Elsewhere customary jurisdiction was untouched. There
was no colonial magistrate in the colony until the arrival of Chief
Justice Liontel; and his inquiries and recommendations marked a
complete break with the judicial *laisser-faire* of the previous decade.

Liontel's first act was to constitute an Appeal Court at Cotonou,
presided over by himself, which began to examine and reverse a
number of decisions made by the French justice of the peace (who had
handled criminal cases beyond his competence). Next he turned to his
main task which was to examine and report on justice in the colony
for the Ministry for the Colonies. As a magistrate from the West
Indies he was dismayed at the combination of administrative and
judicial powers exercised by officials in Africa; as a French-educated

---

[1] P.N., Départ, Confidentielle, 1908–11, Marshal to Ponty, 13 Feb. 1908.

creole coming from an older part of the French empire, he was offended by the distinction between French jurisdiction and the customary and 'fetish' courts. He made it clear that his aim was no less than the rapid extension of French laws to French citizens and French protected subjects alike. Very soon he was at loggerheads with Acting-Governor Pascal who argued that the Appeal Court could not hear all criminal cases from the interior—which would have necessitated bringing witnesses from as far as the Niger down to Cotonou, 'c'est-à-dire dans certains cas des villages entiers'.[1] Pascal defended the custom of domestic slavery, bride price, and debt-pledging of relatives, the existence of which was condemned by Liontel. Moreover, he opposed Liontel's plan to bring in coloured magistrates from the French Antilles: even if the local budget could pay for them, argued Pascal, such officers should be Europeans 'qui ne considéreront pas les noirs si primitifs encore de la Colonie exclusivement comme des frères opprimés par des blancs . . .'. Finally, Pascal charged Liontel with stirring up racial tension and undermining the prestige of the administration in the eyes of Brazilians and Gun alike and asked for his removal.

Governor Liotard, who arrived in September 1900, took up the campaign against the magistrate where Pascal left off. He refused to disband King Tofa's tribunal of native assessors which was under attack from Brazilian creoles and Muslim Yoruba in Porto-Novo. And he continued to deny to creoles elsewhere in the colony the right to apply for French citizenship (and therefore the right to have their cases heard in the French court at Cotonou). When Liontel went ahead and forwarded his plan for a complete reform of the administration of justice in Dahomey, the governor rejected most of it as premature.[2] He considered that administrators acting as justices of the peace were sufficient for the annexed territory; he agreed with the suggestion for a permanent professional magistrate for the Appeal Court; but he emphasized that such a court should not be empowered to revise cases heard according to customary law or reverse judgements given by administrators in the protectorate. Otherwise the head of the judiciary in the colony, as Liotard put it, 'aurait une situation fort délicate vis-à-vis du gouvernement surtout s'il avait la tendance à donner la protection des lois françaises aux

[1] M.F.O., A.O.F. viii, Pascal to Decrais, 22 Aug. 1900.
[2] M.F.O., A.O.F. viii, Liontel to Liotard, 11 Jan. 1901, encl. in Liotard to Decrais, 13 Jan. 1901; Liotard to Decrais, 31 Dec. 1900.

indigènes traités d'après les coutumes locales' by chiefs or by French Residents.[1]

Liontel's project to give the Appeal Court and its judge control of all district courts throughout Dahomey was not accepted by the Ministry for the Colonies. But in 1901 the sentences of native courts presided over by administrators were limited in civil cases to one year's imprisonment. At Porto-Novo the native tribunal continued to deal with civil and criminal cases and passed sentences which included capital punishment. The tribunal was formally abolished in August 1902; but in practice Liotard allowed it to continue for civil cases and minor police offences.

At the end of this debate the pattern of native and European courts in the colony was settled by the government-general, and the elaborate system of district and canton courts prescribed in a decree of 10 November 1903 was adopted in Dahomey as in the rest of French West Africa. For minor police offences district chiefs were empowered to judge according to local customs,[2] impose fines of up to 15 francs or a sentence of up to five days' imprisonment. The canton courts composed of a chief and two native assessors appointed by the governor and presided over by an administrator on tour, dealt with all civil and criminal cases entailing sentences up to five years imprisonment. Judgements given in the canton courts were open to appeal to the District courts—meaning the *Commandant de cercle*. Finally the Appeal Court at Cotonou was reserved for cases from the interior involving sentences in excess of five years and all cases involving French citizens. After eight years of trial and experiment the whole system was revised again in the Government-General Council in 1911.[3] The village (or native) courts were retained, but their power over police matters was reduced. The Appeal Court for all the French West African colonies was located at Dakar. The lieutenant-governor was empowered to set up a special tribunal for creoles. Henceforth, the district courts under administrators applied French laws, the village and canton courts customary law. A special clause provided for the replacement of assessors in the minor courts where, as was frequently the case in southern Dahomey, they were party to the land cases they heard.

[1] Ibid., Liotard to Decrais, 2 Mar. 1901.
[2] 'En tout ce qu'elles n'ont pas de contraire aux principes de la civilisation française'. Decree, 10 Nov. 1903, Art. 75.
[3] Government-General, Dakar, 5 E 26–29, Conseil du Gouvernement Général, Minutes, 24 June 1911.

Though the relationship between Lagos administrators and the Yoruba protectorates was less close and exacting than between the French and the Fon, it had one advantage: the political protection exercised from the colony was not bedevilled by the necessity to extract large amounts of direct taxes through indigenous authorities. The governors of the 1890's, and to a certain extent Egerton and his successors, were able, before 1914, to conduct their relations with the Egba as ambassadors. The critical years between the pacification, after the example of Ijebu Ode, and the completion of the railway which linked the south-west with central and northern Nigeria, were bridged by two administrators of considerable imagination. One of them brought to the new protectorates experience acquired in the Malay States, and the other a fair understanding of the financial implications of his predecessor's theories of local government.

But the ease with which south-western Nigeria was assimilated into the protectorate of Southern Nigeria and finally into the amalgamated colony in 1914, should not obscure the fact that the real tests of rule in the Egba and Ibadan states were postponed, not avoided. The riots that accompanied the introduction of head-taxes in 1918 would undoubtedly have occurred earlier, had the experiment been tried.[1] Moreover, the term 'protectorate' did not entail the exclusion of sizeable forces of Hausa militia from Ibadan and Ijebu which were a permanent reminder that the conditions of peace in the hinterland could not be jeopardized with impunity. The only shock to the complacency with which the Yoruba states were ordered before 1913 was the bombardment of Oyo in 1895, after the *Alafin* had enforced his judicial prerogatives in criminal cases. The garrison was removed from Oyo and 'uncivilized' punishments on the part of the *Alafin* were prohibited.[2]

Coming from Malaya, Governor McCallum was struck by the poor development of representative assemblies in the colony and the Yoruba states. The Legislative Council, he thought, had been treated as a 'nonentity' by his predecessors, and no attention had been given by Denton or Carter to the problem of introducing conciliar bodies into the heavily populated urban communities of

[1] For an account of the troubles at Abeokuta and Ibadan after 1914 see Margery Perham, *Native Administration in Nigeria* (Oxford, 1937), pp. 76–78; Burns, pp. 227–8.

[2] C.O. 147/113, Denton to Chamberlain, 10 Apr. 1897; *Lagos Weekly Record*, 16 June 1894, 23 Nov. 1895; Burns, pp. 218–19. An adulterer from Okeho had been sentenced by the *Alafin* and gelded.

Abeokuta or Ibadan.[1] This problem would soon become acute, once traders, following the railway, demanded some representation among the Egba chiefs through a British official. The resident at Ibadan had no power over the *Bale* in a town whose population had grown to about 170,000. At Abeokuta, in 1897, there was no British representative at all, though McCallum ascertained that the *Bashorun* and the *Alake* were not opposed to receiving one. He did not underestimate the difficulties of getting the Yoruba authorities to meet regularly with an official, whatever his title.

Anyhow it appears to me that we must treat the situation delicately, but find a favourable opportunity of establishing a protectorate over these countries, engage the Chiefs in Administration and make them happy, retain Native Customs and gradually introduce the same Residential system as rules in Perak and Selangor.[2]

As a step forward Lieutenant-Governor Denton was ordered to Abeokuta in August 1897 to promise government support for the *Alake* as head of an Egba council, in return for Egba labour to lay a telegraph to the north and build the foundations of the railway line.[3] The *Alake*, Denton found, could do little on his own initiative; but with Denton's backing he dismissed a number of refractory chiefs and convened a council of seven—the traditional *obas*, representatives of the Christians and the Muslims, and the Egba trade association.[4] It was essentially an advisory council for discussing and approving measures proposed by the *Alake* and the secretary of the Egba United Government—a position first filled in 1902 by the Rev. J. Henryson Samuel, an Egba Methodist pastor. By then the Lagos administration had appointed a railway commissioner to Abeokuta who became, in effect, a permanent resident.

It was fully intended by McCallum and his successor MacGregor that the Egba Council should be responsible for the internal revenues and expenditure of the Egba state. Apart from government loans for public works, increasingly supervised by European officials, these revenues came mostly from tolls on consumer goods and goods in transit passing from Northern Nigeria to Lagos. Despite opposition from Lagos traders and temporary suspension of tolls on the order

[1] N.R.O., Miscellaneous, ADM/91373, McCallum to Wingfield, 13 May 1897.
[2] Ibid., McCallum to Chamberlain, 5 May 1897.
[3] Ibid., McCallum to Denton, 21 Aug. 1897.
[4] S. O. Biobaku, 'The Egba Council 1899–1918', *Odù Journal of Yoruba and Related Studies*, No. 2 (1955), pp. 18–19

of the Colonial Office, the principle was maintained.[1] As MacGregor explained to the chiefs of Lagos and the Western and Central Districts, there could be 'no good, sound and authoritative provincial administration . . . without money'; and in the absence of general head-taxes this could only come from trade.[2]

The second stage in the definition of the relationship between Abeokuta and Lagos came in 1904 with the Egba Jurisdiction Ordinance, after signature of an agreement between MacGregor and the *Alake*, by which the Egba agreed to cede to the colony (the Supreme Court) their powers of jurisdiction over all non-natives of Egbaland, and over all cases of manslaughter and murder. Provision was also made for the establishment of a Mixed Court of the resident and two members of the Egba Council with powers of jurisdiction over civil cases involving non-Egba under the same terms as the District Commissioners' Courts.[3]

The final aspect of Egba relationships with Lagos was the effort of the administration to define the boundaries of the 'Abeokuta Province' as a unit of government within the Western Province. The task was undertaken by the commissioner of lands in 1905. According to later surveys it was badly done.

The boundary satisfied neither the Egbas nor the Ibadans. A large area north of Opeji, inhabited entirely by Egbas, who all owned houses in Abeokuta, was included in the Ibadan Division, though the Bale of Ibadan never exercised efficient administrative control over it. Similarly, a considerable number of Ibadans lived and farmed in an area near Ilugun and paid taxes both to Ibadan and Abeokuta.[4]

The remainder of the old Western District and Egbado formed

[1] Baillaud, pp. 217–30.

[2] U.C.I., 'Central Native Council Minutes', entry 5 June 1903.

[3] *Laws of the Colony of Southern Nigeria*, i. 254–6; Elias, *Groundwork of Nigerian Law*, p. 97. The Order in Council of 24 July 1901 defined Lagos protectorate so as to include Egba territory, but this is not expressly stated in the clauses of the Jurisdiction Ordinance.

[4] *Legislative Council. Sessional Papers* (1928), No. 1, p. 4. The Egba boundaries had been first defined by agreement with the *Alake*, 5 Jan. 1894. In the east the limit was from Orichi, a town on the Ogun, as far down as Otta. 'The boundaries between the Ilaro kingdom and Egba must be determined by the position of the Towns and Farms held under the King of Ilaro, which kingdom was formerly tributary to Egba, but all Egbas who may have farms in the territory now known as the Ilaro kingdom, may continue to work them as here to fore, any complaints upon either side being made to the Travelling Commissioner for the District, through the Officer in charge of Ilaro.' *Ordinances and Orders and Rules thereunder, in force in the Colony of Lagos* (London, 1894), p. 987.

a large triangle between Egba territory and the Dahomey border. It was not an easy area to administer, given on the one hand the uncertainty about which villages came under the laws of the colony, and on the other, changes in political relationships among the Egbado themselves. The main business of the Badagri commissioner was to impose fines for smuggling—occasionally as high as £100— on the border settlements, and to arbitrate in disputes arising from rivalries between the Egbado over forest reserves and new farm land.[1] The towns of Ilaro, Ilobi, and Okeodan were composed of as many as four or five wards, some of eighteenth-century origin, and others founded later by refugees from the Fon or the Egba. There was a strong tendency on the part of the Ilaro wards to claim other Egbado towns as 'dependencies' after Ilaro itself had been freed from Egba tutellage by seeking British protection in 1891. For example, in 1899, during a dispute between Egoa and Ilaro over rights to the forest between the two towns the latter claimed that the former, founded by refugees from Ketu, was in a tributary relationship; and this claim was upheld by the district commissioner. Later a more serious conflict of authority arose between Ilaro and Okeodan. In the 1890's Okeodan had four wards, each with Ilaro, Awori, Ilobi, and Erinja Yoruba respectively. The town *Oba*, called the *Elerinja*, was provided by the Erinja ward.[2] The dispute with Ilaro in 1905 centred around the right of the *Obi* of Ilaro to appoint a head chief to the town of Ajilete. This was contested by the *Elerinja* of Okeodan who affirmed that only he and the head chief of Ilobi had that right. Furthermore, the *Elerinja* refuted claims laid by the chiefs of Ilaro to farm lands on the Ajilete and Ilaro boundary.

As a background to the dispute there was a certain traditional contempt on the part of Ilobis and Erinjas for Ilaro which had long been under Egba control; there was the fact that both Okeodan and Ajilete contained a high proportion of Ilaro Yorubas who sided with the *Obi* of Ilaro; finally there was the policy of the administrators of the Western Province who invariably upheld the claims of the *Obi*, appointed in 1900, and the *Bales* of Ajilete who were of Ilaro descent. Coupled with this was the steadfast assumption on the part of the administration that Ajilete was part of the Ilaro division, and not an

---

[1] N.R.O., Badagri, 'District Commissioner's Diary, 1897–1901', entries for 31 May 1897, Sept. 1897, Dec. 1898, Apr. 1899.

[2] U.C.I., E. V. S. Thomas, 'Historical Survey of the Towns of Ilaro, Ilobe, Ajilete and Ilashe in the Ilaro Division' (1933), p. 28.

independent town. Such had been claimed by the Ilaro Yoruba at the time of the 1891 protectorate; and historically it was true. But the ethnic groups composing Ajilete had been considerably modified by the influx of Egbado during the previous half-century; and between 1858 and 1891, Ilaro rule over Ajilete had been interrupted by the Egba. What was really at stake was not merely the chieftainship of Ajilete, but control of farm lands between Ajilete, Okeodan, and Ilaro.

The *Bale* of Okeodan and the *Olobi* of Ilobi took action, while Ilaro authorities hesitated, and were fined by the district commissioner for putting up trespass notices on land blocks lying between the Yewa river and the Ilaro–Addo road. The *Elerinja* of Okeodan then persuaded Erinja and Ilobi groups at Ajilete to assert their claims to these blocks; and for their pains both the *Elerinja* and the *Olobi* of Ilobi were arrested and gaoled for unlawful assembly. Finally, the position of the Ilaro in Ajilete was strengthened when *Bale* Akindale (an Ilaro) came to be officially regarded as the *Olu* of Ilaro's representative or overlord of the Ifemo land blocks.[1]

The whole episode reflected the determination of British officials after the turn of the century to uphold the paramountcy of one town as a safeguard against factional divisions and to avoid the necessity of constantly intervening to settle petty disputes.

In the south, throughout the Badagri District, the demise of the ward chiefs was recognized, but nothing was done to remedy it. District Commissioner Pennington in 1899 summed up the position:

> The old authority of the Chiefs and Bales has been practically taken away from them. For years we seem to have been breaking down the old order of things and have placed nothing in its place. A great part of the District is in the Colony of Lagos and here of course English law is in force supported by a few constables or Hausas scattered here and there in the bush. The net result in the bush districts is chaos. You cannot administer the niceties of English law in the middle of the West African Jungle.[2]

Governor MacGregor's policy, influenced by Pennington's report, aimed at restoring the position of the hereditary lineage chiefs. Revenues, he argued, were not sufficient to pay for the number of officials and police needed to supervise all aspects of administration in the protected areas of western Yorubaland; nor could the

---

[1] N.R.O., Badagri, 'Political Notes, 1903–1913'.
[2] N.R.O., ADM/91383, Pennington, Report, 12 Oct. 1899.

administration expect the greater paramountcies at Abeokuta, Ibadan, or the ruling house of Ife to tolerate such close supervision, even if it were available. It was important, therefore, to shore up the position of the smaller *Bales* and *Obas* of the Egbado and Awori towns.

Those that learn to read and write; those that go to other countries and return here; and especially the men who serve as soldiers and come back to their own districts, are all ready to challenge the authority of the chiefs. The chiefs have also lost power and prestige by the establishment of Residents and District Commissioners among them; by the abolition of the slave trade; and by the modifying or abolishing of tolls.[1]

To remedy this the Native Councils Ordinance of 1901 (which applied only to the Western Province) prescribed a Central Native Council under the presidency of the governor at Lagos, and District Councils under the 'person who is recognized by the Governor as the principal ruling Chief of the District or Province'.[2]

But in Badagri and in most of the Western Province the ordinance was a dead letter. The Badagri Council, constituted in the *Gazette* in 1902, never met till 1913, and then only at the convenience of the commissioner, when its attention was confined to ways and means of clearing roads. The intelligence reports for the Western District reveal that the commissioners had no confidence in the abilities of the hereditary ward chiefs to take over 'all matters of internal administration', as recommended in the 1901 Ordinance. In Badagri itself, by 1906, only the *Possu* and Adigbe *Wawu* of Ahoviko ward received stipends; and when the *Wawu* died the same year his successor's stipend was discontinued. The only other stipends paid in the Badagri District in 1906 were:

The *Bale* of Mowo £22	The *Bale* of Koja £18
The *Bale* of Iworo £36	The *Olu* of Ilaro £60
The *Oba* of Appa £36	The *Oba* of Ipokia £60
The *Bale* of Igbessa £24	The *Oba* of Addo £50
The *Bale* of Ajilete £18	*Seriki* Abassi £30

By 1913 only the *Oba* of Addo, the *Bale* of Igbessa and Abassi were still in receipt of annual payments. The rest had been discontinued. In contradiction to MacGregor's policy the commissioners preferred to work through one individual rather than Native Councils.

[1] N.R.O., Government House Archives, 'Administrative Policy in Yoruba States (Western Province) 1912–1913', MacGregor to Chamberlain, 11 Nov. 1891.
[2] *Laws of the Colony of Southern Nigeria*, ii. 1261–5.

The most important of the chiefs for the administration of the Egbado towns was Abassi, whose rise to power was noted with wonder and approval by the district commissioners. He was given the title *Seriki* at Okeodan in 1897, when the commissioner was present for the ceremony; and by 1906 his influence was 'enormous and inexplicable both in Badagri and the North of the District'.[1] If the *Seriki*'s sources of income are examined, however, his position as head of the Yoruba Muslims and as paramount chief of the Egbado is not so surprising. First he was a government chief, trusted by the administration. He was the founder of Aiyetoro, where he ruled the country west of Egba territory—'and does it well so far as any one can see'—saving the Badagri commissioners a good deal of travel and unnecessary interference.[2] In addition to his stipend he collected about £84 per annum as landlord to the trading firms of Gaiser and Witt & Busch at Badagri where he owned a section of the waterfront. He had a government lease to collect coconuts around Badagri town and owned a plantation on the opposite shore (originally part of the Topo Mission plantation), 'out of which he is said to make £1,000 per annum'. Finally, he was an astute trader and moneylender.

With wealth went political ambition. In founding Aiyetoro as the capital of Egbadoland between Mekko and Abeokuta and encouraging immigrants to move there from Egoa, Igolo, Sawampa, and other refugee centres, Abassi was attempting to reverse the historical process of the previous century which had seen the dispersal of the Egbado under pressure from the Fon and Egba alike. With the power of Abomey at an end and the Egba contained within a defined boundary and forbidden to raid for slaves, there was a chance for the Egbado to consolidate as a sub-tribe, under new leadership, on farm-lands no longer threatened by constant devastation. Inevitably, as the settlement at Aiyetoro increased, friction occurred between Egba and Egbado villages. After a rough boundary had been drawn between dependencies of Aiyetoro and Abeokuta, it was found in 1907 that some of the Egbado farm-lands still remained in Egba territory. Abassi promised his supporters to drive the Egba out of the farms concerned; and a commissioner from Badagri, sent to look into the matter, unwisely gave the *Seriki* permission to call on police protection when the Egbado harvested their crops. At the first attempt a clash occurred and seven of the Egbado farmers were seized

---

[1] N.R.O., District Commissioner's Diary, entry 27 Sept. 1897.
[2] N.R.O., Badagri, 'Political Notes, 1903–1913'.

by police of the *Alake* of Abeokuta.[1] A series of reprisals followed. Abassi's police force was disbanded, and the border farms were handed over to the Egba.

But the *Seriki*'s position was unaffected by this small setback. In December 1913 he was made official paramount chief of Badagri in recognition of his importance and the fact that for the previous decade he had been the only chief of the Western District ever to take his place in MacGregor's Central Native Council at Lagos. And two years later his position was upheld by the administration against attempts on the part of the chiefs of Lagos to contest his right to hear commercial disputes and supervise the construction of court houses at Addo, Igbessa, Ilaro, and Ipokia. In February 1915 Chief Obanikoro of Lagos informed the Badagri commissioner than these towns acknowledged himself as 'overlord'; and reports from these places told him of 'strange things'—namely that Abassi was supervising their civil affairs.[2] The Lagos chiefs were told, in reply, that if they had jurisdiction in the area, they should reside for at least four months of every year in the towns concerned; otherwise they were to keep out of the Badagri District 'paramountcy'.

In 1919 Abassi died without a successor. 'Since his death', noted a commissioner, 'the Badagri Council has continued to exercise a measure of authority throughout the present Badagri District, but no longer far into the Ilaro Division.'[3] He had been the answer to the problem of administering an area equal to about three districts in the neighbouring colony of Dahomey and at least two in southern Togoland with very slender means. But his position had been the antithesis of Native Council policy advocated by MacGregor.

By the time of amalgamation the only long-lived example of MacGregor's theory had also come to an end. The Central Native Council which first met at the end of 1901 touched on every important problem of native policy concerning the colony and the protectorate, and had power to solve none of them.

As constituted by MacGregor, the council consisted of some twenty-five chiefs from Lagos and the old Western, Central, and Eastern Districts of the colony. It held a dozen meetings between December 1901 and December 1903, during which time MacGregor used it

[1] N.R.O., Badagri, 'Duplicate Correspondence', Punch to Wood, 24 Feb. 1906; Aiyetore chiefs to Wood, 22 July 1907.
[2] N.R.O., Badagri, 'Duplicate Correspondence', Obanikore to Wood, 9 Feb. 1915.
[3] N.R.O., Badagri, 'Intelligence Reports, 1913–1934'.

as a means of sounding out Yoruba opinion of measures to be presented to the Legislative Council, and as a forum and court for
sitting in judgement on matters concerning the position and status
of Yoruba chiefs. Much of its effectiveness depended on the tact
with which the governor, as president, listened to its advice and
allowed the council to perform tasks which undertaken by the administration alone would have been resented as undue interference.
The outstanding example of this was the case of the *Elepe* of Epe
which arose in 1902 when the Yoruba successor to this title at Epe
assumed the right to wear a crown of state without permission of the
Oni of Ife. MacGregor, unsure of the rights and wrongs of the matter,
permitted the council to decide and flattered it by calling from Ife
the *Oni* himself to deliver judgement against the offending chief.[1]
Again in 1903 MacGregor, during his stand against the Legislative
Council and local traders on the question of the Egbas' right to levy
tolls on traffic from the interior, kept the chiefs in his confidence and
won their support. On the other hand, they made no bones about
opposing the Forestry Ordinance of 1903 which was aimed at the
creation of reserves to prevent the over-exploitation of rubber and
mahogany; and they were wary of accepting the administration's
offer of free seeds for kola-nut plantations, fearing some form of
tax or duty on the produce.

Under Governor Egerton the role of the Central Native Council
became less and less an advisory body of informed opinion about
native policy and more an unofficial opposition to every measure
designed to extract contributions from the Lagos population to meet
the cost of public works. Much of the mutual confidence built up
by Egerton's predecessor was lost when small requests on the part
of the council for an agenda, or for more frequent meetings, were
refused. Consequently there was little co-operation on larger issues.
The council objected strongly to a plan to improve the sanitation of
Lagos which involved the compulsory purchase of latrine pails for
every compound.[2] They refused to sanction a head-tax (2*d.* per week)
to help defray the cost of a £130,000 scheme for a better water-supply
for the town. In 1908 the council furiously debated the rumour that
a house-tax was to be imposed, and Egerton, while denying the

[1] U.C.I., 'Central Native Council Minutes', sessions, 28 Feb. 1902, 19 Apr.,
21 May 1902, 24 Feb. 1903. The *Oni* 'sat on the right hand of the Governor and
had his back turned to the Members of the Council'. Only the *Akarigbo* and the
Awujale had the right to a crown in Ijebu.

[2] Ibid., 5 June 1903. 'A tax on what is a call of nature . . .'.

rumour, accused the vice-president of the council, the Prince *Eleko*, of using his position as head of the house of Docemo to organize resistance to the administration at Lagos.[1] The final dispute which terminated the effective life of the council was over the Seditious Offences Ordinance of 1909, which the chiefs objected to on the general ground that it was designed to muzzle any criticism of the administration and would bring a crop of malicious accusations, and for the particular reason that Egerton refused to have the Bill translated into Yoruba for them to read until it had already been passed by the Legislative Council.[2] In the heat of the debate they challenged the assertion of the deputy-governor, Thorburn, that the three unofficial members of the Legislative Council 'represented' the colony more adequately than themselves; and one chief, voicing the sense of political frustration felt by them all, posed the question that had received no answer since 1901: 'Is it a fact that this Council has no power to make or prohibit laws? If so why are we all here? Apparently there is a higher Council than this who make the laws.'[3]

After this outburst the chiefs met together only twice—once in 1910 and for the last time in 1913, when the Colonial Secretary, four members of the Legislative Council, and the Political Secretary, Major E. J. Lugard, were present.[4] In the face of a number of purposeful Bills—a Building Ordinance, prohibiting mud houses, a Mosquito Ordinance, demanding an end to open drains, an ordinance for impounding wandering livestock—they capitulated, requesting only that they should be consulted from time to time: 'for they could not read and write like the educated party and had no voice in the laws'. They were not called again.

In view of the fact that MacGregor attached such importance to Native Councils as institutions of local government and sought to provide funds for them, it is important to ask why this policy had so little success outside the great urban centres of Abeokuta and Ibadan. The Forestry Ordinance which established a revenue system from licences for the councils had to be dropped, not only in the face of opposition from the European and literate African block in Lagos (both inside and outside the Legislative Council), but also because of

---

[1] *Eleko* Eshugbayi. For his later clashes with the administration, see Perham, pp. 265–6.

[2] U.C.I., 'Central Native Council Minutes', sessions, 5 Oct., 18 Nov. 1909. For the reaction of literate Africans at Lagos, Coleman pp. 181–2.

[3] U.C.I., 'Central Native Council Minutes', Chief Alli Balogun, 18 Nov. 1909.

[4] Ibid., 14 Mar. 1913.

the difficulty of appointing effective 'guardians of the forest' in Egbado and Egba territory where their notices defining reservations and listing licence fees were torn down by the rubber-tappers and wood-cutters.[1] Tribute and internal tolls—the only other major source of income for native authorities—were the prerogative of the heads of great Yoruba confederations, not the village and smaller ward chiefs whose status was to be restored. And this latter group the commissioners of the Western District held in scant respect, preferring the well-established system of limited stipends that could be withheld for unsatisfactory behaviour, or increased in the case of outstanding individuals for meritorious service. There remained the possibility of making over to the council fees from court cases. But MacGregor's ordinance, in its vagueness, did not prescribe a judicial role for the convocations of village and ward chiefs; and the Native Courts proclamation of 1900 which instituted minor courts did not apply to the colony and protectorate.

After the amalgamation of 1906 and the creation of the colony and protectorate of Southern Nigeria, the Native Court system of 1900 was supervised more closely by the Supreme Court and the difficult task of extending it to the old Lagos protectorate (Western Province) was undertaken. The Egba Jurisdiction Ordinance of 1904 which had set up a Mixed Court at Abeokuta for non-natives and which extended the laws of the colony to cases of murder and manslaughter in Egbaland, remained unaltered.[2] Similarly, a divisional court for civil and criminal cases was established at Oyo under the presidency of the resident in 1907. And gradually, at other centres in western Yorubaland Native Courts were introduced alongside the Commissioners' Courts, composed of chiefs of the former Native Councils—and like the council either convened by British officials, or meeting on their own initiative.

Memoranda written by Sir Edwin Speed and by Chief Justice Osborne on the judiciary in Southern Nigeria concurred in condemning the Native Courts for their powers and for their independence from the Supreme Court.[3] Speed's opinion was that with the exception of Egbaland, the Crown had acquired such jurisdiction by treaty in the protectorate that it could legislate for Europeans and Yoruba

[1] N.R.O., Dispatches, 20, Report by Commissioner Punch, 9 Feb. 1899, encl. in Denton to Chamberlain, 16 Feb. 1899; C.O. 147/157, MacGregor to Chamberlain, 11 Nov. 1901; Baillaud, pp. 196–7.

[2] Elias, p. 105; and above, 190.

[3] See the excellent short analysis in Elias, pp. 107–8.

alike. But the Native Courts—whether presided over or not by a commissioner—had greater powers than the Commissioners' District Courts; and the commissioner was absolved from any responsibility for their decisions, though he could, and sometimes did transfer land cases to his own court, but for administrative rather than judicial reasons.[1]

Behind the confusion over jurisdiction in the protectorate lay the difficulty about what was meant by 'protectorate' itself.[2] Treaties cited by Speed (most of them dealing with rights over a ribbon of land along the railway line) to back up his case for Crown authority in Yorubaland did not cover the whole of the protectorate of Lagos. This 'protectorate' had been defined by an Order in Council of 24 July 1901 as an area of British 'influence' exercised (in the phrase of the Order) 'in view of international negotiations and the establishment of the Protectorate of Northern Nigeria'. But within the international and Northern Nigeria boundaries there were large gaps where the uncertainty of the legislators was only filled in by the initiative of the travelling commissioners. True, the *Oni* of Ife and the *Awujale* of Ijebu Ode had, like the Egba, signed away in 1904 and 1908 certain powers of jurisdiction to the Crown, but how were these powers to be exercised by administrators—as officers responsible to the Supreme Court, or as presidents of Native Courts? And what of Ibadan and Abeokuta where, as a Colonial Office memorandum admitted, the administration possessed '*de facto* jurisdiction greatly in excess of that which has been acquired *de jure*'?[3]

In short, outside Lagos there were by 1913 four types of 'protectorate': territories at Badagri and Epe over which the Crown had acquired complete jurisdiction by treaty and through the District Commissioners' Courts since the 1870's; territories between these points to a depth of about fifteen miles—the old Western and Central Districts of Lagos protectorate—where the laws of the colony were enforced by encroachment; the Yoruba states—Egba, Oyo, Ibadan—where limited jurisdiction was exercised; and finally, Ondo, Ilesha

[1] 'The anomaly existed that though the District Court was the higher tribunal, it had the lesser powers. Sitting as a commissioner of the Supreme Court, the district commissioner's powers were strictly limited, and his cases were subject to review by the puisne judge, while as president of the Native Court he could award a sentence of two years' imprisonment or £100 fine, however junior his rank.' Lugard, *Political Memoranda*, pp. 266–7.

[2] Burns, p. 225 n.

[3] N.R.O., 'Administrative Policy in Yoruba States (Western Province) 1912–1913', Memorandum, 1 Aug. 1911.

and Mekko where the rights of the Crown were in every respect extremely doubtful. The provincial commissioners, when asked for their views, recommended purely and simply the extension of the powers of the Supreme Court and the laws of the colony to every quarter hitherto untouched. As Commissioner Barnes pointed out, such an extension would in some cases have been a recognition of administrative practice.[1] At Ibadan, Oshogbo, and Ijebu Ode, the District Commissioners' Courts were already applying the laws of the colony to natives and non-natives alike—in civil as well as criminal cases; at Oyo there were occasional sessions in the name of the Supreme Court held by the resident and close supervision of the *Alafin*'s court. At all these places there was a Native Council, used by the resident official as a supplement. In Ondo the district commissioner sat in the Native Council for murder and manslaughter cases; but no records were kept for civil cases when he was not there, and fees collected were subject to no kind of audit. At Ilesha the Native Council was left to its own devices. At Badagri, Epe, and Ikorodu there never had been Native Councils for judicial purposes. Throughout the Western Province, reported Barnes, 'bribery and extortion is rampant' in the Native Courts where, too often, the native clerk and interpreter assumed a role far in excess of his prescribed functions.

Finally, there was the problem posed by Chief Justice Liontel in Dahomey, and no less true of Southern Nigeria by 1913. If the commissioners presided over Native Councils, could officers of the professional judiciary reverse their decisions? The answer given by Chief Justice Osborne differed radically from that of the creole judge. On the whole Osborne was opposed to extending civil jurisdiction of the Supreme Court either directly or through a system of appeals to a people unfamiliar with English law and legal process— for much the same reason as Governor Liotard: there was a risk of 'needless friction with the executive' where decisions might have to be reversed. In Dahomey there had been a compromise system evolved which ran counter to the French principle of separation of powers—not unlike the Provincial Court system practised in Northern Nigeria. For both colonies, whatever the distinction between subjects and citizens and however much the difference in approach to

[1] N.R.O., 'Administrative Policy in Yoruba States (Western Province) 1912–1913', Barnes, Memorandum, 14 Mar. 1913; Provincial Commissioner James, Memorandum, 12 Feb. 1913.
[2] Lugard, *The Dual Mandate*, pp. 540–1.

the problem of the codification of customary law, there was a basic 'collaboration des professionnels et des non-professionnels dans les tribunaux répressifs' which stemmed from a common recognition of the fact that administrators were judges, trained, advised, and if necessary, corrected, by a colonial judiciary.[1]

By 1913, when the commissioners felt themselves able to administer the laws of the colony and were more in favour of a massive increase of the powers of the Supreme Court than the chief justice of that court himself, Lugard had already arrived as governor-general with instructions to amalgamate the heterogeneous provinces of Southern Nigeria with Northern Nigeria. In 1914 the process by which contiguous colonies under different European administrations were drawn into wider political units was complete. Amalgamation and federation, as Lugard later pointed out, raised separate administrative problems;[2] but there were similar considerations behind the creation of A.O.F. between 1898 and 1904 and the unitary colony of Nigeria a decade later. The need to remove internal tariff barriers and make over a share of revenue levied at the coast to the administration of the interior was one. Lugard's own principles of 'decentralization and continuity'—either at the level of the colonial capital (as opposed to the distant metropolis), or at the level of the provincial residency (as opposed to the colonial capital)—were others.[3] A third consideration was the desire for an all-embracing native policy.

After 1914 the Southern Provinces became a testing-ground, particularly in the west, for principles deduced from practice in the emirates. But this was only in part a result of Lugard's own approach to the task of encouraging co-operation from indigenous authorities. A tendency to fix on and expand a paramountcy as a suitable vehicle for passing on orders to subordinate authorities had already existed in the practice of administrators in the Western Protectorate before 1914.

The capital example was the *Alafin* of Oyo whose position both in relation to the provincial commissioner and Lagos, on the one hand, and the *Bale* of Ibadan, on the other, was strikingly modified in the course of two decades. Carter in 1893 had noted that Oyo was only the 'sentimental' capital of Yorubaland, and the *Alafin* its recognized head, so long as he did not interfere with the war

[1] Louis Rolland et al. (eds.), *Législation et finances coloniales* (Paris, 1930), p. 131.
[2] Lugard, *The Dual Mandate*, pp. 98–99.
[3] Ibid., pp. 94 ff. Also all the French West African colonies were contiguous territories at some point of their boundaries.

chiefs at Ibadan.[1] In 1904 when Supreme Court jurisdiction was extended to Ibadan, care was taken to obtain the sanction of the *Alafin*, though it was understood that the only basis for a confederation in the Oyo area was the military alliance between Ogbomosho, Ikirun, Iwo and Ede, under the *Balogun* of Ibadan. Nevertheless, MacGregor's policy was to build up the *Alafin*'s authority as a counterpoise; and in 1904 Parsons, as acting-resident at Ibadan wrote, in compliance with the governor's views:

A settled policy should, I respectfully submit, be prescribed to the Resident (or Residents) and Commissioners in the *hinterland* in pursuance of which both the general authority of the Alafin of Oyo, as King of Yoruba land, and the more vaguely traditional influence of the Oni of Ife, as the fetish head-centre of the country, or a sort of Pagan archbishop, should be steadily fostered. Both these chiefs are more willingly amenable to our influence than are either the turbulent municipality, or old war-camp of the Ibadan chiefs, or the corrupted and almost disloyal sub-nationality of the Egbas.[2]

This rash assessment contained the seeds which were carefully cultivated by Commissioner Ross, posted to Oyo in 1906, who requested the *Alafin*'s stipend be increased to make up for the unwillingness of the Ibadan Yoruba to pay tribute. The following year the *Bale* of Ibadan was severely reprimanded and put on 'probation for six months' for usurping certain of the *Alafin*'s traditional prerogatives and for preventing cases from being heard at his court. The idea of Oyo as the head of a Yoruba federation received a salutary check in 1911 when Captain Elgee pointed out that Ibadan, Ijebu, Ilesha, Ondo, and Mekko, had only ceremonial relations with Oyo, while the intransigent Egba treated the *Alafin* as an equal 'brother ruler'. But by 1914 the seed planted by MacGregor and tended by Parsons and Ross was nourished by the example of the emirates. *Bale* Irifin was deposed for organizing a petition against the *Alafin*, and Provincial Commissioners Grier and Ross, backed by Lieutenant-Governor Boyle 're-established' the principle that Ibadan and its subsidiary villages owed tribute to Oyo. Lugard was more hesitant, indicating that the policy of twenty years of 'disintegration' of paramount authority was to be reversed only 'very gradually'. But in 1916 Deputy-Governor Temple defined the *Bale* as 'a District Head under the *Alafin* of Oyo' who had been allowed to break away

[1] C.O. 147/89, Carter to Ripon, 11 Oct. 1893.
[2] N.R.O., ADM/91383, Parsons to Moseley, 23 July 1904.

by earlier and uncomprehending officials, and who needed no more than 'a little stronger push' to become 'just as amenable to the orders of the *Alafin* as any District Head is to his Emir in the N.P.'.[1] The principle of the paramountcy of Oyo was then adopted by the governor-general himself and enshrined in the *Political Memoranda*.[2] An uprising in Ibadan and at Iseyin and Okeho in 1916 against the introduction of courts whose revenue went to Oyo was suppressed; and by 1925 the *Bale* and three senior chiefs in the largest town in West Africa were appointed and confirmed by the *Alafin* at provincial headquarters thirty miles to the north.

The irony of indirect rule in the Yoruba states was that it had to be enforced by direct interference. But Nigeria was not alone in providing examples of the search for principles of uniform application. As the period of expansion and experiment passed into the era of the governors-general with their plethora of technical services, complex budgets, over-burdered secretariats, and extensive powers of co-ordination, pragmatism gave way to administration by precedent. The day of Lugard or Brévié was also the day of the *Memoranda* and the *Circulaires*, those lengthy and enormously competent fiats whose phrases left much room for interpretation, but little for disagreement. They began slightly earlier in French West Africa than in the British colony. The first of significance for French policy (and the antithesis of Lugard's principles) was issued by Governor-General Ponty in 1909. It laid down what Ponty called 'une politique des races', by which he meant that great paramountcies were to be broken up by a policy 'qui consiste, non à morceler notre autorité sur la masse de nos sujets mais à la rendre plus tutélaire en établissant un contact plus direct entre l'administrateur et l'administré'.[3] Backed up by a second circular in 1911, this policy received its final touches in

---

[1] Cf. C. L. Temple's *Punch*-like, but acute, *Native Races and their Rulers. Sketches and Studies of Official Life and Administrative Problems in Nigeria* (Cape Town, 1918), pp. 67, 76–77.

[2] Lugard, *Political Memoranda*, No. 5, Jan. 1917, p. 177. 'The question of the future status of the Balès of the great cities, such as Ibadan, is one which merits special consideration. The course most in consonance with the history and traditions of the country, and the one most likely to result in a sound administrative organisation would seem to be that the whole of Ibadan and other divisions of Yoruba-land should be divided into districts under Headmen directly responsible to the Alafin, and hence independent of the Balè, who himself would rank as a District Head, responsible, in the case of Ibadan, for a city with a population of some 360,000 souls.' And ibid., No. 9, Nov. 1918, p. 305.

[3] Government-General, Dakar, 17 G 38, Ponty, 'Circulaire sur la Politique Indigène', Sept. 1909.

1913. Dahomey already provided examples of systematic removal of paramount chiefs, and much of Ponty's directive had been foreshadowed by Lieutenant-Governor Liotard between 1900 and 1901. But the major objection to a 'politique des races'—shortage of personnel to make closer contact with the population at village level —was felt in Dahomey as everywhere in A.O.F. and was aggravated by the First World War.

The war, accompanied by a campaign of forced recruitment, provided some serious shocks to the Dahomey administration. Though the bulk of the population in the south gave little trouble and practised passive resistance to recruiting, the Anago and Dje (Holli-Yoruba) of the Pobe area were in open revolt by 1915 and were only suppressed after two expeditions.[1]

Besides the realization that the native policy of Ponty was not universally applicable, administrators also learned by experience that even when it was applied they could not be certain that appointment of chiefs was a sure method of eliminating traditional lineage authorities. Even in such a closely supervised *cercle* as Porto-Novo an assistant administrator doubted the effectiveness of previous policy by 1918:

Les chefs de village sont choisis au petit bonheur. A part quelques exceptions ils n'ont aucune autorité. Très souvent le chef de village est le plus miséreux de la localité; quelquefois un ancien captif que le propriétaire du sol a conservé sur son terrain qu'il continue à travailler, et pour s'éviter les tracas de l'administration exigeante, l'a élevé au rang du chef. Quelle autorité peuvent-ils avoir après cela? Ils sont chefs pour les blancs et n'ont qu'une fonction—recevoir les instructions des deux côtés. Il faut reconnaître que lorsqu'on lui inflige une amende, c'est la collectivité qui paie; mais s'il est puni de prison c'est lui seul qui en souffre. Il existe cependant dans chaque village un chef véritable. Celui-là est rarement connu par nous et ne tient aucunement à se faire connaître.[2]

---

[1] P.N., Noufflard, 'Rapport d'ensemble de l'Année 1915', ff. 5–8. Chief Otutubiodjo was arrested and exiled to Mauretania for ten years. Others who fled to Nigeria were sent back by the British administration. Ibid., f. 10.

[2] P.N., Michelangeli, 'Rapport sur la situation administrative et politique du secteur Porto-Novo-Banlieue', 1918, ff. 5–6. Cf. Robert Delavignette, *Freedom and Authority in French West Africa* (Oxford, 1950), pp. 71–84. This dual-authority structure at village level is less true of chiefs at canton level, even after 1918, in French West Africa.

Governors, Commissioners, Administrators, &c.

Settlement of Lagos

1862	Governor	H. S. Freeman
1863	Lieutenant-Governor	Capt. W. R. Mulliner
1864	,, ,,	John H. Glover, R.N.

Administrators, settlement of Lagos, subject under commission, 19 February 1866, to the governor of the West African settlements, Sierra-Leone

1866	Administrator	Rear-Admiral C. G. E. Patey
1866	,,	John H. Glover, R.N.
1870	Acting-Administrator	H. T. Miles Cooper
1870	Administrator	John H. Glover, R.N.
1870	Acting-Administrator	W. H. Simpson
1871	,, ,,	J. Gerrard
1872	,, ,,	Henry Fowley
1872	Administrator	George Berkley
1873	Acting-Administrator	C. C. Lees
1873	Administrator	Capt. G. C. Strahan
1874	Acting-Administrator	John Shaw

Lieutenant-governors of Lagos, subject under letters patent, 24 July 1874, to the governor of the Gold Coast Colony

1874	Lieutenant-Governor	C. C. Lees
1875	Acting-Administrator	John D'A. Dumaresq
1878	,, ,,	F. Simpson, M.B.
1878	,, ,,	Malcolm J. Brown
1878	,, ·,,	C. A. Moloney
1880	Lieutenant-Governor	W. Brandford Griffith, C.M.G.
1880	Acting-Administrator	C. D. Turton

Deputy governors of Lagos under letters patent, 22 January 1883

1883	Deputy Governor	C. A. Moloney, C.M.G.
1883	,, ,,	Fred Evans, C.M.G.
1883	,, ,,	W. Brandford Griffith, C.M.G.
1884	,, ,,	Comr. R. Murray Rumsey
1884	,, ,,	Capt. R. Knapp Barrow, C.M.G.
1885	,, ,,	C. Pike

Governors of Lagos Colony, under letters patent, 13 January 1886

1886	Governor	C. A. Moloney, C.M.G.
1886	Administrator	Fred Evans, C.M.G.
1887	Governor	C. A. Moloney, C.M.G.
1889	Administrator	Capt. G. C. Denton, C.M.G.
1890	Governor	Sir C. A. Moloney, K.C.M.G.
1890	Administrator	Capt. G. C. Denton, C.M.G.
1891	Governor	G. T. Carter
1893	Administrator	Capt. G. C. Denton, C.M.G.
1893	Governor	Sir G. T. Carter
1895	Administrator	Capt. G. C. Denton, C.M.G.
1896	Governor	Sir G. T. Carter
1896	Administrator	F. Rohrweger
1896	,,	W. B. Griffith
1896	,,	Capt. G. C. Denton, C.M.G.
1897	,,	Lieut.-Col. Sir H. E. McCallum
1898	,,	Capt. G. C. Denton, C.M.G.
1899	Governor	Sir W. MacGregor
1900	Administrator	Sir G. C. Denton, K.C.M.G.
1901	Governor	Sir W. MacGregor
1902	Administrator	H. Reeve
1902	,,	C. H. H. Moseley
1903	Governor	Sir W. MacGregor
1904	Administrator	C. H. H. Moseley
1904	Governor	W. Egerton
1906	Administrator	J. J. Thorburn
1906	Governor	Sir W. Egerton

Governors and administrators of the colony and protectorate of Southern Nigeria, 1 May 1906

1906	Governor	Sir W. Egerton
1906	Administrator	W. F. W. Fosbery
1906	Governor	Sir W. Egerton
1907	Acting-Governor	J. J. Thorburn
1907	Governor	Sir W. Egerton
1908	Acting-Governor	J. J. Thorburn
1909	Governor	Sir W. Egerton
1910	Acting-Governor	J. J. Thorburn
1910	Governor	Sir W. Egerton
1911	Acting-Governor	A. G. Boyle
1911	Governor	Sir W. Egerton
1912	Acting-Governor	F. S. James
1912	Governor	Sir F. J. D. Lugard

Residents of the territory of Cotonou, attached in 1879 to the colony of Gabon, and in 1886 to the Guinea establishments

1883	Resident	B. Colonna de Lecca
1883	,,	Henry Guilman

Residents of the Territory of Cotonou and the Protectorate of Porto-Novo, French establishments in the Gulf of Guinea

1883	Resident	D. Germa
1884	,,	Léopold Maignot
1884	Military Resident	Colonel D. Dorat
1885	Commandant Cotonou	Lieutenant Roget
1886	Military Commandant	Colonel D. Dorat
1886	,, ,,	Lieutenant Roget

Lieutenant-governors on mission and residents, French Guinea establishments, by decree 16 June 1886, under the governor of Senegal and dependencies

1886	Lieutenant-Governor	Jean Bayol
1887	Resident and Commandant	Dr. Pereton
1887	,, ,, ,,	Victor Ballot
1888	Administrator	De Beckmann
1889	,,	Dr. Tautain

Lieutenant-governors on mission and residents, by decree 1 August 1889, under the lieutenant-governor of the South Rivers possessions (residing at Conakry)

1889	Lieutenant-Governor	Jean Bayol
1890	Resident	Ehrmann
1892	Lieutenant-Governor	Victor Ballot
1892	Commander-in-Chief	Colonel Dodds

Governors of Dahomey and dependencies by decree, 10 March 1893, and decree, 22 June 1894

1893	Governor	Victor Ballot
1900	Acting-Governor	Pascal

Lieutenant-governors of Dahomey, by decree, 1 October 1902, and decree, 18 October 1904, under the governor-general, French West Africa

1900	Governor	V. Liotard
1902	Lieutenant-Governor	Liotard
1906	,, ,,	Marchal
1908	,, ,,	Peuvergne
1909	,, ,,	Mallan

1911 Lieutenant-Governor   Merwart
1912–17   ,,   ,,   Ch. Noufflard

Commissioners, Landeshauptmänner, *and governors of Togo*

1885 Commissioner   E. Falkenthal
1889   ,,   Jesko von Puttkamer
1893 *Landeshauptmann*
1895   ,,   ,,   ,,   ,,
1898 Governor   August Köhler
1905   ,,   ,,   ,,
1911   ,,   Julius Graf Zech
1912–14   ,,   Edmund Brückner
                             Herzog zu Mecklenburg

APPENDIX II

The Togo Protectorate Treaty[1]

Bagida, July 5th 1884

THE Consul General of the German Empire, Dr. Gustav Nachtigal, in the name of H.M. the Emperor of Germany and Mlapa, King of Togo, represented by Plakkoo, bearer of king Mlapa's stick, for himself and his heirs and chiefs, have made on this day the following agreement.

1.

King Mlapa of Togo, desirous to protect the legitimate trade made in this country principally by German merchants, and to guarantee them full security of life and property begs the protection of H.M. the German Emperor, so that he may become able to maintain the independency of his territory, situated on the West Coast of Africa from the eastern frontier of Porte Seguro to the western frontier of Lome or Beybeach.

H.M. the German Emperor grants his protection provided all legal rights of others [sic].

2.

King Mlapa will not ceed any part of his territory with rights of sovereignty to any foreign power or person nor will he make treaties with foreign powers without previous consent of H.M. the German Emperor.

3.

King Mlapa grants every protection and free trade to all German subjects and protegees residing in his country and will never give to any person of other nations more facilities, favors or protection than those bestowed on German subjects or protegees.

King Mlapa will not raise any other duties or taxes than customary till now, without previous agreement with H.M. the German Emperor, i.e. one shilling for each ton of Palmkernels one shilling for each cask of Palm Oil payable to the respective local chiefs.

4.

His Maj. the Emperor of Germany will respect all previous commercial treaties between King Mlapa and others and will not incumber in any way the free trade now existing in king Mlapa's territory.

[1] A microfilmed copy of this treaty is available at the *Bundesarchiv*, Koblenz, in RI/I, No. 8, 31–33. The above is from a photostat of an authorized copy in the possession of Sebastian D'Mlapa, Chief of Togoville, by courtesy of Dr. G. Jantzen, Handelskammer, Hamburg.

5.

H.M. the Emperor of Germany will not interfere with the practise of collecting duties which has been followed until now by King Mlapa and his chiefs.

6.

The contracting parties reserve to themselves their future agreement about matters, questions etc. of mutual interest, not included in this treaty.

7.

This treaty will enter into power at once provided the ratification by the German Government.

In faith of which we have hereunto set our hands in presence of the undersigned witnesses.

Witnesses

J. J. Salu ⎫	Chief Plakkoo
⎬ as interpreters	X his mark
J. B. Ahjevon ⎭ .	Chief Adey of Bey
	X his mark
H. Randad	Coodayee
	X his mark
Dr. Max Buchner	Nadzi, 2d Chief of Beye
	X his mark
Mandt	Okloo
Lieutenant z. See	X his mark
	King Garsa of Bagida
	X his mark
	Nakoo
	X his mark
Josua Lenze	Dr. G. Nachtigal
	Consul General, Imperial
	Commissioner for the West
	Coast of Africa.

Mit dem Original übereinstimmend
von Hagen,
Kaiserlicher Kommissariats-Sekretär.

Export of Palm Products

Lagos Colony

	Palm oil (tons)	Palm kernels (tons)
1862 . .	1,763	..
1863 . .	4,538	2,665
1864 . .	3,878	4,511
1865 . .	3,800	2,630
1866 . .	6,397	7,216
1867 . .	5,473	13,619
1868 . .	4,869	15,498
1869 . .	5,903	20,394
1870 . .	5,841	15,894
1871 . .	5,961	19,375
1872 . .	4,337	25,870
1873 . .	3,208	16,410
1874 . .	4,610	25,192
1875 . .	6,009	26,455
1876 . .	6,641	30,306
1877 . .	11,016	30,675
1878 . .	5,133	27,874
1879 . .	8,231	26,841
1880 . .	4,988	29,632
1881 . .	6,024	20,801
1882 . .	8,791	28,591
1883 . .	6,571	25,820
1884 . .	7,942	29,802
1885 . .	8,859	30,805
1886 . .	10,322	34,812
1887 . .	8,354	35,784
1888 . .	8,225	43,525
1889 . .	7,830	32,715
1890 . .	10,669	38,829
1891 . .	14,016	42,342
1892 . .	8,194	32,180
1893 . .	13,576	51,456
1894 . .	11,311	53,534
1895 . .	12,754	46,501
1896 . .	10,514	47,649
1897 . .	6,196	41,299
1898 . .	6,277	42,775
1899 . .	10,976	49,501
1900 . .	9,926	48,514
1901 . .	11,013	57,176
1902 . .	17,466	75,416
1903 . .	10,580	63,568
1904 . .	10,654	69,288
1905 . .	9,219	45,177
Southern Nigeria		
1906 . .	57,260	113,347
1907 . .	65,473	133,630
1908 . .	65,460	136,558
1909 . .	82,130	158,849
1910 . .	77,000	173,000
1911 . .	79,000	176,000
1912 . .	77,000	185,000
1913 . .	83,000	175,000

Dahomey

	Palm oil (tons)	Palm kernels (tons)
1891 .. .	6,616	16,254
1892 . .	5,045	15,597
1893 . .	7,500	20,823
1894 . .	8,318	24,063
1895 . .	12,438	21,178
1896 . .	5,525	25,152
1897 . .	4,077	12,875
1898 . .	6,059	17,991
1899 . .	9,650	21,851
1900 . .	8,920	21,986
1901 . .	11,291	24,212
1902 . .	12,676	29,778
1903 . .	6,937	21,685
1904 . .	8,369	25,997
1905 . .	5,637	17,480
1906 . ,	6,378	18,825
1907 . .	7,835	18,811
1908 . .	9,521	23,036
1909 . .	15,016	33,224
1910 . .	14,628	34,784
1911 . .	15,252	39,346
1912 . .	11,917	37,296
1913 . .	7,971	26,375

Togo

	Palm oil (tons)	Palm kernels (tons)
1892 . .	1,537	7,117
1893 . .	2,959	6,802
1894 . .	2,460	8,175
1895 . .	2,466	9,022
1896 . .	566	6,320
1897 . .	294	2,498
1898 . .	445	3,667
1899 . .	1,944	5,818
1900 . .	2,199	6,330
1901 . .	2,998	7,756
1902 . .	2,973	9,443
1903 . .	1,025	4,831
1904 . .	939	5,658
1905 . .	425	3,200
1906 . .	469	3,434
1907 . .	998	4,346
1908 . .	1,359	5,121
1909 . .	2,779	8,013
1910 . .	3,696	8,216
1911 . .	4,013	13,286
1912 . .	3,337	11,639
1913 . .	1,174	7,139

APPENDIX IV

Revenue and Expenditure

Lagos Colony

	Revenue (£)	Expenditure (£)		Revenue (£)	Expenditure (£)
1862 . .	7,130	6,510	1889 . .	57,633	57,488
1863 . .	16,708	15,837	1890 . .	56,340	63,700
1864 . .	21,335	22,805	1891 . .	78,624	66,388
1865 . .	24,081	24,095	1892 . .	68,421	86,513
1866 . .	23,816	23,602	1893 . .	115,317	101,251
1867 . .	29,974	30,195	1894 . .	137,017	124,829
1868 . .	33,895	33,711	1895 . .	142,049	144,483
1869 . .	40,438	39,431	1896 . .	179,754	168,444
1870 . .	41,638	42,379	1897 . .	177,953	182,668
1871 . .	45,612	45,611	1898 . .	206,444	203,802
1872 . .	41,346	41,346	1899 . .	192,791	223,289
1873 . .	52,240	52,225	1900 . .	209,205	200,336
1874 . .	39,335	37,297	1901 . .	238,536	224,927
1875 . .	43,336	44,379	1902 . .	364,154	225,490
1876 . .	46,448	45,170	1903 . .	333,370	310,090
1877 . .	59,389	42,305	1904 . .	338,124	325,188
1878 . .	50,889	49,736	1905 . .	379,684	414,633
1879 . .	54,939	45,934		Southern Nigeria	
1880 . .	47,987	55,475	1906 . .	1,088,717	1,056,290
1881 . .	42,421	45,461	1907 . .	1,459,554	1,217,337
1882 . .	44,636	44,039	1908 . .	1,387,915	1,357,763
1883 . .	50,558	37,879	1909 . .	1,361,891	1,648,681
1884 . .	57,932	44,693	1910 . .	1,933,235	1,592,282
1885 . .	63,504	40,313	1911 . .	1,956,176	1,717,259
1886 . .	53,507	55,383	1912 . .	2,235,412	2,110,498
1887 . .	51,346	78,610	1913 . .	2,668,198	2,096,311
1888 . .	57,057	60,840			

Dahomey

	Revenue (Fr.)	Expenditure (Fr.)		Revenue (Fr.)	Expenditure (Fr.)
1890 . .	325,220	[1]	1902 . .	5,764,918	4,825,799
1891 . .	460,523	[1]	1903 . .	5,280,481	4,959,760
1892 . .	639,005	[1]	1904 . .	4,499,952	4,555,987
1893 . .	1,046,067	[1]	1905 . .	3,207,704	2,950,125
1894 . .	2,021,082	[1]	1906 . .	4,420,981	4,338,558
1895 . .	1,695,207	[1]	1907 . .	3,538,946	3,462,204
1896 . .	1,673,474	[1]	1908 . .	3,289,507	3,070,086
1897 . .	1,914,515	2,163,922	1909 . .	3,469,679	3,467,717
1898 . .	2,409,915	2,418,644	1910 . .	3,599,566	3,434,719
1899 . .	2,709,511	2,143,796	1911 . .	4,462,995	4,181,861
1900 . .	3,414,237	2,991,528	1912 . .	4,916,746	2,901,736
1901 . .	4,513,611	2,785,039	1913 . .	4,923,202	4,541,770

[1] Incomplete before 1897.

Togo

	Revenue (M.)	Expenditure (M.)		Revenue (M.)	Expenditure (M.)
1885 . .	..	48,300	1900 . .	753,000	1,157,000
1886 . .	..	98,300	1901 . .	1,878,000	1,422,000
1887 . .	46,300	93,400	1902 . .	1,650,000	1,021,000
1888 . .	97,700	108,400	1903 . .	2,249,000	1,702,000
1889 . .	94,400	123,300	1904 . .	5,268,000	4,709,000
1890 . .	96,000	129,400	1905 . .	5,441,000	5,413,000
1891 . .	150,900	167,400	1906 . .	2,847,000	2,660,000
1892 . .	220,400	204,400	1907 . .	2,201,000	2,075,000
1893 . .	221,700	245,700	1908 . .	2,610,000	2,980,000
1894 . .	376,600	410,200	1909 . .	3,110,000	2,719,000
1895 . .	382,000	388,700	1910 . .	2,457,000	2,451,000
1896 . .	303,100	345,500	1911 . .	3,216,000	3,216,000
1897–8 . .	301,000	492,000	1912 . .	3,150,000	3,150,000
1898 . .	384,000	692,000	1913 . .	4,031,000	4,201,000
1899 . .	856,000	851,000			

List of Sources

THE following list is no more than its title suggests. It includes only archive series and publications cited in notes to the text and works that have been of substantial help to me.

I. PRIMARY

(a) Unpublished Manuscripts in European and African Archives

BRITISH

Public Record Office, London

Admiralty I: In-Letters, 1816–63, from officers of the West African Squadron; surveys; charts; correspondence from traders and consuls.

C.O. 96: Gold Coast, Original Correspondence, 1874–86.

C.O. 147: Lagos, Original Correspondence, 1861–1906.

C.O. 151: *Blue Books*, prior to 1879.

C.O. 806: Africa, Confidential Prints.

F.O. 2: Consular Correspondence.

F.O. 84: Slave Trade, General Correspondence, 1816–92.

F.O. 403: Africa and Slave Trade, Confidential Prints.

Methodist Missionary Society Archives, London

Correspondence from missionaries on the West Coast of Africa, and journals under 2/4. Also uncatalogued: Thomas Birch Freeman, ['History of West Africa'], n.d., an untitled typescript of the original.

Nigerian Record Office, Ibadan

Badagry Letter-Books, 1871–99; Badagry Minute Book, 1887–9; Duplicate Correspondence; Badagry Intelligence Reports; Political Notes; District Commissioners' Diary, 1897–1901, 1913; Badagry: Record of Cases in the Petty Debt Court holden at Badagry in the Settlement of Lagos; Civil Commandants' Court Record Book, 1867–77; Gold Coast Commissioners' Civil Court Record Book, 1878–87; Badagry Criminal Record Books, 1878–88.

Consulate Letter-Book, 1855–60, and 1856.

Dispatches to Secretaries of State, 1861–99; Confidential Dispatches, 1881–93.

Government House Archives: Administrative Policy in Yoruba States (Western Province) 1912–13; Miscellaneous ADM/91373, and 91383; Papers relating to the Opening Up of Lagos Protectorate, 1890–1906.

Governor's Letter-Book, 1862–70; Secretariat Letter-Book, 1872–84.

CMS. ECC. 1/524, Instructions of the Committee to missionaries.

CSO. 33/1776, Herbert Macaulay, Inquiry into the House of Decemo.

University College, Ibadan

Central Native Council Minutes, 1901–13; Egba Documents.

PUGH, J. C., 'The Porto-Novo–Badagri Sand Ridge Complex', in 'Research Notes', No. 3, Department of Geography.

THOMAS, E. V. S., 'Historical Survey of the Towns of Ilaro, Ilobi, Ajilite and Ilashe in the Ilaro Division' (typescript, 4 January 1933).

FRENCH

Government-General Archives, Dakar

Affaires Financières T. 30; Conseil de Gouvernement de l'A.O.F. 5 E 26–29; Politique indigène 17 G 38; Régime fiscal, Impôts S 15; Statistique 22 G 11–31.

Ministère des Affaires Étrangères, Paris

Mémoires et documents, Afrique: Établissements Français du Golfe de Guinée 51–54, 76–83, 125–7 (1838–94); Possessions Anglaises de la Côte Occidentale 55–57, 86, 128–31 (1819–94); Possessions Allemandes de la Côte Occidentale 95–96, 134 (1884–95).

Affaires diplomatiques, Angleterre, Freetown, Sierra Léone 11, 27, 53, 70–74, 81–82, 107 (1864–93).

Correspondance commerciale, Sierra Léone 2–4 (1867–1901).

Ministère de la France d'Outre-Mer, Paris

Afrique: Affaires diplomatiques VI; Expansion territoriale et Politique indigène IV; Justice VIII.

Dahomey: Affaires diplomatiques, Allemagne, Angleterre VI; Correspondance générale I; Expansion territoriale et Politique indigène IV; Travail et main-d'œuvre XV.

Gabon: Affaires diplomatiques VI; Commerce et industrie XIII; Correspondance générale I.

Sénégal et Dépendances: Affaires diplomatiques VI; Commerce et industrie XIII; Statistique XX.

Missions Africaines de Lyon, Rome

Dahomey Préfecture 12/80200 (1899–1901), correspondence and missionary journals.

Porto-Novo Archives (Institut Français d'Afrique Noire), Dahomey

[The archives are not catalogued. The following titles refer to folders and bound volumes of MSS.]

Correspondances adressées au Gouvernement-Général, 1900–2; Correspondance avec le Ministère des Colonies, 1895–1901; Correspondance Confidentielle, 1900–4; Correspondance télégraphique, 1899–1902; Correspondances, 1899–1904; Correspondance du Commandant Supérieur, 1893–7.

Rapports d'ensemble, 1901–14; Rapports mensuels: Abomey, 1891–1924; Allada, 1908–13; Affaires politiques, Abomey, Porto-Novo, 1893–1919.

Documents du Protectorat, I, II.

Manifestations, 1907–10.

GERMAN

Afrika-Verein, Hamburg

Protokolle des Vorstandes des Vereins Westafrikanischer Kaufleute, 1–3 (1902–34).

Auswärtiges Amt, Politisches Archiv, Bonn

[Microfilms of the following captured documents were consulted]

Deutsche Botschaft, London, 1199: C. Allg. Kolonialpolitik 1–5 (1885–7); C. Deutsche Kolonialpolitik (1888–90).

Bundesarchiv, Koblenz

R 1/1, 3, and 8, Instructions to Nachtigal, 1884; Treaty with King Mlapa, 1884.

[By permission of Dr. v. Vietsch,] Dr. W. H. Solf, 'Mittelafrikanisches Reisetagebuch' (28 August–13 October 1913).

Handelskammer, Bremen

KO/Colonisation: 1–2, 2a, 3, 5, 7, 8, 11, 16, 18–21, 23, 25, 26, 29; D 184; K 5/318, 344; A 302; Hp/II/100, III/D1; B 349, 390, 470. General commercial and colonial correspondence, Minutes, &c.

Handelskammer, Hamburg

84/A/1/1–3; 85/A/1/1–8; 85/A/3/3. Commercial and colonial correspondence, Minutes, Government circulars, &c.

Norddeutsche Missions-Gesellschaft, Bremen.

Missionary correspondence, Togo, 1a–98 (green series); 33, 41 (red series).

Staatsarchiv, Bremen

J. K. Vietor Papers; Adolf Lüderitz Papers (uncatalogued).

Staatsarchiv, Hamburg

CL. vi, No. 2, 4a/2/16; CL. vi, No. 15, 6/2 and 4, 5, 5b; No. 4, XIX. C. 19; XIX. B. 7/16/1e; No. 7, XIX. B. 7/1; XIX. B. 7.7/1. Correspondence with Hamburg traders in Lagos and Whydah; correspondence with the German Government; Minutes of meetings; Togo Protectorate; correspondence with Hanseatic Embassy, Berlin.

(*b*) *Government Publications, Historical Records, Newspapers*

African Trade Section of the Incorporated Chamber of Commerce of Liverpool. Reports. Liverpool, 1892–5.

Afrika. Berlin, 1897–1901.

Amtsblatt für das Schutzgebiet Togo. Lome, 1906–14.

Blue Books of Lagos Colony, 1879–1905.

British and Foreign Anti-Slavery Reporter, The, i–v, 1839–44; New Series, i–viii, 1845–50.

British Cotton Growing Association Correspondence. Oldham, 1902.

Bulletin de Renseignements sur la situation économique et politique de l'Afrique Occidentale Française. Dakar, 1921.

Chemins de fer de l'A.O.F. Paris, 1931.

Colonial Office List. London, 1862–1914.

Colonial Reports, as under:
1891, [C. 6837], No. 58, Lagos, Annual Report.
1899, [Cd. 3], No. 284, Lagos, Annual Report.
1901, [Cd. 788], No. 348, Lagos, Report for 1900–1.
1905, [Cd. 2648], No. 507, Southern Nigeria (Lagos).
1906–14, Southern Nigeria.
1922, [Cmd. 1698], Report on the British Mandated Sphere of Togoland for 1920–1.
1925, [C. 452 f.], Rapport annuel du gouvernement français sur l'administration sous mandat des territoires du Togo pour l'année 1924.
1925, Colonial No. 14, Report on the Administration under Mandate of British Togoland for the Year 1924.

Church Missionary Intelligencer, i–v. London, 1850–5.

Compte définitif des recettes et des dépenses du budget des fonds de l'emprunt de 65 millions, 1909–1912. Dakar, 1914.

Compte définitif des recettes et des dépenses du budget des fonds des emprunts de 65 et 100 millions. Dakar, 1917.

Dahomey. Rapport d'ensemble. Porto-Novo, 1895–1906.

Deutsches Kolonialblatt. Berlin, 1890–1918.

Deutsche Kolonialzeitung, i–xxxi. Frankfurt and Berlin, 1884–1915.

Deutsche Kolonialpolitik, I: Deutschland in Afrika und in der Südsee. Leipzig, 1885.

Deutschen Schutzgebiete in Afrika und in der Südsee, Die. Amtliche Jahresberichte, Reichs-Kolonialamt. Berlin, 1911–14.

DONNAN, E. (ed.), *Documents Illustrative of the History of the Slave Trade to America.* 4 vols. Washington, 1930–5.

Entwicklung unserer Kolonien, Sechs Denkschriften: I, Togo. Berlin, 1892.

FITZNER, RUDOLF (ed.), *Deutsches Kolonial-Handbuch.* Berlin, 1896.

FRANÇOIS, M. G. (ed.), *Le Gouvernement Général de l'Afrique Occidentale Française.* Paris, 1908.

50 Jahre Deutsche Kolonialgesellschaft (1882–1932). Berlin, 1932.

Haushalts-Etat für die Schutzgebiete. Berlin, 1907–14.

HERTSLET, SIR E. (ed.), *Treaties between Great Britain and Foreign Powers.* 31 vols. London, 1835–1926.

—— *The Map of Africa by Treaty.* 3 vols. London, 1894 and 1909.

Histoire dahoméenne de la fin du XIXᵉ siècle à travers les textes. Études dahoméennes, ix, Institut Français d'Afrique Noire. Porto-Novo, 1953.

JACOB, E. G. (ed.), *Deutsche Kolonialpolitik in Dokumenten.* Leipzig, 1938.

Jahresbericht über die Entwicklung der Deutschen Schutzgebiete. Berlin, 1895–1912.

Koloniale Rundschau, Monatsschrift für die Interessen unserer Schutz-gebiete und ihrer Bewohner. Berlin, 1909–14.

Kolonialwirtschaftliches Komitee. Deutsch-Koloniale Baumwoll-Unter-nehmungen, i–xii. Berlin, 1901–10.

Kolonialwirtschaftliches Komitee. Die Arbeit des Kolonialwirtschaftlichen Komitees, 1896–1914, Berlin, 1914.

Lagos Government Gazette, 1887–1905.

Lagos Observer. Used for 1882–8.

Lagos Times and Gold Coast Colony Advertiser. Used for 1880–95.

LUGARD, F., LORD, *Political Memoranda. Revision of Instructions to Politi-cal Officers on Subjects chiefly Political and Administrative, 1913–1918.* London, 1919.

MEINECKE, GUSTAV (ed.), *Koloniales Jahrbuch*. Berlin, 1888–97.

Missions catholiques, Les, used for nos. 281–2025. Paris, 1883–1908.

Nigeria. Legislative Council Sessional Papers, No. 1. Lagos, 1928.

Parliamentary Papers, as under:

  1842, xi, xii (551), Report: West Coast of Africa.

  1847–8, xxii (272), (366), (536), (623), Select Committee reports on the Slave Trade.

  1849, xxx, (169), Copy of Dispatches received from Captain Winniett, Lieutenant-Governor of Her Majesty's Settlements on the Gold Coast, relating to Recent Missions to Certain Princes in the Vicinity of those Settlements.

  1852, liv (221), Papers Relative to the Reduction of Lagos by Her Majesty's Forces on the West Coast of Africa.

  1854, lxv (296), Quantities of Palm-oil imported into the United King-dom, 1844–53.

  1862, lxi (339), Papers relating to the Occupation of Lagos.

  1865, xxxvii (170), West Coast of Africa, Colonel Ord's report.

  1865, v (412), Report of Select Committee on State of British Settlements on the West Coast of Africa.

  1870, 1 (444), Gambia, Correspondence on proposed cession to France.

  1874, lxx, [C. 1038], Statistical Tables Relating to the Colonial and other Possessions of the United Kingdom.

  1876, lii, [C. 1343], West Africa, Papers *re* H.M. possessions.

  1884, lvi, [C. 4052], Gold Coast, Further Correspondence.

  1890, li, [C. 5905], Anglo-French West African Agreement, 1889.

  1893–4, lxii, [C. 7227], Lagos, Report by Carter on Interior Expedition, 1893.

  1905, lvi, [Cd. 2325], Papers *re* construction of railways in Sierra Leone, Lagos, and Gold Coast.

PAYNE, O. (ed.), *A Lagos Almanack and Diary*. Lagos, 1877 and 1892.

Proceedings of the Church Missionary Society, for Africa and the East. Used for 1850–2. London, 1852.

Reichskolonialministerium. Deutsche und französische Eingeborenen-behandlung. Berlin, 1919.

Revue Coloniale. 2e série, xvi. Paris, 1856.

SCHEFER, CHRISTIAN (ed.), *Instructions générales données de 1763 à 1870 aux gouverneurs et ordonnateurs des Établissements français en Afrique occidentale.* 2 vols. Paris, 1927.

Southern Nigeria Handbook. Lagos, 1912.

SPEED, EDWIN ARNEY (ed.), *Laws of the Colony of Southern Nigeria.* 2 vols. London, 1908.

Togogebiet und Biafra-Bai. Bundesrath, No. 117, 1884. Berlin, 1884.

Tropenpflanzer, Der. Zeitschrift für tropische Landwirtschaft. Berlin, 1899–1914.

West African Year Book, 1901. London, 1901.

(c) Maps and Charts

CORTESÃO, ARMANDO, and TEIXEIRA DA MOTA, AVELINO (eds.), *Portugaliae Monumenta Cartographica*, i–iv. Lisboa, 1960.

FAGE, J. D., *An Atlas of African History.* London, 1958.

KAMAL, YOUSSOUF, *Monumenta Cartographica Africae et Aegypti.* 5 vols. Cairo, 1926–51.

MERCIER, PAUL (ed.), *Cartes ethno-démographiques de l'Afrique occidentale.* Institut Français d'Afrique Noire, No. 5. Dakar, 1956.

SILVEIRA, LUIS, *Portugal: Colonies. Collections of Plans and Views.* London, 1956.

'Carte de la Côte des Esclaves dressée par F. Borghero, Missionnaire, d'après ses reconnaissances et les documents les plus récents. 1865. Dédiée à Mr d'Avezac, Membre de l'Institut.' 1:920 000.

'Carte du Bas Dahomey et des Établissements Français du Golfe de Bénin par Alexandre L. d'Albéca, Administrateur Colonial, Officier d'Académie.' 1:200 000. 1889.

'Carte ethnographique et administrative du Dahomey.' 1:150 000. 1922.

'Côte des Esclaves dressée par l'Abbé Pierre Bouche.'   No scale. [1880?]

'Dahomey.' 1:200 000. 1914.

'Karte des Schutzgebietes Togo.' 1:125 000. 1913.

'Le Dahomey par Édouard Foà. Carte gravée par E. Morieu d'après les documents les plus récents.' 1:500 000. 1890.

Le Herissé, A. [Ethno-historical map of Dahomey.] No scale. 1911.

'Lome . . . von Heinrich Klose.' 1:7000. 1896.

'Map of the Colony of Lagos and Neighbouring Territories.' [With insets of Lagos and Abeokuta.] Intelligence Division, War Office. 1:506 880 1888.

Metzger, DR. O. F., 'Übersichtskarte der Kolonie Togo.' 1:1650 000. 1914.

'Northern and Southern Provinces of Nigeria.' War Office, No. 2437. 1:200 000. 1910.

'Plan de la ville de Porto-Novo.' 1916.

'Sketch Map of the Town of Lagos.' W. G. Lawson, Act.-Colonial Surveyor. No scale. 1884.

Spieth, 'Übersichtskarte von Süd Togo.' [Ethnic and linguistic distribution.] 1:100 000. 1906.

Trierenberg, 'Übersichtskarte von Togo und seinem Hinterlande.' 1:600 000. 1894.

'Victoria Lagoon.' F.O. 971. No scale. 1883.

II. SECONDARY

ADAMS, CAPT. JOHN, *Remarks on the Country extending from Cape Palmas to the River Congo, including observations on the Manners and Customs of the Inhabitants.* London, 1823.

—— *Sketches Taken During Ten Years Voyages to Africa between the years 1786–1800.* London, 1822.

AKINDÉLÉ, A., and AGUESSY, C. (eds.), *Contribution à l'étude de l'histoire de l'ancien royaume de Porto-Novo.* Mémoire de l'Institut Français d'Afrique Noire, No. 25. Dakar, 1953.

ALBÉCA, A. L. D', *Les Établissements français du Golfe de Bénin.* Paris, 1899.

ALMEIDA PRADO, J. F. DE, 'Les Relations de Bahia (Brésil), avec le Dahomey', *Revue d'histoire des colonies*, xli (1954), 167–226.

ARANJO, ANTÓNIO JOSÉ DE, *Colonies portugaises d'Afrique. Colonisation, émigration, déportation.* Lisbon, 1900.

ASMIS, DR., 'Die Stammesrechte des Bezirks Atakpame (Schutzgebiet Togo)', *Zeitschrift für Vergleichende Rechtswissenschaft*, xxv (1910), 67–130.

—— 'Die Stammesrechte der Bezirke Misahöhe, Anecho und Lome-Land (Schutzgebiet Togo)', *Zeitschrift für Vergleichende Rechtswissenschaft*, xxvi (1911), 1–133.

AVOSEH, T. OLA, *A Short History of Badagry.* Lagos, 1938.

AVRIL, ADOLPHE D', *La Côte des Esclaves: le Yoruba, le Dahomey.* Paris, 1889.

BAILLAUD, E. *La Politique indigène de l'Angleterre en Afrique occidentale.* Paris, 1912.

BALTZER, F. *Die Kolonialbahnen mit besonderer Berücksichtigung Afrikas.* Berlin, 1916.

BANDINEL, J., *Some Account of the Trade in Slaves from Africa as connected with Europe and America.* London, 1842.

BARRET, PAUL, *L'Afrique occidentale, la nature et l'homme noir.* Paris, 1888.

BASCOM, WILLIAM R., and HERSKOVITS, MELVILLE J. (eds.), *Continuity and Change in African Cultures.* Chicago, 1959.

BAUDIN, R. P. NOËL, 'La Guerre civile à Porto-Novo', *Les Missions catholiques*, Nos. 297, 298 (1875), pp. 82–83, 95–96.

BERBAIN, SIMONE, *Le Comptoir français de Juda (Ouidah) au XVIIIᵉ siècle.* Mémoire de l'Institut Français d'Afrique Noire, No. 3. Paris, 1942.

BERTHO, J., 'Adja-Tado. Races et langues du Bas-Dahomey et du Bas-Togo', *Notes africaines*, No. 26 (1945), pp. 22–24.

—— 'La Parenté des Yoruba aux peuplades de Dahomey et Togo', *Africa*, xix, No. 2 (1949), pp. 121–32.

BEURDELEY, G., 'Les Populations indigènes du Bas Dahomey', *A travers le monde*, Nos. 40, 46, 47, 48. Paris, 1901.

BIOBAKU, SABURI O., 'An Historical Sketch of Yoruba Traditional Authorities', *Africa*, xxii, No. 1 (1952), pp. 35–49.

—— *The Egba and their Neighbours 1842–1872*. Oxford, 1957.

—— 'The Egba Council 1899–1918', *Odù Journal of Yoruba and Related Studies*, No. 2 (1955), pp. 14–20.

BLAKE, JOHN W., *European Beginnings in West Africa 1454–1578*. London, 1937.

BOLD, LIEUT. EDWARD, R.N. (ed.), *The Merchants' and Mariners' African Guide; containing an accurate description of the Coast, Bays, Harbours, and adjacent Islands of West Africa*. London, 1822.

BOLLMANN, J., *Konzessionen und Monopole in den deutschen Schutzgebieten. Ein Rechtsgutachten*. Hannover, 1902.

BONNASSIEUX, PIERRE, *Les grandes compagnies de commerce. Étude pour servir à l'histoire de la colonisation*, Paris, 1892.

BOSMAN, WILLIAM, *A New and Accurate Description of the Coast of Guinea*, in John Pinkerton (ed.), *A General Collection of the Best and Most Interesting Voyages and Travels in all Parts of the World*, xvi. London, 1814.

BOUCHE, ABBÉ PIERRE, *Sept ans en Afrique occidentale. La Côte des Esclaves et le Dahomey*. Paris, 1885.

BOUËT-WILLAUMEZ, E., *Commerce et traite des noirs aux côtes occidentales d'Afrique*. Paris, 1848.

BRICOURT, J. DUCHÉ DE, *L'Évolution de la question douanière du Sénégal et dans ses anciennes dépendances (Guinée Française, Côte d'Ivoire, Dahomey et dépendances)*. Paris, 1902.

BRUNET, L., and GIETHLEN, L., *Dahomey et dépendances*. Paris, 1900.

BUELL, R. L. *The Native Problem in Africa*, i. New York, 1928.

BURNS, A. C., *History of Nigeria*. 3rd ed. London, 1942.

BURTON, R. F., *Abbeokuta and the Cameroons*. 2 vols. London, 1863.

—— *A Mission to Gèlele King of Dahome*. 2 vols. London, 1864.

—— *Wanderings in West Africa: from Liverpool to Fernando Po*. 2 vols. London, 1863.

BUTLER, J. R. M., 'Imperial Questions in British Politics, 1868–1880', in E. A. Benians, J. R. M. Butler, P. N. S. Mansergh, E. A. Walker (eds.), *The Cambridge History of the British Empire*, iii (Cambridge, 1959) 17–64.

CARTER, SIR GILBERT, 'The Colony of Lagos', *Proceedings of the Royal Colonial Institute*, xxviii (1896–7), 275–304.

COLEMAN, JAMES S., *Nigeria Background to Nationalism*. Berkely and Los Angeles, 1958.

CORDIERO, LUIANO (ed.), *Viagens, Explorações e Conquistas dos Portuguezes 1574–1620. Da Mina ao Cabo Negro segundo Garcia Mendes Castello Branco.* Lisboa, 1881.

—— *Viagens . . . 1516–1619. Escravos e Minas de Africa,* Lisboa, 1881.

—— *Viagens . . . 1607. Estabelecimentos e Resgates Portuguezes na Costa Occidental de África.* Lisboa, 1881.

CROOKS, J. J., *A History of the Colony of Sierra Leone Western Africa.* London, 1903.

DALZEL, ARCHIBALD, *The History of Dahomey, An Inland Kingdom of Africa; compiled from Authentic Memoirs; with an Introduction and Notes.* London, 1793.

DAVIES, K. G., *The Royal African Company.* London, 1957.

DELAVIGNETTE, ROBERT, *Freedom and Authority in French West Africa.* Oxford, 1950.

DENHAM, MAJOR, CLAPPERTON, CAPT., and OUDNEY, DR., *Travels and Discoveries in Northern and Central Africa in 1822, 1823, 1824.* 4 vols. London, 1831.

DENNÉE, J., *L'Afrique au XVIᵉ siècle et le commerce anversois.* Anvers, 1937.

DIEHN, DR. OTTO, 'Kaufmannschaft und deutsche Eingeborenenpolitik in Togo und Kamerun. Von der Jahrhundertwende bis zum Ausbruch des Weltkrieges.' (Unpublished doctoral thesis), Hamburg, 1956.

DIKE, K. O., *Trade and Politics in the Niger Delta, 1830–1885.* Oxford, 1956.

DOMINIK, HANS, *Kamerun.* Berlin, 1901.

DU CASSE, ANDRÉ, *Les Négriers ou le traffic des esclaves.* Paris, 1938.

DUNCAN, JOHN, *Travels in Western Africa in 1845 and 1846, comprising a Journey from Whydah through the Kingdom of Dahomey to Adofoodia in the Interior.* 2 vols. London, 1847.

DUNGLAS, E., 'Contribution à l'histoire du Moyen-Dahomey (Royaumes d'Abomey, de Kétou et de Ouidah)', *Études dahoméennes,* xix, xx, xxi. Institut Français d'Afrique Noire, Porto-Novo, 1957–8.

EGHAREVBA, CHIEF J., *A Short History of Benin.* Lagos, 1953.

ELIAS, T. OLAWALE, *Groundwork of Nigerian Law.* London, 1954.

EPSTEIN, K., 'Erzberger and the German Colonial Scandals, 1905–1910', *English Historical Review,* lxxiv, no. 293 (1959), pp. 637–63.

FAULONG, L., *Les Rapports financiers de la métropole et de l'Afrique Occidentale Française depuis 1825.* Paris, 1910.

FOÀ, ÉDOUARD, *Le Dahomey.* Paris, 1895.

FORBES, COMMANDER F. E., *Dahomey and Dahomans.* 2 vols. London, 1851.

FORDE, DARYLL, 'The Cultural Map of West Africa: Successive Adaptations to Tropical Forests and Grasslands', *Transactions of the New York Academy of Sciences,* Series II, xv (1953), 206–19.

FORTES, M., *The Dynamics of Clanship among the Tallensi.* Oxford, 1945.

FRANKEL, S. HERBERT, *Capital Investment in Africa its Course and Effects.* Oxford, 1938.

FREEMAN, T. B., *Journal of Various Visits to the Kingdoms of Ashanti, Aku, and Dahomi, in Western Africa.* 2nd ed. London, 1844.

FULL, A., *Fünfzig Jahre Togo* (*Koloniale Fragen im Dritten Reich*). Berlin, 1935.

GEARY, SIR W. N. M., *Nigeria under British Rule*. London, 1927.

GEAY, J., 'Origine, formation et histoire du royaume de Porto-Novo d'après une légende orale des Porto-Noviens', *Bulletin commercial et historique et scientifique de l'A.O.F.* vii (1924), 619–34.

GIESE, DR. F., 'Die Rechtsverhältnisse des aufgelösten Kolonialrats', *Zeitschrift für Kolonialpolitik, Kolonialrecht und Kolonialwirtschaft*, x, no. 5 (1908), pp. 339–41.

GOLLMER, CHARLES, *Life and Missionary Labour in West Africa*. London, 1889.

HAGEN, DR. A., 'La Colonie de Porto-Novo et le Roi Toffa', *Revue d'ethnographie*, vi (1887), pp. 81–116.

HAGEN, M. VON, *Bismarcks Kolonialpolitik*. Stuttgart, 1923.

HAZOUMÉ, PAUL, *Le Pacte de sang au Dahomey*. Transactions et Mémoires de l'Institut d'Ethnologie, XXV. Paris, 1937.

HELFFERICH, DR., *Zur Reform der kolonialen Verwaltungs-Organisation*. Berlin, 1905.

HENRICI, E., 'Das Volksrecht der Epheneger und sein Verhältniß zur deutschen Colonisation im Togogebiete', *Zeitschrift für Vergleichende Rechtswissenschaft*, xi, no. 1 (1892), pp. 131–53.

HERSKOVITS, MELVILLE J., *Dahomey An Ancient West African Kingdom*. 2 vols. New York, 1938.

—— and FRANCES S., *Dahomean Narrative*. Northwestern University Press, 1958.

HERVET, G., *Le Commerce extérieur de l'Afrique Occidentale Française*. Paris, 1911.

HIEKE, ERNST, *G. L. Gaiser Hamburg–Westafrika*. Hamburg, 1949.

—— *Zur Geschichte des deutschen Handels mit Ostafrika, I, Wm. O'Swald & Co. 1831–1870*. Hamburg, 1939.

HUTCHINSON, T. J., *Impressions of Western Africa*. London, 1858.

HUTTON, J. A., *The Work of the British Cotton Growing Association*. Manchester, 1904.

ISERT, PAUL ERDMANN, *Voyages en Guinée et dans les îles caraïbes en Amérique*. Paris, 1793.

JÖHLINGER, OTTO, 'Deutschlands Kolonialwirtschaft im Jahre 1912', *Koloniale Rundschau*, No. 1 (1913), p. 44.

JOHNSON, REV. SAMUEL, *The History of the Yoruba From the Earliest Times to the Beginning of the British Protectorate*. 4th ed. Lagos, 1957.

KADE, DR. EUGEN, *Die Anfänge der deutschen Kolonial-Zentralverwaltung*. Würzburg, 1939.

KLOSE, HEINRICH, *Togo unter deutscher Flagge*. Berlin, 1899.

KOHLER, J., 'Das Togorecht', *Zeitschrift für Vergleichende Rechtswissenschaft*, xxvii, no. 1 (1912), pp. 134–41.

KOSCHITZKY, MAX VON, *Deutsche Kolonialgeschichte*. 2 vols. Leipzig, 1888.

KÜAS, RICHARD, *Togo-Erinnerungen*. Berlin, 1939.

KUCZYNSKI, R. R., *The Cameroons and Togoland, A Demographic Study*. London, 1939.

LABARTHE, P., *Voyage à la Côte de Guinée, ou Description des Côtes d'Afrique, depuis le Cap Tagrin jusqu'au Cap de Lopez-Gonsalves*. Paris, 1803.

LABOURET, HENRI, and RIVET, PAUL (eds.), *Le Royaume d'Arda et son évangélisation au XVIIᵉ siècle*. Transactions et Mémoires de l'Institut d'Ethnologie, VIII. Paris, 1929.

LAFITTE, ABBÉ, *Le Dahomé souvenirs d'un voyge et de mission*. Tours, 1876.

LAIRD, MACGREGOR, and OLDFIELD, R. A. K., *Narrative of an Expedition into the Interior of Africa*. 2 vols. London, 1837.

LAMBINET, COLONEL E., *Notice géographique, topographique et statistique sur le Dahomey*. Paris, 1883.

LANDER, RICHARD and JOHN, *Journal of an Expedition to Explore the Course and Termination of the Niger*. 3 vols. London, 1832.

—— *Records of Captain Clapperton's Last Expedition to Africa*. 2 vols. London, 1830.

LE HERISSÉ, A., *L'Ancien Royaume du Dahomey*. Paris, 1911.

LLOYD, C., *The Navy and the Slave Trade*. London, 1949.

LOMBARD, J., 'Cotonou ville africaine', *Études dahoméennes*, x (1953).

MACLEOD, JOHN, *A Voyage to Africa with Some Account of the Manners and Customs of the Dahomian People*. London, 1820.

McPHEE, ALLAN, *The Economic Revolution in British West Africa*. London, 1926.

MAGUET, EDGARD, *Concessions domaniales dans les colonies françaises*. Paris, 1930.

MANOUKIAN, MADELINE, *The Ewe-speaking People of Togoland and the Gold Coast*. Ethnographic Survey of Africa, *Western Africa*, part VI. London, 1952.

MARTIN, GASTON, *Nantes au XVIIIᵉ siècle. L'Ère des négriers (1714–1774) d'après des documents inédits*. Paris, 1931.

MATHIESON, W. L., *Great Britain and the Slave Trade 1839–1865*. London, 1929.

MAUPOIL, BERNARD, *Contribution à l'étude de la géomancie dans l'ancienne côte des esclaves*. Paris, 1937.

MAYER, BRANTZ (ed.), *Captain Canot; or, Twenty Years of an African Slaver. Being an Account of his Career and Adventures on the Coast, in the Interior, on Shipboard, and in the West Indies*. New York, 1854.

METZGER, DR. O. F., *Unsere alte Kolonie Togo*. Neudamm, 1941.

MEYER, HANS (ed.), *Das Deutsche Kolonialreich*, ii. Leipzig, 1910.

MÜLLER, G., *Geschichte der Ewe-Mission*. Bremen, 1904.

MÜLLER, KARL, *Geschichte der Katholischen Mission in Togo*. Styler Verlagsbuchhandlung, 1958.

MONNET, A. (ed.), *La Mise en valeur de l'A.O.F. et du Togo*. Casablanca, 1955.

NEWBURY, C. W., 'A Note on the Abomey Protectorate', *Africa*, xxix, No. 2 (1959), pp. 146–55.

—— 'The Development of French Policy on the Lower and Upper Niger, 1880–98', *Journal of Modern History*, xxxi, No. 1 (1959), pp. 16–26.

NORRIS, ROBERT, *Memoirs of the Reign of Bossa Ahadee, King of Dahomey, An Inland Country of Guiney*. London, 1789.

PERHAM, MARGERY, *Native Administration in Nigeria*. London, 1937.

PLIMPTON, GEORGE A. (ed.), *The Journal of an African Slaver, 1789–1792*. Worcester, Mass., 1930.

RÉPIN, A., 'Voyage au Dahomey, par M. le Dr. Répin, ex-chirurgien de la marine impériale, texte et dessins inédits', *Le Tour du monde, nouveau journal des voyages*. Paris, 1863.

ROUSSIER, PAUL (ed.), *L'Établissement d'Issiny 1687–1702*. Paris, 1935.

RUDIN, H. R., *Germans in the Cameroons, 1884–1914*. London, 1938.

RYDER, A. F. C., 'The Re-establishment of Portuguese Factories on the Costa da Mina to the mid-eighteenth century', *Journal of the Historical Society of Nigeria*, i, no. 3 (1958), pp. 157–83.

SCHACK, F., *Das deutsche Kolonialrecht in seiner Entwicklung bis zum Weltkriege*. Hamburg, 1923.

SCHANZ, MORITZ, *West-Afrika*. Berlin, 1903.

SCHLETTWEIN, A., 'Kodifikation des Eingeborenenrechts in Togo', *Zeitschrift für Vergleichende Rechtswissenschaft*, xliii, No. 1 (1927), pp. 248–52.

SCHLUNK, M., *Die Evangelische Ewe-Kirche in Süd-Togo*. Bremer Missionsschriften, No. 35. Bremen, 1912.

SCHMIDT, ROCHUS, *Deutschlands Kolonien, ihre Gestaltung, Entwicklung und Hilfsquellen, II, West-Afrika und Südsee*. Berlin, 1895.

SCHRAMM, P. E., *Deutschland und Übersee*. Göttingen, 1950.

SCHREIBER, A. W. (ed.), *Bausteine zur Geschichte der Norddeutschen Missions-Gesellschaft*. Bremen, 1936.

SKERTCHLY, J. A., *Dahomey as it is; Being a Narrative of Eight Months' Residence in that Country, with a Full Account of the Notorious Annual Customs, and the Social and Religious Institutions of the Ffons*. London, 1874.

SPIETH, J., *Die Eweer, Schilderung von Land und Leuten in Deutsch-Togo*. Bremen, 1906.

—— *Die Ewe Stämme. Material zur Kunde des Ewe-Volkes in Deutsch-Togo*. Berlin, 1906.

—— *Die Rechtsanschauungen der Togoneger und ihre Stellung zum europäischen Gerichtswesen*. Bremen, 1908.

—— *50 Jahre Missionsarbeit in Ho*. Bremen, 1910.

TALBOT, P. A., *The People of Southern Nigeria*. 4 vols. London, 1926.

TOWNSEND, MARY E., *The Rise and Fall of Germany's Colonial Empire 1884–1918*. New York, 1930.

TRIERENBERG, GEORG, *Togo, die Aufrichtung der deutschen Schutzherrschaft und die Erschliessung des Landes.* Berlin, 1914.

VENN, H., *West African Colonies.* London, 1865.

VERGER, P., in *Les Afro-Américains.* Mémoire de l'Institut Français d'Afrique Noire, No. 27. Dakar, 1953.

VIETOR, J. K., *Geschichtliche und kulturelle Entwicklung unserer Schutzgebiete.* Bremen, 1913.

VOGT, AUGUST, *Westafrika in vorkolonialer Zeit. Freuden und Leiden eines Bielefelder Kaufmannes vor 50 Jahren in Togo, der früheren Sklavenküste in den Jahren 1873–1877.* Bielefeld, 1923.

WALCKENAER, A. (ed.), *Collections des relations de voyages.* 21 vols. Paris, 1842.

WHITFORD, S., *Trading Life in West and Central Africa.* Liverpool, 1877.

WINKELMANN, G., 'Die Eingeborenenrechtspflege in Deutsch-Ostafrika, Kamerun und Togo unter deutscher Herrschaft', *Zeitschrift für Vergleichende Rechtswissenschaft*, liii, No. 2 (1939), pp. 189–221.

WOOD, Rev. BUCKLEY, *Historical Notices of Lagos, West Africa.* Lagos, 1878.

ZAHN, F. M., *Der Westafrikanische Branntweinhandel.* Gütersloh, 1886.

ZIMMERMANN, A., *Geschichte der Deutschen Kolonialpolitik.* Berlin, 1914.

Index

Abeokuta, town and province, 35, 44, 45, 52, 72; and Lagos trade, 73, 75, 90; authorities in, 91; French mission in, 99; annexation of, planned, 110; embassy to, 138–9; population of, 143; boundaries of, 190–1, 194; British jurisdiction over, 199.

Abomey (Agbomey), town and district, foundation of, 10, 13; royal lineage of, 13–14, 15; expansion of, 23; court politics at, 129–30; under French rule, 133, 181–3.

Abson, Lionel, director at Whydah, 25.

Adandozan, king of Dahomey, 14, 37.

Addo, 36, 45; and British protection, 69, 70; 138.

Addo river, 70, 71, 75.

Adele, Ologun of Lagos, 36, 46.

Ademola, Alake of Abeokuta, 91.

Adja lineages, 5–6; origins of, 7–8, 9; title succession among, 13–14, 15.

Adja-speaking peoples, 3–4; see also Abomey, Allada, Ewe, Fon, Gun.

Adimola, ancestor of the Adja, 8.

administration; British, 66–67; personnel, 78, 79, 174–5; judiciary, 81–82, 83–84; French, 126–7; personnel, 175, 183; resistance to, 184, 204; German, 112–14, 140, 151, 175–6, 178–9; see also agriculture, chiefs, finance, jurisdiction, railways.

African Barter Company, 87.

African Steamship Company, 57.

Agaja, king of Abomey, 1, 14; attacks on coastal markets, 23.

Agassu, ancestor of the Adja, 8.

Agbanlin, ancestor of the Gun, 9, 10.

Agbomey, see Abomey.

Agoli-Agbo (Goutchili), king of Abomey, 14, 133, 181–2.

Agonglo, king of Abomey, 14, 27.

Agorigan, Fon chief of Cotonou, 126.

agriculture and plantations, in Togo, 150–4; in Dahomey, 155; in Nigeria, 156.

Aiyetoro, 171, 194.

Ajarra market, 142.

Ajohon market, 142.

Ajilete, 137; rivalry for chieftainship of, 191–2.

Ajuda, slave mart, 41.

Akarigbere, lineage chiefs, 46.

Akitoye, Ologun of Lagos, 47, 48, 49, 54, 56.

Akran, chief of Badagri, 30, 47 and n., 63 n., 70; under British rule, 83, 85.

Akwamu, Ewe, 97.

Alafin of Oyo, 35, 72, 170, 171, 188, 200, 201–2.

Alake, 91; of Abeokuta, 189, 190 195.

Alaketu of Ketu, 15 and n.

Allada (Ardra), town and district, first charted, 2, 3; foundation of, 7; early European contact with, 17–18, 19; rivalry with Whydah, 21; defeated by Abomey, 23; under French rule, 133, 181.

Allada-Tadonu (Adja-Tadonu), 8, 133.

Allemand, Rear-Admiral, 104, 106.

American cotton planters, in Togo, 152 and n.

Anecho (Little Popo), 18, 28, 38, 42, 55, 99, 101, 102, 110, 112, 114, 117.

Anglo-French Conference on West Africa, 135–6.

Anlo, Ewe, 97.

Appa, annexation of, 69, 70; under British protection, 77; relations with Porto-Novo, 93; French rivalry for, 109; divided by boundary, 171.

Ardra, see Allada.

Ardra river, see Weme.

arms traffic, 72–73, 89 n., 90, 130 and n., 159.

Ashipa, Ologun of Lagos, 46.

Association of West African Traders (Verein Westafrikanischer Kaufleute), 151–2 and n., 153.

Atakpame, 35.

Austin, W. J., trader, 61 n.

Awori, 35, 36, 48, 70, 191–2, 193.

Badagri, town and district, 27; foundation of, 30–31; 36, 44, 45; disorders at, 47, 48, 54; British post at, 50,

PRINTED IN GREAT BRITAIN
AT THE UNIVERSITY PRESS, OXFORD
BY VIVIAN RIDLER
PRINTER TO THE UNIVERSITY